THE HISTORY OF
THE FACULTY OF ACTUARIES
IN SCOTLAND
1856-1956

A series of towers rising from a palace on the plain to a castle in the air

THE HISTORY OF
THE FACULTY OF
ACTUARIES IN SCOTLAND
1856-1956

BY

ANDREW RUTHERFORD DAVIDSON,
F.F.A., F.I.A.,

Past President of the Faculty

THE FACULTY OF ACTUARIES
23 St. Andrew Square
EDINBURGH
1956

PRINTED IN GREAT BRITAIN BY
WILLIAM HODGE AND COMPANY, LIMITED, GLASGOW.

Dedicated
to the Memory of
WILLIAM THOMAS THOMSON
who has been called
" The Founder of the Faculty "
and
to my Wife,
who has helped me.

FOREWORD

by the President

When the Council decided that to mark the Centenary a history of the Faculty should be written the selection of an author presented no difficulty. The choice of Mr. Andrew R. Davidson was immediate, unanimous, confident. Mr. Davidson had a fine record of service to the Faculty. From personal experience I can vouch for it that he was an inspiring tutor who spared neither himself nor his students. He had shown not only by his earlier papers to the Faculty and his contributions to the discussions but also by his scholarly Presidential Address and by his philosophical essay on probability contributed during his term of office as President that he had an imaginative independence of outlook and a faculty of clear and forceful expression. As a member of Council, in whatever capacity, he had proved himself to be a doughty champion of the Faculty, ever ready to defend its rights yet always eager that it should face up to its responsibilities. And he had a knack of being there when things were done. He was first Chairman of the Students' Society ; he was first Secretary of the Board of Examiners ; he was Secretary of the Faculty when the present premises were secured ; he was President when the Grant of Arms was made. It is quite in character that he should be historian of the first hundred years.

Mr. Davidson says somewhere in his book that he is a lazy man but his service to the Faculty does not bear this out, particularly when it is remembered that he was at the same time engaged in a strenuous business life which led in due course to the managership of the largest Scottish life office. And certainly no lazy man would have undertaken the research involved in writing a history. The reading of all the minutes of the Faculty is in itself no light task and it is clear that he has done much more. For me, he has made the past live and it gives me the greatest pleasure to commend this book to my actuarial brethren and to that wider public which is interested in Scottish affairs.

K. K. W.

CONTENTS

ILLUSTRATIONS

PREFACE

" When at first I took my Pen in hand
  Thus for to write; I did not understand
  That I at all should make a little Book
  In such a mode; "
                                    —JOHN BUNYAN.

" There is properly no history—only biography."
                                    —EMERSON.

During the autumn of 1951, the Council honoured me
with the suggestion that I should prepare some account of
the Faculty of Actuaries in Scotland, covering the first
hundred years of its existence. The task was entirely to
my liking, particularly since, as the result of indifferent
health, I had but recently retired from active business life.
No doubt I should have paused, " letting *I dare not* wait
upon *I would* ", so that some abler mind might have been
devoted to the work ; but the subject lay too close to my
heart and it has kept me from " idlenesse, the nourse of
sin " ! If I bring no other qualification, I have at the least
an enthusiastic admiration for the Faculty and for the
important work that it has accomplished and I have done
what I could in this little volume to tell what should be
a very human story. I trust it may serve in some measure
as a grateful acknowledgement of the debt I owe to the
Faculty and to my many friends amongst its Fellows.

In submitting the completed volume, I may express the
hope that the members of my profession will take some
pleasure in reading it. The " little Book " has not turned
out quite as I expected ; books, I suspect, gradually develop
a certain personality and take command of the author.
William de Morgan used to say that he was always interested
and excited as to what his characters would do and say
when he took up his pen to continue one of his novels

and, although all I have to record has been said and done in the past, I have felt myself moved by the ambitions and hopes of the men who made the Faculty. The story is in part the story of the actuarial profession, of the development of actuarial science and of the ever-increasing sphere of its usefulness in modern affairs ; but it is also, and perhaps should be mainly, the story of those men who, during the last hundred years, have devoted their lives to actuarial work under the aegis of the Faculty and whose achievements and characters have moulded its destiny. It is unlikely that many (or any) who are not actuaries will pick up this book and it may be that not many actuaries will read it through ; the latter may feel that it is sufficient that the record has been made and that no duty lies upon them to pore over it. On the other hand, it is a record of human endeavour and, as I think, achievement ; the fault lies not in the subject, but in the author, should it prove but a dull record of a dead past.

The history is, in a sense, a reflection upon a small scale of the history of our nation during the last hundred years ; the Faculty begins its career as a typical Victorian aristocracy. The original leaders are important men and they are aware of it ; they are highly conscious of their position and influence and they are not to be trifled with. Their benevolence, for they are benevolent, is not unmixed with condescension ; they are men who have worked hard and who expect the younger generation to do likewise. Strong, upright, tireless men, who put a premium on success, they are not prepared to spend their lives coddling weaklings or failures. Their attitude to lack of success has no sentimentality about it—the blame lies squarely upon the individual ; laziness, slackness, lack of application or a wavering devotion to one's life's work are anathema to them and incomprehensible. The desire for leisure and early retirement to a life of ease are not their preoccupations. In a word, they are Victorians— magnificent Victorians. One may feel that they take themselves full seriously ; but they are not figures of fun, for with all their failings they are *par excellence* men. To-day it is not uncommon to jeer at the Victorians—rather a presumptuous attitude, I think—and who are we to dare ? With its perpetually " laid-on " entertainment, its emphasis on the wish to escape from realities, its noise, its restlessness, its canned food and its canned music and mainly its lack of high moral purpose, we shall be fortunate if our modern age does not go down to history as the Age of Vulgarity, as the Age in which people were afraid to be left alone with their thoughts. We laugh at the hypocrisy of the Victorians and we pride ourselves on calling a spade a spade. But their hypocrisy was a measure of their aspiration ; if they were not always virtuous, they paid homage to virtue and it is an impudent fellow indeed who goes abroad without pretence. Who amongst us has not something that he wishes to hide—or, out of respect for others, should wish to hide ?

Nearly fifty years of the story of the Faculty lies in the Victorian era and it seems that its character showed no great change during that period and for some years after ; but latterly it becomes more democratic ; the junior members obtain more influence in its affairs and their voices are raised in discussion. The Chairman's word is no longer law and in the end the President is the Prime Minister of a small State who must needs walk warily and count votes. To-day all national questions, however complex, are to be decided by counting heads and it is an axiom that one must not enquire as to what the heads are made of ; but so far as the Faculty is concerned, the modern view that democracy is a distribution of prizes rather than a sharing of responsibilities has not gained credence and one dare hope is unlikely to do so—for our Fellows may surely be presumed to be reasonably intelligent. The emancipation (it is not too strong a word) of the junior members which has taken place particularly over the last forty years will, one need not doubt, be a source of strength to the Faculty in the future. For, in a relatively small body, enthusiasm is an essential ingredient of success.

Latterly we have relied upon our younger members to keep it glowing and fortunately we may look to them to do so in the future. One may be confident that the greatly-increased and ever-increasing influence which falls to the lot of the more junior Fellows will carry with it a deep sense of responsibility and tradition and of gratitude to the Faculty and to the men who made it. Perhaps in our institution, we may dare to be democrats.

The preparation of this work has involved a surprising amount of research into the records and the collection of evidence in connection with even the most distinguished figures in the Scottish actuarial past has not always been easy. " The life of man is a little thing ; and a little thing is the corner of the earth that is his home ; and a little thing is the most enduring renown." It is astonishing how completely some of the men—great figures in their sphere —have been forgotten and how seldom we think of our predecessors and of the debt we owe to them. I am, of course, no historian and, inexperienced as I am, the process of collecting evidence has been to me a source of great interest and some amusement ; I had not before realised how much more a witness tells about himself than about the subject of the enquiry. No doubt " in the multitude of counsellors there is safety," but sometimes, when I have been able to consult more than one individual as to the character and influence of an actuarial personage of the past, their accounts have reflected so exactly their own characters and experience as to render the portraits they give quite unrecognisable as applying to the same individual. And obituary notices are notoriously unreliable as the basis of any history which pretends to impartiality. If history be a " distillation of Rumour " then perhaps this is history ; but since I have no particularly dark deeds to write of, no stories to tell that might have sent delicious shivers down the spines of my readers and made them glance warily at the lengthening shadows, it certainly does not come within Gibbon's caustic definition—" the register of the crimes, follies and misfortunes of mankind." However, I have studied the records, listened to the rumours and have sifted the evidence with such skill and industry as I can command ; I can only trust that my judgements and my account have done injustice to no one. Included in the minutes and other records there is naturally a great deal of detailed information and it has been necessary to be selective, for " *l'art d'ennuyer c'est tout dire* " and I have no wish to bore my readers. In a volume such as this, however, the important facts must be recorded and I hope my choice has been judicious and that no milestone has been left unmarked. It is, I suppose, out of the question that all will agree with my selection of data—" men's thoughts are much according to their inclination "—and it is impossible for one who has spent his whole working life as a member of the Faculty, to view it quite objectively. It is a question for the learned whether an entirely objective history has ever been written and it is another question whether anyone can bear to read it if it has. For a record of the lives of men written with complete detachment must lack the vigour bred of enthusiasm and represent their story as a sluggish backwater rather than a swiftly-flowing river moved by every chance and change upon its rocky course.

In order to avoid encumbering the text with detail, I have given in Appendices such information as it appears to me should be recorded in any history of the Faculty, but which need not form part of the narrative. The first two Appendices give the names respectively of the Presidents and of the Vice-Presidents and other Honorary Officials, and the third of the Honorary Fellows of the Faculty ; the others are referred to in the text as occasion arises.

I find that it is out of the question that I should mention here each and all of those who have helped me, for I have met on all hands the greatest kindness and co-operation ; but there are several to whom the degree of my indebtedness is such that I wish to record my particular thanks. I am naturally greatly obliged to Mr. R. C. Simmonds, whose valuable History of the Institute of Actuaries has proved a mine of information and to Mr. Edward Waugh, Secretary of the Faculty, whose unfailing helpfulness and courtesy as well as the assiduity with which he and his staff have answered the numerous enquiries I found it necessary to make rendered the compilation of the work both possible and pleasant. For information as to a past rather more remote than comes within my personal recollection I am particularly grateful to Messrs. Alexander Fraser*, J. R. Armstrong, J. A. Thomson and S. F. M. Cumming ; but no statement or remark in the text should be credited (or debited !) to any individual, for others have helped me and in any case the responsibility is solely mine.

I must record my special indebtedness to my friends G. H. Recknell, A. R. Reid, J. B. Dow, A. Bateman and H. A. Fraser, each of whom has read the manuscript and made valuable suggestions. I have to thank Mr. A. C. Stalker for so kindly and efficiently preparing the index. Particularly, I am obliged to Mr. D. A. B. Scrimgeour, who was entrusted by the Council of the Faculty with the onerous task of supervising the actual production of the printed book ; he has been most helpful and quite unsparing of his time and energy.

The frontispiece, an original painting by James Riddel, R.S.W., of Old Edinburgh as seen from the Queen's Park, is taken from *Traditions of Edinburgh* published by Messrs. W. and R. Chambers, to whom grateful acknowledgement is made both for permission to reproduce and for assistance in the reproduction.

Finally, I am grateful to the President for his courtesy in contributing a Foreword to this Centenary Volume.

A.R.D.

---

* Unfortunately Mr. Fraser died in June, 1955, when the book was in an advanced state of preparation.

WILLIAM MORGAN, F.R.S.

"the father of the actuarial profession"

(from the portrait in the possession of the Equitable Life
Assurance Society, London)

CHAPTER I

INTRODUCTORY

"One of the hardest tasks that an expert in
any subject can undertake is to try to explain
to the layman what his subject is and why he
makes such a fuss about it."
—C. C. DARWIN.

IT is a matter of doubt whether it is necessary to
describe the nature and scope of the profession in a
history of the Faculty; but perhaps it is desirable
to give some sketch, however slight, of its origins
at least. For the Faculty itself was born of the need
for an actuarial profession and to describe this need
is to define the foundations upon which our
institution was built. If I give some indication of
what an actuary is and does this Chapter, should it
serve no other purpose, will prove a timely warning
to any layman who should by chance turn these
pages. Such a warning is certainly required; it
would be such a pity if anyone seated himself in his
favourite chair (in front of such fire as the Government of the day may permit) with a view to an
evening's reading, but under a misapprehension as
to the subject. This might well occur; for to this
day, should one shoot down the first hundred people
one meets in a busy thoroughfare in any important
city, it is in a high degree unlikely that there would
be lost to the world any individual having the
remotest idea of the meaning of the word " actuary."

Within the last few years one of my daughters,

answering an enquiry from a French correspondent as to the occupation of her father, made use of the word " *actuaire*." She was assured politely, but quite firmly, that there was no such word and that her father was, without doubt, an accountant. In my earlier life, having been accused (if that be the word) by a lady of being a lawyer, I let the matter rest ; it was too difficult. Perhaps the lady suffered from the effects of a classical education and may have assumed that the meaning of the modern word " actuary " should correspond in some degree to that of *actuarius*, an official who recorded the acts of the Roman Senate and who might, I suppose, be regarded as being a member of the legal profession. It would lend a great air of respectability to the profession were we able to trace our descent from the *actuarii* ; but actuaries are quite normally respectable anyway and should one achieve the difficult task of putting a plausible case for such professional antiquity, one might deserve a stricture resembling that contained in the opening sentence of a well-known biography of the Earl of Beaconsfield—" The romantic story of his ancestry which Benjamin Disraeli composed and possibly believed, throws a light on his character but leaves his lineage obscure " ! When in 1864 Archibald Hewat, who became in due time an important figure amongst Scottish actuaries, was offered an appointment in the Scottish Equitable Life Assurance Society with a view to becoming an actuary, he consulted an ancient dictionary in his father's library and found—" Actuary—a registrar or clerk." To quote his own words—" Neither registrar nor clerk appealed to the ambition of one who had fondly dreamt of being a Boanerges in some pulpit ! " However, after obeying his father's injunction to "consult the Home Secretary" (his mother), he accepted the offer.

When the Equitable Society was founded in 1762 the chief executive official received the title "Actuary" and it has been remarked that the use of the word was "probably an antiquarian whimsy" on the part of the person who prepared the Society's deed of co-partnership. A man of great character and ability came to occupy the post of Actuary to the Society and, as suggested in the Institute of Actuaries Year Book, it was almost certainly due to the prominence and high example of William Morgan, F.R.S. (Actuary to the Society from 1775 to 1830), that the title came into general use. William Morgan " may justly be regarded as the father of the actuarial profession."

An actuary has been described as one who applies the theory of probability to practical problems. This description may be held to be based on sound authority since the Diploma issued by the Faculty to the persevering individual who has completed his examinations uses these words—" having been examined . . . as to his knowledge of the Doctrine of Probabilities . . . ". This form has some traditional justification, apart from the fact that it appears to have been used in substance since the Faculty was instituted, because the actuarial profession undoubtedly had its roots amongst those mathematicians who were investigating the theory of probability and applying their results to practical financial problems in the latter part of the eighteenth century ; but the description is hardly satisfactory. An actuary is one who uses the records of the past as a basis for estimates of future occurrences. It is true that, in the beginning, the members of the profession were largely concerned with calculations of a financial nature involving contingencies of life and death ; but the scope of the profession has greatly broadened since those early days. Although to this day a majority of actuaries are employed by life assurance societies or kindred institutions, many are otherwise engaged and the young actuaries made a great name as practical statisticians during the " Unnecessary War," as Sir Winston Churchill called it.

In my view, therefore, the subject of this book is the foundation and development of an association of persons whose profession involves the employment of the statistics of the past as a measure of the occurrences of the future, but whose preoccupation in the early days was entirely—as it is to an extent to-day—with life contingencies.

In the latter part of the eighteenth and in the earlier years of the nineteenth century many institutions were founded, the conduct of whose affairs required the estimation of future rates of mortality. Societies for granting annuities, Government activities of a similar nature and institutions for granting assurances on lives called for the solution of certain practical arithmetical problems. It was natural that those responsible for promoting such schemes (in so far as they were not mere swindles of the " Anglo-Bengalee " type) should apply to the mathematicians of the time for guidance. Very much earlier than this the practice of granting annuities or " rents for life " in consideration of the payment of sums of money had been a common practice ; but there was little attempt at scientific accuracy in calculating the prices. Towards the end of the seventeenth century the British Government, " with the mighty brain of Sir

4

Isaac Newton at its disposal," was granting life annuities without reference to the age of the proposed annuitant at the rate of £14 in respect of each £100 subscribed. The problems were to calculate the present value of a life annuity and later, when life assurance began to be appreciated, the premium for a capital sum payable at death. These problems are still fundamental in actuarial work and perhaps it would not be too much to say that, whilst modern methods shew a great advance as compared with the early efforts, solutions that are entirely satisfactory are still to seek. The vitality of the people is improving—the average length of life is increasing—and this process has been going on for many years; the early efforts to sell annuities were consequently not profitable from the point of view of the seller as past experience (so far as it was statistically available) was employed rigidly as an estimate of future mortality rates; but for exactly the same reason early life assurance ventures tended to flourish. The difficulties of the one type of enterprise and the success and growing popularity of the other drew the attention of many eminent mathematicians to the underlying problems and in due course gave rise to the profession of actuary.

Gradually, through the years, the scope of the profession grew with the public appreciation of the great variety of fields in which the training of an actuary might prove useful. To-day there are many actuaries in private practice, dealing with a wide range of problems. There is the Government Actuary's Department, the establishment of which may, perhaps, be said to have set the seal upon the importance and wide influence of the profession on the background of modern life; in many aspects of demography the authority of the profession is recognised ; and to an ever-increasing extent its representatives are to be found in commercial life. Some of these latter appointments appear at first sight just a little surprising. I well remember an English friend telling me that two young actuaries had found employment with a large firm which made women's clothes. I expressed astonishment and surmised, having a well-known mathematical process in mind of course, that no doubt they would be employed in " curve-fitting." The Englishman replied " No, actually they do statistical work."

In the old days, the word " actuary " was employed rather loosely, and the first President of the Institute of Actuaries remarked in 1848 that " at present every little clerk of a Savings Bank called himself an actuary " ; but by now long usage and the authority of several Acts of Parliament have tended to confine the title to the legitimate members of the profession, although it is true that to this day the chief officers of Savings Banks (not little clerks !) see fit to employ the title.

That the profession has grown greatly in numbers as well as in scope is a satisfactory state of affairs, and, in view of the high requirements stated as being necessary for an actuary by the *Post Magazine* at the time of the founding of the Institute, it is not a little astonishing that there are so many superlatively fine fellows available. The magazine said : " The requirements in the character of an actuary are—a high degree of mathematical knowledge, the most unspotted integrity and a practical acquaintance with the management of large accounts, so as to present the most involved details in the simplest form ; he must be capable of hearing opposition without irritation and of supporting the views which he believes to be just, without arrogance—he must possess a thorough command over himself, a complete acquaintance with the world and that suavity of manner which enables a man to perform a difficult duty without imputation, but to meet with patience the objections of the ignorant or the schemes of the interested."

CHAPTER II

THE STAGE

" When shall I see Scotland again ? Never shall I forget the happy days I passed there, amidst odious smells, barbarous sounds, bad suppers, excellent hearts and the most enlightened and cultivated understandings."
—SIDNEY SMITH, 1814.

THE Faculty of Actuaries in Scotland was established in 1856 ; but the seeds from which it sprang are to be sought earlier, in the " Augustan days " of Edinburgh, when Scott, Hogg (The Ettrick Shepherd), Wilson (Christopher North of the *Noctes Ambrosianae*, —the " grog-drinking, cudgell-playing professor of moral philosophy ") and others famous in their time lent colour to the scene. In the beginning of the nineteenth century the citizens of Edinburgh held European reputation in many departments of thought and the good name of our lovely old City stood high indeed ; no doubt we have fallen from that pinnacle of achievement, but the pompous impudence of a London weekly which, in 1950, referred to the " dying prestige " of the City, is nonsense of course. The City, old in years, is youthful indeed in outlook and enterprise—its reputation has fortunately not rested upon the barren and shifting foundation of politics ; it is in the spheres of learning and of the arts, in its great tradition and in its beauty that Edinburgh has stood pre-eminent. What more noble cradle could have been found for our Faculty ?

It has been said that after the Jacobite uprising of

1745 a general spirit of improvement began to be shown in Scotland; but up to the end of that century Edinburgh was still " a series of towers rising from a palace on the plain to a castle in the air," although the " New Town " was developing and had reached Castle Street by 1790. The City, since the advent of the " New Town "—the " draughty parallelograms " —has been called " east-windy and west-endy "; the prevailing wind is the west wind, however, as witness the fact that a gentleman, who had commissioned the building of a house in Princes Street, " took the builder bound " to erect another to the west to protect him from the gales. On the other hand, when an east wind does sweep over the northern parts of the City, it can be bitter, and soon obliterates the memory of the milder, but more frequent, breezes and no doubt the virulent conduct of a few gave rise to the tradition of " west-endiness". By 1800 a further extension of the northern part of the city was decided upon and the Old Town, within the next few decades, changed its character completely —so far at least as its residents were concerned. The " nobility and gentry", the professional classes— the " writers " and such—had removed themselves. So late as 1825, however, one reads of a life assurance company establishing its office in the High Street— only to depart to what had become a more " respectable " address within a year or two. Gradually the older parts were deserted by their more prosperous inhabitants; the glory departed from the High Street, the Canongate, the old closes and wynds and they were left to their smells and their beauty. Many consider plumbing and civilisation to be synonyms; but what was once the odoriferous squalor of the Old Town of Edinburgh can still present a silhouette of breath-taking loveliness. To stand in Princes Street when a harvest moon looks over Arthur's Seat and illumines the scene through a gentle haze brings an enchantment from which long acquaintance cannot steal the poignancy.

The life of the City in the middle of the nineteenth century was naturally very different from that of to-day; in Edinburgh, as elsewhere, great changes have arisen in the name of progress. Although one may not be inclined to go as far as the old gentleman who, seated in the hall of one of the Edinburgh Clubs, was asked his opinion of the new swing-doors and replied, " I have lived a long time ; I have seen many changes—all of them for the worse", there was a quiet dignity about the old City, which has passed and which one may regret in these restless days. The Capital was, from one point of view, " not so much a small City as the largest of small Towns " and it was scarcely possible to pass unnoticed or to remain anonymous within its comparatively narrow boundaries. There were green fields a-plenty and views of the sea and of the snows on Ben Ledi from the City's towering crags ; the Pentland hills, apparently more distant than to-day, looked down quietly from the south-west, no longer battlefields or the hiding-place of hunted men. Surely it was a peaceful and a quite enchanting medley of a City in Victorian times, with its so striking contrast of the ancient and modern—facing each other across the valley—and its contented, or perhaps it may be, somewhat complacent citizens with their background of law, University, finance and beer. In those days and even into the early years of the twentieth century, no new-fangled ideas about the need for incessant entertainment had encroached upon the Scottish

Sunday—that great and impressive religious ceremony —with streets deserted, except by the demure stream of churchgoers in their Sabbath black ; a day of rest indeed and worthy of a people who treasured such resources in their minds that solitude and restful leisure meant neither boredom nor terror for them. It was to an extent more of a self-contained and self-sufficient community than to-day, when modern transport has made us citizens of the world and when an event in Timbuctoo (if that City is so unfortunate as to have events) is known the world over within the hour. What happened in Edinburgh was mainly what mattered to the people and the affairs of church and state, of the theatre and the arts, were viewed from a more local stand-point than now. The feeling that what the people of Edinburgh thought mattered supremely was at the root of all discussion.

The actuarial profession arose in Scotland, as elsewhere, from the requirements of the life offices ; but the Scottish institutions of that description were late in the field as compared with their friends in England. Fire insurance business, from the nature of its contracts, involved no abstruse consideration of theories of probability. No impetus was given, therefore, to the birth of an actuarial profession by the establishment of a fire Office in Edinburgh in 1720 ; it was called the Edinburgh Friendly Insurance Office and was absorbed by the Sun Fire Office (its senior by only 10 years) in 1847. Nor is it to the oldest existing Scottish insurance office that we must attribute the honour of sowing the first seeds. The Caledonian Insurance Company, amongst whose directors was the painter Raeburn, was established in 1805 and had its first office at No. 7 Hunter Square, in premises belonging to a firm of ironmongers and general merchants, but did not commence life business until 1833, by which year several others had entered upon the stage. It is to the Scottish Widows' Fund and Life Assurance Society that this honour belongs, for this institution was discussed in a pamphlet published in 1812 and in 1815 it commenced operations under the title of " The Scottish Widows' Fund and Equitable Assurance Society," with a crack of the whip well worthy its high destiny, for its twenty-five patrons included two Dukes, a Marquis and a few Barons! For some years this Office operated in splendid isolation, but in 1823 the Edinburgh Life was established, followed by the North British and the Scottish Union—of which last office Sir Walter Scott was first Governor. Curiously enough Sir Walter was also connected with the Edinburgh for, according to his diary, on 13th December 1825 he attended the yearly Court of that Company and remarked that he was " one of those graceful and useless appendages, called Directors Extraordinary." The entry continues " . . . an extraordinary director I should prove had they elected me an ordinary one. There were three moneyers and great oneyers, men of metal—counters and discounters—sharp, grim, prudential faces—eyes weak with ciphering by lamp-light—men who say to gold, Be thou paper, and to paper, Be thou turned into fine gold. Many a bustling, sharp-faced, keen-eyed writer too . . ." He was Governor of the Scottish Union from 1824 until his death in 1832 and during his last sad journey to Abbotsford in July 1832 he spent a night in Edinburgh at Douglas's Hotel, 35 St. Andrew Square—the present address of the Scottish Union and National

Whilst it was, as we shall see, due to the initiative of the officials of the life offices in England and in Scotland that the actuarial profession was formally established, the need for actuarial advice was there before the life offices, so far as Scotland was concerned at least. As early as 1743, we find " The Church of Scotland Ministers' and Scottish University Professors' Widows' Fund " being established and it is a tribute to its founders and to their native caution that this fund, which was amalgamated with another in 1928, is still in robust and healthy existence. That institution is, however, a mere infant when compared with the United Incorporations of St. Mary's Chapel, Edinburgh, which was instituted on 15th October 1475 and is still active as a widows' fund. Other widows' funds were started by professional bodies early in the nineteenth century and by the banks for the benefit of their employees ; there was also a great variety of friendly societies, which provided relief to their members in sickness or on superannuation. In 1820, no fewer than seventy-nine of these friendly societies provided data for a report upon their activities at the request of the Highland Society of Scotland. All these bodies required actuarial advice and no doubt in Scotland, as in England, consulted those available who were skilled in mathematics. Quite recently, I heard of a small assurance company overseas, which, having no actuary, had taken advice from the local school-master, and probably these early funds and friendly societies may in some cases have had recourse to a similar fount of learning. Many of these institutions flourished and are alive and well to-day ; probably they were instituted by men of substance who had their due share of caution and one can imagine the founders of the older funds in a murky room in the Old Town discussing their affairs and their claret in an equally conscientious and responsible spirit. It would be claret of course, for one may quote John Home's lines on the Claret Duties -

> Firm and erect the Caledonian stood
> Old was his claret and his mutton good ;
> " Let him drink port " an English statesman cried—
> He drank the poison and his spirit died.

In the conduct of the affairs of the friendly societies, the doctrine of *laissez faire* was not given entirely free rein—they took such steps as the circumstances permitted to see that their members should not behave so as to render their experience unfavourable. In one Society, members found drunk on the Sabbath were to be excluded or, if forgiven, were to be fined five shillings ; and a similar penalty was exacted from any member who, " at the annual meeting or six hours after should be the first in stirring up mischief, fighting or breeding any riot." Swearing during a meeting cost sixpence.

And so the seed was scattered and whether the soil was to prove fertile, the tale I have to tell should say. The professional men of the old days in Edinburgh set themselves a high standard both at desk and at table and it will, I think, appear that, in its sphere, the Faculty has maintained the professional tradition of Scotland. It is a well-established jest that Scotsmen are to be found the world over in positions of influence ; however that may be, it is indeed true that, due in part to the limitation of opportunities at home, the Scottish seats of learning have sent overseas many whose contributions to the development of the lands of their adoption have been striking and beneficent. The records of the Faculty are rich in actuarial pioneers, who in the early days helped to establish sound actuarial practice overseas and who have, latterly, guided the destinies of great institutions ; in this respect the Faculty has been true to its heritage.

CHAPTER III

THE BIRTH PANGS

" Well," said I, " I do not see why the
dispute, if dispute there be, should not be
settled in the ring."
—BORROW, " LAVENGRO."

THE Association of Managers of Life Offices in
Scotland was founded about 1833 and is the senior
association of its kind in point of years ; it flourishes
to-day under the name of the Associated Scottish
Life Offices. It is no part of my commission to relate
the history of that Association ; but it was the first
link in the chain of circumstance which led to the
foundation of the Faculty. The second and vital
link was of course the foundation of the Institute of
Actuaries in 1848. It would be a work of super-
erogation to attempt a description of the founding of
that great institution ; an account in much detail is,
as all actuaries very well know, to be found in the
admirable volume written by R. C. Simmonds to
celebrate its centenary. Simmonds remarks that
" The record of the Institute of Actuaries begins . . .
at least partly with a Scotsman," and describes a
meeting on 15th April 1848 in the London Office of
the Standard Life Assurance Company (then situated
at 82, King William Street) when W. T. Thomson,
of that Company, was requested by the Chairman,
Griffith Davies of the Guardian, to give some
account of the activities and regulations of the
Association of Managers in Scotland. G. H. Recknell,

Bust of WILLIAM THOMAS THOMSON
in the Hall

". . . it was on him the newly-formed Faculty of Actuaries relied,
as its chief strength and support."—*Deuchar*

in his account of the Actuaries' Club, describes this meeting as "convened by a Scot, on Scottish soil, in London." Thomson had apparently suggested that a similar association might with propriety be started in England; but, in the event, it was not until many years later (1889) that his idea bore the fruit he expected. Actuaries in England had been meeting informally long before 1848, and the idea of a society of some kind had been in their minds. Suffice it to say that the discussions which followed the meeting of 15th April 1848 led to the foundation of the Institute of Actuaries—a professional and academic body and in no sense an association of life offices or of their chief officers. Peter Hardy, during the discussions, appears to have suggested the establishment of a "College of Actuaries" and perhaps one may shed a sentimental tear over the thought that his idea was adopted without the delightful name. The Actuaries' Club (the direct descendant of the informal meetings already referred to) was founded later in the same year as the Institute, and the Life Offices' Association in 1889. The Actuaries' Club has been the subject of an interesting and pleasant monograph by my old friend, G. H. Recknell, but neither the Associated Scottish Life Offices nor the Life Offices' Association, its English counterpart, have so far allowed themselves to be subjected to the remorseless scrutiny of the historian.

There was some controversy in those early days between the Institute and the Club of which the details do not concern us here; although the profession in London was in fact divided until 1884, for many years they have performed their respective and distinct functions in the closest accord and amity and with incalculable advantage to the profession.

The debt which actuarial science and actuaries in general owe to the premier professional body cannot be exaggerated.

That the Institute was of an entirely different nature from the Association of Managers in Scotland was evident from the beginning, and Scottish actuaries were admitted to membership. Clearly the necessity for two distinct bodies—one professional and the other of a business nature—was early appreciated in the North at least, for individual actuaries were members of both.

By 1853 the Scottish members of the Institute represented no less than one-third of the total and were putting forward suggestions " to extend to the Scottish members some of the advantages enjoyed by those resident in London . . . " Prior to this date and immediately afterwards, there was evidence of some lack of satisfaction with their position on the part of the Scottish members, which had resulted in controversy from time to time. The personal relations between those in London and the members in the North appear, on the other hand, to have been excellent ; David Deuchar refers to a " notable dinner " held in a London coffee-house, when " several able and eloquent speeches were made in the course of the evening, resulting from the proposal of the health of the Scottish members and other toasts." The evening was a success ; " the company did not separate until a late hour." In 1850 a number of members of the Institute, fortunately including John Finlaison, the President, were entertained to dinner in Barry's Room, Edinburgh, under the chairmanship of Sheriff Gordon, son-in-law of " Christopher North " and " himself renowned for geniality and eloquence." Again the party went with a swing; the Sheriff claimed Finlaison as a brother Scot, who had left the land of his birth some forty-six years previously—and this is an honour which we in Scotland must not forget, for the first President of the Institute made a great figure in his day. On this occasion, Finlaison said that " it was to the actuaries of Scotland that the Institute was indebted for its existence." This was courteous indeed, particularly in view of the fact that twenty years before the foundation of the Institute he himself had cherished the idea of some such association in London.

But dining, perhaps unfortunately, is not the only business of life and differences of opinion arose from time to time between the Southern and Northern members. Of the course of these differences Simmonds has given a typically generous account, and for record purposes there is given in Appendix IV the Reports of the proceedings at two General Meetings of the members of the Institute resident in Scotland held in November 1853 and February 1854 as well as copies of correspondence between members of the Council of the Institute resident respectively in Scotland and in England. If in the differences of opinion which appear from the records of the past had lain the real difficulty in the way of co-operation, then I think the advice of George Borrow quoted at the beginning of this chapter would have formed an admirable solution. What a page of history has been lost to the literature of fisticuffs ! Had a champion from amongst the actuaries of each country met over fifteen rounds in a sequestered spot near London or Edinburgh, what a hilarious and amicable dinner would have followed the decision of the conflict ! And to crown the event, the course of the " discussion " might have been reported by Thackeray or

De Quincey according as the venue (to copy the modern sports writers) happened to be in England or in Scotland ! But the disputes between the Scottish and English actuaries—small matters in reality—were not, whatever the individuals concerned at the time may have thought, the cause of Scottish dissatisfaction ; they were symptoms of a trouble the source of which lay deeper.

In 1856 the Caledonian Railway Company ran a train which left Lothian Road Station, Edinburgh (the station is still in the same place, but is now called Princes Street Station) at 9.30 a.m. and was advertised as an express train, having first and second class accommodation, which reached Euston Station, London, at 9.30 p.m. Whether it ever did reach its destination at 9.30 p.m. I have no idea. There were, of course, no facilities on the train, but on this route stops were made at Beattock, Carlisle, Birmingham, Rugby and Wolverton for refreshments (where no doubt the " railway sandwich " made its tentative bow to the public) ; so that, should a traveller take full advantage of his opportunities, he would be refreshed indeed by the time his long journey was concluded. There were other trains and another route. By way of the east coast from Waverley Station a train for third-class travellers left at 8 a.m. and was billed to arrive at King's Cross at 9.30 p.m. ; but for the plutocrats who could afford to travel first or second class a train left at 9.50 a.m. and was expected to arrive at the same time as the train which had left at 8 a.m. Again, there were five stops for " refreshment " and for the alleviation of boredom— Berwick, Newcastle, York, Doncaster and Peterborough. For some reason that is quite incomprehensible to me, a train left Edinburgh, Waverley

JAMES BORTHWICK

first Chairman of Council (1856)

(from the portrait by Colvin Smith, R.S.A., in the Board Room of the
North British and Mercantile Insurance Company, Edinburgh)

Station, at 2 p.m. and landed the unfortunate passenger at King's Cross at 4.30 a.m. Is there any place from China to Peru where one would not rather be than King's Cross at 4.30 a.m.?

There was no heating system for railway carriages in those days and sleeping cars had not been introduced. The fares were not greatly different from what they are to-day—nominally at least, although they were payable in real money!—but the numerous stops and the obvious necessity to maintain one's powers of endurance no doubt added quite a little to the expense. One journey from Edinburgh to London and back would have absorbed more than a year's salary for the young aspirant to actuarial honours in 1856.

Deuchar is partly right when he observes that the real reason for the secession of the Scottish actuaries from the Institute and for the consequent establishment of the Faculty was a geographical one. It was sad that the break should occur in the way it did and that the parties did not appear to appreciate the fundamental reason why their marriage was a failure; but it was from the first inevitable. The geographical difficulty was (is, for that matter) quite insurmountable, for who but the fortunate (if " fortunate " be correct) few were in a position to undergo the rigours of the journey and to participate in the deliberations of the Institute, held as they were in London? One may as well also face the fact that there was more than four hundred miles of boredom to it; Scottish actuarial affairs were already important and, perhaps, it must in honesty be said, most important of all, Scotland is Scotland with its own habit of life and particularly its own great and world-wide insurance interests.

The Faculty of Actuaries in Scotland was founded then as a result of the secession of Scottish members from the Institute in 1856 and in the following chapters we may consider its domestic affairs, trace its growth in importance, and note the service it has been so fortunate as to render to actuarial science.

CHAPTER IV

ADOLESCENCE

> " I live alone, preferring loneliness
> To the companionable suffocation of an aunt."
> —CHRISTOPHER FRY, " The Lady's not for Burning."

APART from the fact that, according to those best qualified to judge, the year 1856 was a poor vintage year for claret, it was a very satisfactory one for Britain. The war in the Crimea ended and England entered upon an " era of muscular Christianity, strenuousness and cold baths." None of these were bad things and they all helped to make the magnificent Victorians what they were. The quotation refers, of course, to England and I have made this clear since I am not sure to what extent cold baths impinged upon the culture of the people of Scotland.

In this happy and propitious environment, a meeting was held at 45 George Street, Edinburgh on 4th January 1856, at which the Faculty of Actuaries in Scotland was constituted ; the Scottish actuaries had decided to live alone. Mr. Balchin in his " The Anatomy of Villainy " says " It is one of the most sublime of all human illusions that time is on the side of truth . . . " ; however, he admits that there is something in the idea. Looking back over one hundred years, it seems to be beyond doubt that the course taken by the Scottish members was correct, if it be admitted that their duty lay in the encouragement of actuaries and actuarial science in their own country. The resignation of the Scottish members of the Council of the Institute took place in February and March 1855 and was followed in April of that year by the resignations of other members ; against the names of two of these, " defaulter " (an unusual word for one who has used what must have been his undoubted right to resign) was entered in the Minutes of the Institute Council with what Simmonds describes, rather curiously, as " pathetic precision." Simmonds quotes from the Report of the Institute Council to the Annual General Meeting of 7th July 1855, as follows :—

> " The Council will regret this secession the less if the contemplated measure (of establishing an independent Actuarial Body) be carried out, and if it be the means of raising up in Scotland an efficient school of professional study."

This sensible and benevolent minute—typical of the attitude which the Institute has, for so many years now, shown towards the Faculty—strikes at the root of the matter. It is difficult to comprehend why the necessity for two separate bodies was not understood earlier and why the Faculty—an institution indispensable to Scotland and Scottish actuaries—should have been regarded as the fruit of differences amongst friends. It is easy, of course, to be wise after the event and when irritation is long forgotten.

At the meeting of 4th January, the Chairman was W. T. Thomson and a prospectus of the suggested body, which had been prepared and signed beforehand by thirty-eight actuaries, was submitted for consideration and adopted. The signatories of the prospectus became the original members of the Faculty and the new body was declared to be constituted. John M. McCandlish and Robert Balfour were appointed interim Honorary Secretaries and a committee was set up to prepare a formal Constitution. The " Constitution and Laws," dated 1856 and giving the names of the office-bearers and original Fellows, is reprinted in Appendix V.

An enquiry into the qualifications of the first office-bearers of the Faculty reveals that they were pre-eminently business men ; their approach to the actuarial problems with which they were confronted had a strong practical bias and it is not generally as theorists that they are to be remembered. One does not find that our science, as such, benefited directly to any great extent from the originality or genius of these men ; the fruits of their labours, of their sound practical judgment and of their indefatigable assiduity are with us to-day in the institutions—life assurance offices, widows' funds, friendly societies and so on— which they helped to found and which they set upon the way of greatness and guided in their formative years.

It was not until 1887 that the office of President was instituted, but for the first five years of the Faculty's existence a chairman of Council was appointed, who held office for one year. This practice was abandoned, however, for the years 1861 to 1883, when at each meeting of Council a chairman was appointed to preside for the occasion of that meeting only. For the years 1884-5-6, the original arrangement was adopted ; but in 1887, John Macgregor McCandlish, an original Fellow and one of the first honorary secretaries, became the first President of the Faculty.

The first Chairman of Council was James Borthwick, who on his retirement in 1858 had held the office of Manager of the North British Insurance Co. for thirty-four years. Borthwick had been a merchant of Leith and was one of the gentlemen who subscribed or signified their intention to take shares in the North British at the time of its foundation. Although his actual association with the Faculty was of short duration—he retired from active affairs within two years of its foundation—he had long been active in the " Managers' Association " and received on his retirement a memorial signed by some thirty of the representatives of Scottish insurance companies in terms which must have warmed his heart and which bear eloquent witness to the beneficent influence which he had upon his colleagues and through them upon the destines of the Faculty of which he was the senior office bearer. The description, Merchant of Leith, is not in itself colourful, particularly to modern eyes ; but James Borthwick, apart from the important part he played in the affairs of his great office, had other distinctions. He and a Mr. Simpson were the first two civilians who crossed the field of Waterloo after the battle and he was asked at a neighbouring farmhouse to speak to a wounded German officer who lay dying. Borthwick was able to speak to him in his own language and received from him his watch, chain and a small picture of his wife and children with the request that they should be forwarded to an address in Germany—a commission which he discharged immediately upon his return to Scotland. His interests were apparently varied ; he did sketching —some of his sketches of Norwegian scenes are still extant—and his grand-daughter remarks " I do remember that he was said to be one of the first of his generation to leave the table sober after a convivial evening." One is left to conjecture whether this is a tribute to his head or to his discretion !

John Mackenzie, Manager of the Scottish Widows'

Fund, was a member of the first Council; he became Treasurer of the Bank of Scotland in 1859 and so, no doubt, ended his immediate interest in the affairs of the Faculty. Another member, William Chalmers, had been Treasurer to the Commissioners of Police in Aberdeen before becoming the first Manager of the Northern. The peculiarly Scottish brand of lawyer—Writer to the Signet—had two representatives upon this original Council, McCandlish, already mentioned, who was Manager of the Scottish National and ultimately of the Scottish Union and National and who was to be the first President and Gilbert L. Finlay, W.S., Manager of the Edinburgh, who had much influence in the Managers' Association and who was a member of the first Council of the Institute of Actuaries. Finlay was Honorary Secretary of the Managers' Association and convened the meetings, which were held in a hotel which stood on the site of the present General Post Office in Edinburgh. These meetings were informal dinner parties— commencing at the dangerously early hour of 4.30 or 5 p.m.—and after dinner, " business was discussed, differences were arranged amicably and the meetings made for peace, harmony and co-operation," or so we are told! Finlay seems to have been a person of great energy and was widely respected. Henry D. Dickie, another member of Council, spent no less than forty-nine years as an official of the Caledonian; he was also a Baptist lay-pastor. He was sixty-six years of age when he became a Fellow of the Faculty.

Apparently the most active member of the Council was William Thomas Thomson, of whom Deuchar said " . . . it was on him the newly formed Faculty of Actuaries relied, as its chief strength and support."

Thomson was in his forties when the Faculty was founded and was a man of an enthusiastic temper and of considerable mental capacity, so that it was not perhaps surprising that, being of a rather younger generation than some of the other members of the first Council, he should take a leading part. Like Finlay, he had the honour of being a member of the first Council of the Institute and took, as Simmonds says, a leading part in its foundation. His obituary notice says that " he stood alike physically and mentally high above many, if not most, of his contemporaries." It seems to be clear that he was more of a technical actuary in the modern sense than some of his colleagues and he contributed the article on " Life Insurance " to a contemporary edition of the Encyclopaedia Britannica. He was a man of strong character and, one gathers from his correspondence, of decided opinions ; to his official colleagues he used the phrase " have the goodness to," very much as Sir Winston Churchill uses the word " pray." It may be that the following sentence taken from one of his letters gives a glimpse of the man across the years—" I shall not enter upon your general arguments as I would require to do so at considerable length to show that they are in many respects fallacious and for this I cannot at present afford the time " ! He was appointed an Honorary Fellow in 1878 and on his death in 1883 a long minute recorded his immense labours for the Faculty and a high appreciation of his character.

I have given some brief particulars of a few members of the Council when the Faculty was founded and no doubt it will appear that, with the exception of Thomson, it was fair comment to say that they were business men rather than actuaries ; it was from these

EDWARD SANG

first official Lecturer to the Faculty

men that the suggestion of forming an association was taken to London ; but it was a business association of insurance managers they had in mind rather than an academic body—and this, such particulars as I have been able to glean of their habit and life would lead one to expect. To the event that the suggestion went from Edinburgh to London, the Institute of Actuaries owes the fact that it was established when it was ; but to the English decision to found an academic rather than a purely business body, the Faculty certainly owes its existence. Here we have a nice state of equilibrium in mutual indebtedness which is quite charming and has proved a very satisfactory foundation for co-operation.

For many years the dominant personalities in the Faculty continued to be business men and one had to wait for the names of a later generation for real technical achievement. On the other hand, the founders were not unmindful of the need for technical training and took steps to train the younger men of their day in the way they should go. It was a fortunate circumstance that there resided in Edinburgh at that time an extremely interesting personality and one of great skill and energy in applied mathematics— Edward Sang—who was appointed Lecturer to the Faculty. Sang's influence on the actuarial aspirants of his day was immediate and all-important and, as it happens, he was the great-uncle of a distinguished Scottish actuary of a much later generation— Alexander Fraser. His career was brilliant and romantic and from him and one or two others came the original impetus for actuarial study and original investigation in Scotland, which has survived amongst us and will, one hopes, long continue to bear fruit. It was in 1805 that Edward Sang was born and there was not wanting early evidence of the great gifts he was to display in later years. The following letter written at the tender age of eleven years to his elder brother gives some idea of his calibre :—

Kirkcaldy,
7th December, 1816.

Dear Brother,

    I have sent with the cart the Algebra, Mechanics and Astronomy. I cannot send the Geometry, Conic Sections or French Dictionary. I do not know whether you wish me to send any Latin Books or not. You may send word in your next letter. I understand what you mean by some of your work; it was a cissoid. I intend to come at New Year, if I get play for a week, if Father consents. Excuse my letter, being the first I have written.

    I am, dear David, your affectionate brother,

Edward Sang.

In 1818, at the age of thirteen, he entered the University of Edinburgh and had to take the second class for mathematics since for that session there was no third or advanced class ! In his time Sang held a number of important appointments both at home and overseas ; for a long period he was engaged as a mathematical lecturer in Constantinople, where he lectured and wrote mathematical text books in the Turkish language. In 1854 he finally settled down in Edinburgh as a teacher of mathematics, actuary and general consultant in a wide variety of subjects involving applied mathematics. Amongst a list of one hundred and twelve scientific works appended to his obituary notice in the *Proceedings of the Royal Society of Edinburgh*, there are several dealing with actuarial subjects which no doubt formed the basis of his lectures to the members of the Faculty. He also constructed tables of actuarial functions—for example, "Life Assurance and Annuity Tables for every Combination of Two Lives"—but modern (or at least fairly modern!) Scottish actuaries know of Sang chiefly for his great volume of logarithms, "faultless as it is believed to be for accuracy," which many of us found a daily companion of great usefulness before the days of the modern contraptions which discourage the schools from effectively teaching arithmetic to their pupils. At the age of 86 Sang died after a long life of great usefulness and of unremitting diligence. On a large telescope which he mounted himself, he inscribed in golden characters in Turkish and in English, his favourite motto— "He rewardeth the searcher and keeper of His Laws." We, in the Faculty, must never forget the debt which we owe to Edward Sang in laying the foundation of a true spirit of scientific study for the Scottish school of actuaries.

One of Sang's pupils, David Chisholm, was on the original Library Committee of which Thomson was Chairman. Chisholm had actually been in the employment of Sang before he joined the North British in 1841. It is recorded in the Company's minutes on 28th May 1885 that "Mr. Chisholm thanked the Directors for allowing him to retire after 44 years' service on full salary, aged 74 years." He was the author of "Commutation Tables for Joint Annuities and Survivorship Assurances"; the work was based upon the Carlisle Table of Mortality and was in use until fairly recent times. Chisholm's book, like modern statistical theory, always seemed to me to supply confident answers to unanswerable questions!

He dedicated his book to the Directors of the North British and to Borthwick, the first Chairman of Council. One copy still in the possession of the Company bears the inscription in the author's own hand "Presented to the actuarial Library of the North British & Mercantile Insurance Co., Edinburgh, by the Author with his best wishes as a memorial of the long and pleasant connection with the Company, being the last copy of the work on hand, Edinburgh November 1886." William Smith, LL.D., was another member of the Library Committee; he was Manager of the English and Scottish Law in Edinburgh and was perhaps more distinguished as a philosopher than as an actuary, although he was a highly competent life assurance man. He translated the works of one or other of the German philosophers who were in vogue amongst Victorians. He seems to have been rather a pompous person or perhaps only awe-inspiring.

The Constitution and Laws prepared by the Committee appointed on 4th January 1856 were adopted at a general meeting of the newly-constituted Faculty held at 45 George Street on 20th March, at which Thomson was again Chairman. The rates of subscription were fixed and the Council appointed for the ensuing year. "The Manager, Actuary or Secretary of any Scottish Life Assurance Institution at its principal establishment and any professional Actuary practising in Scotland" were originally eligible for Fellowship subject to election. Provision was made for Non-resident Members—persons not resident in Scotland, but connected with a Scottish Life Assurance Institution—and for the election by unanimous recommendation of the Council as Fellows or Honorary Fellows of "Gentlemen . . . who may be distinguished by scientific acquirements in subjects connected with the objects of the Faculty or who

JAMES MEIKLE
"the guiding spirit of the Actuarial Society of Edinburgh"

may have rendered important service in promoting these objects . . . " Persons not originally eligible as Fellows might apply before 31st May 1856 for admission to the class of Associates and if in the opinion of the Council their official position or previous education were suitable, their names might be submitted for ballot at the next Quarterly Meeting. Arrangements were made for admission of matriculated students, subject to passing a preliminary examination, and for their admission as Associates on passing two examinations and attending classes and lectures conducted by the Faculty. Associates were eligible for election as Fellows after a period of not less than one year.

The founders of the Faculty had as their principal objects the formation of an association of practising actuaries and the promotion of a satisfactory school of actuarial study and, with a view to forwarding these ideas, the newly-appointed Council met frequently. The first meeting of Council was held at 21 St. Andrew Square on 26th March 1856 and James Borthwick was appointed Chairman for the year. W. T. Thomson and Archibald Borthwick were appointed to confer with Sang regarding examinations, a Library Committee was formed— W. T. Thomson, Convener, with Sang, Chisholm, W. Smith and W. Wood—the question of accommodation for General and Special Meetings of the Faculty was considered and the form of a request for contributions to the funds to be addressed to the Scottish Life Offices was arranged. At a subsequent meeting (23rd July) it was reported that £115 10s. had been received from the Offices. Sang had agreed to give a course of four actuarial lectures and the first examiners were appointed—W. T. Thomson,

A. Borthwick, J. M. McCandlish and E. Sang. Progress was being made in the educational sphere and at a meeting of Council on 21st October it was reported that George Ross, Advocate, had agreed to give a series of law lectures.

The law lectures were on the subject of life assurance law and Mr. Ross received a " piece of plate " as a token of appreciation. Sang's first four lectures were open to the general public as well as to members and students of the Faculty at a fee of 10s. 6d. for the course. These lectures were delivered early in 1857 and it may be of interest to note the subjects chosen :—

1. Outline of the History of Assurance against Casualties. Rise and progress of Tontines, Benefit Societies, Sick Societies and Assurance Associations in General.
2. The Commercial, Moral and Social Influences of Assurances—the applicability of the principle in different circumstances.
3. The History of Unsound and Fraudulent Schemes, and the Characteristics which distinguish them.
4. The data on which the Calculations are founded. Mortality Registers.
Effects of different Rates of Interest and different Mortality Tables, in framing tables of Rates and in making Valuations.

In later years there appeared recurring criticism of the admission of Fellows and Associates by virtue of their official position and without examination. Of course it was inevitable that there should be an arrangement of this nature at the beginning otherwise it is difficult to see how the Faculty would have been started at all. There is always theoretical trouble about originating anything, analogous to the time-honoured problem of priority between the hen and the egg ! It may well be that some of the gentlemen who were admitted on the basis of their professional achievements would have experienced difficulty in passing the examinations ; but, if it is " by their fruits ye shall know them," then the tradition they built up and the institutions they founded and guided point to the conclusion that these early actuaries were generally highly competent practising actuaries and worthy members of our profession. That the rules as to the admission of these Fellows and Associates were rigidly and carefully applied is clear from the Council Minutes ; at a meeting as early as 13th June 1856, out of fourteen applications for admission as Associates only four were regarded as suitable to go forward for ballot at the ensuing Quarterly General Meeting.

A library was being assembled, partly by purchase, but largely in the beginning by presentation. One list of volumes presented is given in the Council Minutes of 23rd July 1856. One of the books was " Dublin Problems " ; one wonders what the problems were ? Dublin has not infrequently been a fruitful source of problems, but my impression has always been that the people of that charming City cherish a preference for solving them by methods more violent than normally come within the scope of actuarial practice. I was delighted to see also from the same list that thus early we had a copy of Quetelet's " Theory of Probabilities." The volume will recall to survivors of the students of my vintage Mr. McLachlan who was Assistant Secretary and Librarian of the Faculty in my early days and who recommended us all to read Quetelet. McLachlan was a delightful, a quite charming man of the old school, who took a rather paternal interest in the young men and deserves to be remembered for the willing help he gave them and his unfailing kindness and courtesy. I do not number his suggestion to read Quetelet as one of his outstanding benevolences, however ; he had never aspired to become a member of our profession and it is only charitable to assume that he had not himself dipped into the volume of which he was such an enthusiastic propagandist.

The meeting of Council of 9th January 1857 was notable ; the result of the first examination of candidates for admission to the class of matriculated students was reported. The examination covered the usual ground of general education and it was particularly stipulated that the candidates were " to give in written answers before leaving the room and without receiving assistance of any kind." The most successful student was Ebenezer Erskine Scott (son of one of the original Fellows who was the author of the well-known tables of five-figure logarithms); he passed his second examination in 1857 and his final in 1860, being admitted Associate in that year. Since he did not enter the class of Fellow until 1869 (there were, and are for that matter, no obstacles in the way of examinations between the classes of Associate and Fellow), he was not the first to become a Fellow by examination. D. Barron, W. F. Birkmyre and Andrew H. Turnbull shared the honour, becoming Fellows together in 1862. The meeting of 9th January 1857 was, however, important for another reason, for thus early the question of a Royal Charter was mooted and it was remitted to A. Borthwick, W. T. Thomson and G. A. Esson to enquire into the steps necessary to obtain a Charter of Incorporation.

In February 1858 it was decided to proceed with the project; the cost had been estimated as between £200 and £250 and the funds of the infant institution were much below the amount required. However, the Council decided that the balance of the cost " be gradually liquidated out of future revenue."

At the Council Meeting in October 1856, it had been suggested that a home for the Faculty might be found at 23 St. Andrew Square—the Faculty's present address—but the project fell through and it was reported in February 1857 that premises had been leased at 45 George Street at an annual rental of £15. It was after seventy-five years that the move was made to a new building at 23 St. Andrew Square; but it is quite an interesting coincidence that after touring about to various addresses in George Street, York Place and Queen Street we should have returned to what was apparently our first love. At 45 George Street there was accommodation for the new library and a large hall for meetings, lectures, classes and so on. The address is well known to the citizens of Edinburgh and to many others in remote parts of the world as that of the premises occupied for so many years by the famous Scottish publishers, Messrs. William Blackwood & Sons, and as the home of Blackwood's Magazine. The new rooms appear to have been reasonably satisfactory as a beginning and enabled the Council to put into effect new plans for a more vigorous prosecution of its educational projects. A review of the progress during the first three years showed gratifying results from this point of view, but it was felt that much might be accomplished by the formation of " a voluntary association having some connection with the Faculty but not incorporated with it, which might meet at regular intervals when papers might be read . . . " In January 1859 the Council were informed by James Meikle of the founding of the Actuarial Society of Edinburgh and the Society was granted the use of the Faculty's Hall and expenses were to be defrayed by the senior body. W. T. Thomson is credited by Deuchar with having suggested the formation of the Society, and in the event he was its first President.

In the light of subsequent occurrences, the idea of founding a Society, separately from the Faculty itself, for the purpose of hearing scientific contributions and for discussion may seem to have been misconceived ; but the step was probably judicious when it was taken. Deuchar says—" It was considered that in this junior society the younger men were more likely to be induced to try their 'prentice hands, at writing papers and engaging in discussion, than would have been the case if they had been required to make the venture in the awful presence of the managers of the companies." There can be no question whatever that in those days there was some truth in this observation, however one may smile at the phrase—" awful presence of the managers." I have had the advantage of discussing this subject with an actuary whose memory goes back a long time —much further than my own—and he considers that, although a change seemed to occur after the first world war, the managers of the old school were very sensible of their dignity. It appears certainly to be true that the younger men stood in awe of their official superiors in those days and it may be that the superiors entertained certain feelings of nervousness or hesitation in entering upon technical discussions with their juniors. After all, the latter had received specific mathematical and scientific training to some extent, and the same could not be said of the original actuaries or even of all their immediate successors. Dignity is not of course a bad thing; it is when it degenerates into pomposity that it becomes objectionable and one gathers that not all the early actuaries escaped the charge of being pompous. However this may be, there seems to have been a gulf fixed between the juniors and the seniors—a mutual shyness, it may be, that was difficult to overcome. Writing of the art of leadership, André Maurois says of the leader— " He must be reserved, even to the point of shrouding himself in mystery. I would not criticize him for fostering a legend." Perhaps the early actuaries subscribed to this proposition; but it has always appeared to me to be slightly Machiavellian and rather silly. One would require to take oneself very seriously indeed to set out in the morning with the intention of shrouding oneself in mystery! The establishment of the Actuarial Society of Edinburgh, whatever the ostensible reason for its superficial separation from the Faculty, was certainly justified by results, for the young men took charge from the first and when, over forty years later, the Society was wound up and its functions were taken over by the senior body itself, complaints of the overbearing manner of some of the seniors were now and then to be heard. All the actuaries in positions of influence to-day have gone through the mill, have added experience to their technical equipment, and in the most theoretical discussion should be worthy of a respectful hearing; but I can myself remember the day when this could hardly be said and when some reverend senior would fulfil his self-imposed task of making a speech at a meeting by explaining with great impressiveness, but a calculated lack of precision, an elementary point "for the benefit of students."

James Meikle was the guiding spirit of the Society in its early years and it and the Faculty were the objects of his fundamental loyalty. He wrote the first paper for the Society and some forty-one years later wrote the last. Meikle was an extremely interesting character; he entered the service of the Scottish Provident Institution at the age of 14 and retired after no less than sixty-three years of service. It might be said of him, as it was of another, that he was of a " diffident but not of a retiring disposition " ! Naturally I shall have more to say of Meikle in the course of this narrative for he was a tremendous worker and became President of the Faculty, having occupied at various times the posts of Examiner, Librarian and Secretary. He was accorded the richly deserved honour of the Presidency of the Actuarial Society on a number of occasions and apart from the two I have mentioned (the first and last contributions to its *Transactions*) he made many other contributions. He was a great help to the young men of his time and was particularly noted for his lucid expositions of actuarial theory. He set himself and others a high— a very high—standard of accuracy and was credited with the remark " Large numbers do not appal me." Essentially a man of great kindness of heart, in his later years of service he withdrew himself and was rarely seen even by his official colleagues, one of whom assures me that the person who saw him most frequently was the office cashier who entered his room on official business once a month ! He was seventy-seven years of age when finally he retired ; he dressed always in a frock coat and tall hat and in the end he left the office very quietly and without ceremony, except that when for the last time he left the building where he had worked so long, he was seen to turn to face it, raise his hat and make a deep bow before passing on his way to his home.

One may say that by 1859—only three years after its foundation—most of the normal activities of the Faculty as we know it to-day were in full swing; surely a wonderful achievement. The junior and affiliated body—the Actuarial Society—gave facilities for original research and for discussion and kept an eye upon the interests of students and the younger men. In February of that year a course of study was prepared by Sang for the members of the Society and some years later its representatives recommended to the Council of the Faculty a revision of the syllabus of examinations on the ground that the subjects should be more clearly defined. When in 1860 the Council agreed to defray the expense of printing Meikle's paper on " The Rationale of Life Assurance Premiums," the *Transactions* were under weigh. Prizes were offered by the Faculty from time to time to encourage original work and the number of students who presented themselves for examination showed a gratifying yearly increase.

The Faculty was officially represented at an International Statistical Congress in London in 1860 and in 1863 it played a part in a Social Science Congress in Edinburgh. It may be that a practical appreciation of the actual nature of the former event is indicated by the fact that it is minuted under the heading " Statistical Society Dinner "; but the minute does go on to refer to official representation at the Congress ! During those years also an investigation into the mortality experience of the life offices was carried out jointly with the Institute.

The Founders must have been content indeed; the initial success of their scheme justified beyond the possibility of argument the wisdom of the course they had adopted and one may surmise that the remarkable progress achieved far exceeded their most sanguine expectations. There were far more actuarial students in Scotland than there would have been had there been no Faculty and there was an up-and-coming school of research and study which would not have existed without it. But the idea persisted that the Scottish actuaries should not live alone and in 1864 an amalgamation was proposed by certain members of the Institute of Actuaries—perhaps they may have felt that the words " of Great Britain " in the title of their Body laid a duty upon them to promote the idea. The matter had been brought to the notice of Thomson when on a visit to London and in the following year a conference was held there at which the matter was discussed. Relations were naturally cordial and the Institute made certain alterations in its Constitution and Laws presumably with the view of facilitating the union. One trusts that these changes were desirable in themselves, because, of course, the union did not take place; in 1867 the Faculty decided finally that junction with the Institute was undesirable, " but that, so far as is consistent with its independent existence as a professional body, the Faculty endeavour to co-operate with the Institute on matters of common interest, such for instance as the investigation now being made into the mortality experience of the British Life Offices." The parties decided not to remarry; there was to be no triumph of hope over experience ! Although for some reason that is more than difficult to follow, the original secession is even to-day referred to as an "unhappy event," this is the last occasion upon which an amalgamation of the two bodies has been officially and seriously considered and I may perhaps be permitted to express the hope that the *status quo* will persist for a very long time indeed. The secession was not an "unhappy event"; it was inevitable and it was the soundest of common sense. We of the Faculty, and our English friends with us, should rejoice that it occurred and that it laid the foundation of an institution in which we take a deep pride—a pride which all our friends will understand and respect.

Since the occasion to which I have just referred, suggestions have from time to time been made as to joint examinations—of course in the utmost good faith; but, with the best will in the world, any such arrangements must inevitably undermine the independence of the Faculty and in time involve a reconsideration of the advisability of its continued existence. There are, of course, arguments for and against such an arrangement. One rather specious view is that there should be one and only one standard of qualification for actuaries in the United Kingdom and it has been held that this view is justified by the relatively small numbers in our profession. But in these days, the numbers are not so small as to lend colour to this proposition and in other professions the distinction between English and Scottish qualifications has been retained with undoubted advantage. There is no reason to expect that the tests should differ in point of severity and the conducting of examinations and the consequent fostering of study being amongst the main *raisons d'être* of the Faculty, the idea, if adopted, must unavoidably have far-reaching consequences. No matter how generous

might be the arrangements suggested by the Institute
(and those suggested when the matter was last
officially considered were very generous) time, geo-
graphy and the invincible logic of the relative size
of the two bodies must have had an irresistible
influence in placing the one in a position at once
inferior to and dependent upon the other. It must
always be carefully borne in mind that the original
conception, when the Faculty was founded, was to
promote and establish a school of actuarial study
and research in Scotland; it had been found by
experience that one United Kingdom body did not
provide this and members of the Faculty must always
keep the original ideal in the forefront and be true
to their heritage. It is only on the basis that Scottish
actuaries do their own work in their own way that
this can be achieved; there is no easy way—" There
is nothing truly valuable which can be purchased
without pains and labour." I shall have occasion to
refer to this subject again in a later chapter; there
were several eminent members of our profession—
both in England and in Scotland—who favoured the
idea, before it received full, and one trusts final,
consideration during the Presidency of Charles
Guthrie.

Meanwhile the library was growing in size and
importance, and, in 1865, the first catalogue was
printed. As illustrating the type of the collection
that was being built up, the following list of works
purchased in May 1865 is of interest :—

Macleod	*Elements of Political Economy*
„	*Theory & Practice of Banking*
Mill	*Elements of Political Economy*
Fawcett	*do.*
Senior	*do.*

McCulloch	*Metallic and Paper Money*
Goschen	*Theory of Foreign Exchange*
Bell	*Commentaries on the Law of Scotland*
„	*Arbitration*
„	*Dictionary of the Law of Scotland*
Thomson	*Bills*
Kinnear	*Bankruptcy*
Menzies	*Conveyancing*
Wallace	*Conic Sections*
Todhunter	*Co-ordinate Geometry*
Playfair	*Geometry*
Leslie	*Geometric Analysis*
De Morgan	*Differential Calculus*
Todhunter	*History of the Doctrine of Probabilities*
Sang	*Life Contingencies*

As one reads the minutes of these years, one comes across names that were to be important in the affairs of the Faculty; for instance, George M. Low and Archibald Hewat were admitted as matriculated students in 1868. An interesting fact emerges also; the Professors of Mathematics at the Scottish Universities were admitted as Honorary Fellows; this gives a foretaste of a fortunate state of affairs— the intimate and happy relation between the University of Edinburgh and the Faculty brought about by G. J. Lidstone and Sir Edmund Whittaker—which was to mature in the then rather distant future.

When one recollects the characters of the men who were chiefly in charge of its affairs it is perhaps natural that the satisfaction engendered by the efforts of the young Faculty should have taken a practical form. As early as 9th January 1857 the idea of a Royal Charter had been discussed and in 1868 the great event took place—Queen Victoria had been pleased to grant a Royal Charter of Incorporation to the Faculty of Actuaries in Scotland. There had been obstacles in the way; the Board of Trade raised objections. However, the views of that body do not seem greatly to have disturbed the Council or its Counsel. How the times have changed; who dare say " boo " to the Board these days ? On the 24th September, 1868 a letter from Messrs. Tods Murray & Jamieson, W.S., was read to the Council intimating that Her Majesty had signed the Warrant for the Charter and at a meeting on 24th October the document itself was submitted. The Faculty is, therefore, the first actuarial organisation to obtain a Royal Charter and it is appropriate that at this point this Chapter should draw to a close. Queen Victoria would hardly be expected to grant such an honour to an institution which she regarded as adolescent and this chapter is headed " Adolescence." If Her Majesty regarded the Faculty as mature, who am I to argue ? In any case, maturity is not a mere matter of years even in a human being; the great Marquis of Montrose went to the University of St. Andrews at the age of twelve and by thirteen Edward Sang knew most of the answers ! It is true, on the other hand, that there are cases where the years do not cure immaturity; a financial expert from the United States once told me that he took a poor view of some of his colleagues—no doubt men well past their youth. He remarked of them, with that passion for accuracy which is the essence of American wit,— " Their mental age is nine—or, give them a break, say eleven ! "

New laws had to be drawn up to conform with the Faculty's improved status and the initial letters F.F.A. were officially adopted for Fellows. At the same time —in the early months of 1869—the design of a Seal by a Mr. Murdoch of North Hanover Street was adopted ; it had been stipulated that the Seal should incorporate the Royal Arms of Scotland and the motto " Ad finem fidelis " and it remained in use until 1904, when alterations were deemed advisable for reasons that will appear in their place. A photograph of the original Charter is reproduced and a reprint of the full text appears for reference in Appendix VI. On 4th March 1869 the Secretary was instructed to " get a box for the Charter."

It has been possible, also, to reproduce a photograph of the first Seal and it may be remarked that, although the Seal itself has twice been changed, the motto of the Faculty has endured. Some years later than the point we have reached, W. T. Thomson, to whom the Faculty owed so much, addressed the members of the Actuarial Society of Edinburgh and concluded with these words—" I conclude with a recommendation that you will never forget the motto of the Faculty of Actuaries—which I hope may also be the motto of the Actuarial Society—*ad finem fidelis*. You could not have a more comprehensive and safer guide in life than the principle expressed in these words. Faithful in small things. Faithful in great things, ever faithful ! No tampering with principle ! No compromise with good faith ; but with all gentleness endeavouring to keep others right ; while you yourself remain faithful to the end."

And so we may pass from the period of " Adolescence " to a new chapter, which it may not be presumptuous to head " Maturity."

CHAPTER V

MATURITY—THE FIRST PHASE
1870-1914

> " Let his lack of years be no impediment to
> let him lack a reverend estimation; for I
> never knew so young a body with so old
> a head."
> —The Merchant of Venice.

THE Faculty entered upon its new era of dignity as
a Chartered Body inspired by the enthusiasm and
energy of its members; but the greater part of these
motive forces was inevitably engaged with more or
less routine matters—examinations, classes and the
like—for it was still not a large body. At this point,
there were 51 Fellows, 12 Associates, and 110
matriculated Students. Naturally, the number of
Associates was small, as the class was only an
unavoidable resting place—a kind of actuarial Pur-
gatory, from which in due time one was translated to
Fellowship. The membership of the Actuarial Society
was 114, practically all members of the Faculty,
either as Fellows, Associates or Students. The
financial position was sound, without being flourishing; Mr. Micawber would have approved, since the
economic condition laid down by that theoretically
wise gentleman as the precedent of happiness was
fulfilled—but only just. In the year I have chosen,
the income was £104 7s. 5d. and the expenditure
£97 11s. 11d. The library was an asset of value,
over £250 had been spent upon it and many important
donations had been received—there were soon more

48

The first Seal—in use until 1904

than 1200 volumes, as well as innumerable pamphlets, reports and so on. In addition there was an investment valued at some £250, so that the native caution of its original crew had steered the ship of the Faculty past the shoals and rocks and had set it upon a clear course out into the unknown sea of the future—ship-shape and Bristol fashion. For many years the journey was safe and sure rather than adventurous. There were no hurricanes or disasters; Britannia ruled the waves and the sea was placid—the merest ripple upon its calm surface was an event. On this voyage of discovery, the landfalls were pleasant rather than exciting and only gradually was new territory explored; there were new lands it is true, but they merged so gently into the old ones as to make it difficult to realise how new they were.

Not even the most partial admirer of the Faculty will deny that during the next forty years or so by far the major share of actuarial pioneer work was done in London, under the aegis of the senior body—the Institute; but for all that, much work—solid, rather than brilliant, it may be—was done in Scotland, as the *Transactions of the Actuarial Society of Edinburgh* are there to testify. From its formation in 1859 until its dissolution in 1900, when its functions were undertaken by the Faculty itself, there were read before the Society 237 papers, of which 104 were printed in its published *Transactions*. The proceedings of the Society were opened with an address by its first President, W. T. Thomson on " The Duties and Qualifications of an Actuary "; but the first published contribution was by Meikle—" The Rationale of Life Assurance Premiums "—and the last was by the same author on " The Preparation of a Table of Mortality from observations of various magnitudes." Meikle contributed no less than sixteen papers to the Society—twice the number of the next most prolific writers in its *Transactions*, David Deuchar and J. M. McCandlish—and gave an inspiring example. I do not wish to enter upon a statistical study of the work of the Society, but, according to the record and always subject to the possibility (probability, if you wish) of an arithmetical indiscretion on my part, it seems that Edward Sang was placed fourth with seven papers. W. T. Thomson gave only three papers—two upon the " Study of Statistical Science "—and his son, S. C. Thomson who followed McCandlish and was the second President of the Faculty, gave a like number. J. J. McLauchlan, W. G. Walton and T. B. Sprague gave six each. It will be remembered that the Faculty made itself responsible for the cost of printing the Society's *Transactions* and it is amusing to note that, when Dr. T. B. Sprague gave his address as President of the Society in 1882, the Council was consulted as to the propriety of printing it " with certain peculiarities of spelling." Dr. Sprague had suggested, presumably by way of compromise, that ordinary spelling be used, " but that such letters as appeared to him to be superfluous should be printed in italic or some other distinctive type " and, although the minutes make it clear that the Council was not disposed to interfere in the matter, this latter idea was adopted. The paper appears with a surprisingly large proportion of italic letters.

There was a good number of contributions of a theoretical nature on mathematical subjects, statistical science and on the theory of probability. In 1891 Professor Chrystal gave a paper entitled " Some considerations regarding the Fundamental Principles in the Theory of Probabilities " and in 1892 Dr. T. B. Sprague made a rejoinder to some extent when he wrote on " Probability and Chance, and their connection with the Business of Insurance." He expressed the opinion that " The business of insurance has little or nothing to do with the mathematical calculation of chances." Of course, we can't have that ; it would take the fun out of actuarial science altogether ! It would remove the pleasant aroma of witchcraft from our work and make our most abstruse calculations into a mere matter of arithmetic and that would never do ! Professor Chrystal was followed in the Chair of Mathematics in Edinburgh by Professor (now Sir Edmund) Whittaker and he and his distinguished successor, Professor Aitken, who at present occupies the Chair, have both contributed valuable and interesting papers on the subject of probability to the *Transactions* of the Faculty. There are certain difficulties as to the foundations of the edifice of the Theory of Probability whenever that theory is applied to practical affairs and perhaps it may not be too much to say that these are not entirely resolved at this day. Many probably feel when thinking of the matter—as Alice did regarding a famous poem—" Somehow it seems to fill my head with ideas—only I don't exactly know what they are " ! So long as this happy state of uncertainty remains, the Faculty may, one trusts, look for contributions on the subject from the mathematical Professors of Edinburgh ; anyway Dr. Sprague did not succeed in " debunking " actuarial science ; or, if he did, no one has noticed.

The Actuarial Society was fortunate in receiving contributions from George King, the author, as all actuaries know, of the first text-book on life contingencies, and from Sir George Hardy of the Institute ;

the former gave four papers, the latter only one. One of King's papers, called "The Theory of Finance," was published in book form and used by students up to my own day as a foundation for the study of compound interest. What a debt actuaries the world over owe to George King for his magnificent work on life contingencies! New matter has had to be recorded and naturally new authors have been required; but the original text-book remains unrivalled—a monument to its author's memory. Surely his name will always have an honoured place in actuarial tradition.

It would be interesting to write at length about the papers included in the *Transactions* of the Actuarial Society, many of which are important. The paper " On the calculation of the Values of the Pecuniary Interests of Heirs of Entail (Scotland) " by H. R. Cockburn and R. Murrie and some writings on fertility statistics—" On the Relative Ages of Husbands and Wives whose marriages are fruitful " by J. Chatham, for instance—were consulted in my active days and may be still for all I know. It is, however, out of the question to spend more time and space on the subject here; but perhaps it will appear from what has been said already that up to the end of the nineteenth century much valuable work was done in Scotland by the Faculty and its subsidiary Society in the way of original research and that the boundaries of knowledge in actuarial science were extended by its Fellows. I cannot forbear from mentioning one paper by Dr. T. B. Sprague however; the title was " Remarks on the Exercise of Independent Thought by the Head of an Office and his Subordinates " and, when one considers the personality of the author, it is certainly intriguing. For it has been said to me

Bust of THOMAS BOND SPRAGUE, LL.D.
(President of the Institute of Actuaries 1882-86 and of the Faculty 1894-96)
in the Hall of the Faculty

that Sprague was a terror and probably his " Subordinates " were not accustomed to feeling fancy
free in his presence!

Reading through Council Minutes one is inevitably
impressed with the brief appearance upon the stage
of the various figures. W. T. Thomson, so active in
his day, retired in due course and his name passes
from the record. He and his son, S. C. Thomson,
were together prominent in the Faculty's affairs for a
number of years and when the father died in 1883 a
long appreciation of his services and character
appeared in the Minutes. S. C. Thomson became the
second President and did much work for the Faculty
in the various offices he held, being President of the
Actuarial Society on three occasions. He was a man
of energy in a variety of fields ; but he was not the
man his father had been. For real solid work and
devotion to the Faculty, no one in those early days
stands before Meikle ; but gradually other names
occur and we find T. B. Sprague, who came from
the Institute and was elected a Fellow in 1874 in
virtue of his office and high achievement and to the
Council in 1877, playing an important part. He
celebrated his appointment as Fellow by making a
most liberal presentation of books to the library.
Having done my best to study the influence upon its
affairs of the members of the Faculty during its long
history, I have come to the conclusion that four men
stand out head and shoulders above the rest, and
these are William Thomas Thomson, James Meikle,
Thomas Bond Sprague and George James Lidstone
—two of them being immigrants from the south.
They were all great actuaries ; as to whether they
were great men must be a matter of opinion. As
Hazlitt puts it, " Greatness is great power, producing

great effects " and " The test of greatness is the page
of history." The name of an important politician
may reach the page of history and so be remembered
for a time at least, either as a benefactor, scoundrel,
charlatan or mere careerist; but this may be due
rather to the public nature of his occupation than to
any character of greatness in the man himself. Sir
Winston Churchill is a great man; he has brought
great talents and an overwhelming character to bear
upon the affairs of the nation—nay, of the world—
with tremendous effect for the benefit of mankind;
but " the finest chess player is not a great man, for he
leaves the world very much as he found it." Probably
George Lansbury was a great man—time will tell—
for who can estimate the ultimate effect of his
transparent virtue ? Caligula was not a great man;
he was a dangerous fool in an important position;
but his name has certainly reached the page of history.
It is all rather difficult and probably the names of the
actuaries I have mentioned will be remembered only
in the rather circumscribed field in which they
exercised their talents; let us be content to repeat
that they were great actuaries and that their influence
upon the Faculty was important and beneficent.

I shall have occasion to write of Lidstone in a later
chapter and I have already referred at some length
to Thomson and Meikle. The latter was the subject
of a minute of Council in 1870, which recorded the
work he had done in connection with the investigation
into the mortality of the Scottish Offices—" The
whole practical working " was done by him—and
acknowledged the debt of gratitude which the
profession owed to him. In 1889, one student did
so well in the first examination, that the question of
passing him " with distinction " arose at a meeting

of Council; the suggestion was quite a new one, for no one had before had honourable mention in the published list of successful candidates. It must have been a proud moment for Meikle when he was asked temporarily to leave the meeting that the discussion might proceed, for the distinguished student was his son, Henry Meikle, who later became Actuary to the Government of India. James Meikle was President from 1896 to 1898 and President of the Actuarial Society in 1869, 1875, 1884, and 1899.

Thomas Bond Sprague was impressive both in character and in appearance. He was strongly built, of medium height and his blue-grey eyes had an unusually penetrating quality. His aspect, with beard and rather heavy eyebrows, was one of rugged strength, as can be seen from the photograph produced here of the bust which stands, with that of W. T. Thomson, on the platform in the Faculty Hall. Surprisingly, for one might have expected the words to boom out from such a countenance, his voice was rather weak, but pleasant. He was a man of over-whelming energy and of a domineering temper one suspects; it has been said of him that he was a martinet, but scrupulously fair. From a long memoir by George King in the Journal of the Institute one may quote :—" It must be admitted, however, that he was sometimes rugged, and a little aggressive and not always easy to get on with; and his earnestness led him on rare occasions to be perhaps over-vehement in his expressions. He had no thought of being personally discourteous or of hurting the susceptibilities of those to whom he was for the moment in opposition. The opinions were attacked and not the persons." Sprague was called to the Bar as a young man and retained a keen interest in the law throughout his active life ; but feeling, it is said, that the legal profession did not yield scope for his mathematical talent (he had been Senior Wrangler) he withdrew and took up, fortunately, the profession of actuary. King says "During his long connection with the Institute of Actuaries he was to a large extent its guiding spirit . . . " He was President of the Institute from 1882 to 1886 and of the Faculty from 1894 to 1896; the only man who has held both these important positions and therefore doubly head of his profession in his day. As a tribute to his energy it should be mentioned that, whilst President of the Institute, he was actually resident in Edinburgh and was (1882) President of the Actuarial Society of Edinburgh. He was President of the Society on three occasions, 1874, 1882, and 1891. In due course his son, Dr. A. E. Sprague, became President of the Faculty and here again we have a record, for this is the only case of father and son occupying the position, although the Thomsons would have achieved it had the office of President of the Faculty been instituted in the days of the elder. It is I think a pity that mention of T. B. Sprague to-day evokes first a smile and a reference to his fad about phonetic spelling ; second thoughts no doubt occur, but they should be first thoughts, for his writings were many and his services to his profession stupendous. The controversy between Sprague and W. S. B. Woolhouse too is always remembered and no doubt it was fun in its day ; but quite unworthy of the protagonists—at least of Sprague. It was concerned with the relative merits of the summation and graphic methods of graduation ; the one, as all know, a process of averaging rough data to achieve smoothness and the other of drawing a freehand curve through them.

They elaborated their methods with great detail and defended them with vehemence ; but it was a storm in a teacup. Both methods are useful in their place and are used to-day ; but there is no great magic or philosophical content in either of them. These little foibles of Sprague—the silly (as I think) fad and the elementary argument—will be forgotten ; but the reputation of so great an actuary will endure with actuarial science.

I have heard stories of him in his office and in his private life and certainly life under T. B. Sprague cannot have been very easy ; even for his day, when generally the heads of offices were not very approachable, he seems to have been rather a terror and one wonders if he had any sense of humour, for overweening self-importance can hardly exist along with it. But in one who was so completely master of his trade and whose abilities were in many ways superlative, some little arrogance may be more readily forgiven than when shown by those who pretend to a knowledge and an ability which are in fact transparently absent. In the records of the Faculty this class does not lack representatives. Perhaps Sprague's sense of humour was there in embryo at least, for on one occasion when he had surprised some young men rolling pennies on the Board Room table, he administered the necessary and expected reprimand and remarked as he left the room " And now, Mr. A., you may come out from under the table." This reminds me of the story of an occasion when an officious person in his office reported to S. C. Thomson (a man of liberal views if ever there was one and Sprague's contemporary, but far from being his peer) that one of the apprentices had been found drinking the Directors' sherry ; Thomson's only comment

was " And didn't he leave any for you, Mr. B. ? "
Sprague received the degree of LL.D. of Aberdeen
University in 1893.

John MacGregor McCandlish was a lawyer, a
Writer to the Signet, prior to his appointment in
1846 to the position of Secretary of the Scottish
National. He became Manager of that Office in 1853,
General Manager of the Scottish Union and National
in 1878 and retired in 1890. As has been said, he was
the first President of the Faculty ; but he was noted
in his day as an " insurance man " rather than as an
actuary. The honour of being the first to occupy
the position of President fell to him rather as a fortunate
accident than as the reward of any particular actuarial
achievement, for his turn happened to come when
the office was instituted. He was one of the first
Honorary Secretaries of the Faculty and he lectured,
it is said, extensively on insurance subjects. Perhaps
he was a colourful individual ; but if he was, the
colour has faded and I have found it impossible to
ascertain very clearly what it was. When, in 1878,
he resigned from the position of Honorary Secretary,
he wrote the following letter, which seems to me to
convey a picture of an individual, courteous, conscientious and probably kindly :—

Edinburgh, 16th January 1878

Gentlemen,

I have to request that in filling up the several
appointments in the Faculty of Actuaries at the
approaching Meeting, you will have the kindness to
elect some other member than myself to be your
Honorary Secretary. I have had the honour of holding
that office since the establishment of the Faculty
about twenty-two years ago, an honour which I have
always very highly appreciated, and it is more than
time that in the interests of the Faculty some change
should take place and that you should have an

opportunity of bestowing this honour on some more worthy member.

The duties of the Office, never very arduous, have been for some years almost nominal, owing to the good service rendered by successive Acting Secretaries. I rejoice in the prosperity of the Faculty and shall continue to feel an unabated interest in its welfare, and to be ready to render it any service in my power.

I beg to thank you very heartily for having so often re-elected me to this office and for the kindness and forbearance I have experienced at the hands of the Council and the other Members, while endeavouring to discharge its duties.

I have the honour to be, Gentlemen,
Your most obedient servant,
John M. McCandlish.

He was elected to the Presidency of the Actuarial Society on no fewer than seven occasions.

Other prominent personalities in this phase of the Faculty's existence were A. H. Turnbull, D. Deuchar, G. M. Low, J. J. McLauchlan, N. B. Gunn, A. Hewat and James Chatham. Turnbull was one of the three who were the first to become Fellows by examination and he was the third to hold the office of President. He was a Borderer—a native of Jedburgh—and even as a youth was outstanding. He was distinguished indeed as a business man and life office manager—he was Manager of the Scottish Widows ; but it would hardly be true to regard him as a distinguished actuary. He followed in the older tradition—although, as has been said, he went through the examinations— but he rendered valuable service to the Faculty. As the reproduction here of his portrait by Sir George Reid, P.R.S.A., shows, he was of an impressive presence and one who was closely associated with him in business has remarked that he held the respect of his staff, but hardly their affection. My informant was present when he gave his address as President of the Actuarial Society in 1900 and still recalls his commanding appearance as he stood, in evening dress, upon the platform of the then Faculty Hall at 24 George Street—now ,with little alteration, the Lecture Hall of the Royal Society of Edinburgh. Turnbull was of simple and austere habits ; normally his lunch, taken at his desk, consisted of a glass of sherry and a piece of dry toast.

G. M. Low, a Fellow by examination—he passed the final in 1871—was also in the old tradition ; he was primarily a business man and, after holding the Managership of the Edinburgh, followed T. B. Sprague as Manager of the Scottish Equitable. Although like Turnbull and others he repaid the debt he owed to the Faculty by serving it in various capacities, he did not do so by original actuarial research. He was the only man to occupy the Presidential Chair on two occasions (1900-1903 and 1915-1919) and his second term was unusually protracted owing to the First World War. He was far-seeing, cautious and immaculate in work ; he has been quoted as remarking —" I cannot understand anyone making a mistake." This is a curious view for a man of experience to take and indicates a certain lack of imagination ; if he got through life without making any mistake he was certainly singular. I tend to subscribe to the view that a man " who never made a mistake, never made anything " and although, as I have indicated, he was a highly successful business man, we are not in his debt as having " made anything " for actuarial science. In the ordinary way, it appears that he did not allow people to know him ; he was dignified to a degree and gave the superficial impression at least of aloofness. One who, as a very young junior, came in occasional contact with him, found him kindly however, and

JOHN MACGREGOR M'CANDLISH
first President (1887-90)

ANDREW HUGH TURNBULL

President, 1892-94

another, who knew him more intimately, has exemplified his cautious attitude to life by giving as an illustration of the kind of remark he would make— " I rather think, and if I am not mistaken, the day will turn out fine " ! Low wrote an article on Annuities for one of the editions of the Encyclopaedia Britannica and was twice President of the Actuarial Society.

David Deuchar, President 1898-1900, and N. B. Gunn, President 1903-1906, were both primarily business men ; but it seems that neither had the personality or sheer business capacity of men like Turnbull and Low. Deuchar wrote a very useful essay on the early actuarial societies to which I am indebted. It would not be fair to run the risk of underestimating him, for, although a doubt has been expressed to me as to his claim to any high competence, a published assessment says of him that he " was a many-sided man of versatile mind and high capacity accustomed to receive with great urbanity the officials who had to consult him " and at the time of his death a publication called " Business " referred to him and said—" A Scotch Actuary is a cross-grained man as a rule ; but David Deuchar lived on the sunny side of the edge. At any rate he was a pleasant actuary to meet not once but often." Deuchar became a Fellow in 1865. The rather uncomplimentary reference to a " Scotch Actuary " reminds one of a definition of the word " actuary " due to a prominent citizen of the United States of America toward the beginning of the present century. There had been an influx of Scottish actuaries and that they had retained an element at least of the older tradition one may surmise from this person's reply when asked what an actuary was—" A Scotsman with some mathematics and a strong business sense " ! Gunn was of impressive appearance and is credited with having had plenty of *savoir faire* ; he had a wide range of business and other interests and held important office in Free St. George's Church (now St. George's West) during the distinguished ministry of Dr. Alexander Whyte.

Archibald Hewat, although like many of his contemporaries in Scotland not in any profound sense an actuarial originator, was more of a technician than many. He was genuinely devoted to the Faculty and was indefatigable in its service. Apart from the important position to which he attained in the life assurance world, he was distinguished as a practising actuary and dealt extensively with the most important widows' funds, friendly societies and kindred bodies. He was the son of an Edinburgh citizen, John Hewat, known to his intimates as " Time-Gun Hewat." This has rather a wild-west flavour (Two-Gun Tony, the Terror of Bloody Gulch !) ; but there was nothing sinister about John Hewat, who was a highly respectable and widely respected person. It appears that the introduction of the " one o'clock gun " in Edinburgh was largely due to his initiative. On a visit to Paris, his attention had been attracted by the time-gun there, which was fired by the action of the sun's rays through the medium of a burning-glass. Although there had been a visual signal at one o'clock in Edinburgh for some time, on Calton Hill, Hewat felt that with the spreading of the City it no longer served its purpose and urged a time-gun in addition to be fired by electricity, since the climate of our northern Capital renders hardly feasible a scheme of setting one's watch by the sun's rays. Both the visual and aural signals are in operation to this day, but with the greatly increased area and population of the

City they serve a comparatively small proportion of its inhabitants; I wonder what John Hewat, were he here, would suggest now? Archibald Hewat was a generous and respected man and a highly popular President from 1906 to 1908; he took a proper pride in occupying the Chair and was sensible of the dignity of the office. He presented to the Faculty the presidential badge of office, consisting of a massive gold medallion with the crest engraved thereon. This badge remains a permanent memorial of one of the Faculty's most devoted Fellows and when, as I shall describe in its place, the Faculty acquired a new Coat of Arms involving naturally a new seal, Archibald Hewat's son, Dr. Fergus Hewat, a distinguished Edinburgh physician, requested and received permission from the Faculty to have the medallion engraved afresh with the new design at his own charge. He felt, he has said, that his father would have liked him to do this.

J. J. McLauchlan and James Chatham were very much actuaries in the modern manner and were more abreast of the actuarial times than many of their contemporaries. The former followed Hewat as President and has left in the *Transactions* memorials of his industry and originality. He was regarded by all who knew him with admiration and respect; he was a kindly and friendly man. He was a son of the Manse; his father was the first minister of the Gaelic Church in Edinburgh and later, in 1876, became the Moderator of the General Assembly of the Free Church of Scotland. Never of robust health, J. J. McLauchlan yet gave ample evidence of his undoubted ability and mental energy and was Secretary of the Scottish Equitable for no less than twenty-eight years, where he served under first Sprague and then Low.

It has been said of James Chatham that he was a friendly man and invariably appreciative of good work in his juniors ; he was himself a tireless worker and studied all new actuarial developments. The first distinguished tutor produced by the Faculty itself, in 1890 he received permission to use the Faculty's rooms " for four or five mornings a week " (not much rest for the students or himself !) for the purpose of tuition. In 1891 he was appointed to give a course of lectures, which were to be free to members and students of the Faculty and to members of the Actuarial Society of Edinburgh. He was given a fee of twenty guineas for the course and the subjects dealt with were as follows :—

1. Mortality Tables and Experiences.
2. Life Assurance Finance and Practice.
3. Friendly Societies and Widows' Funds.
4. Law of Life Assurance.

A comprehensive course indeed ! Chatham was an authority on life office book-keeping and was probably instrumental in introducing the addressograph into general use amongst the life offices ; but he did important work also in the more strictly actuarial and statistical fields. Some say that he tended to believe what he wanted to believe—a tendency to prejudge the issue and stick to his first opinion I suppose—and this is a serious fault in an actuary or statistician. Chatham could apparently be difficult on occasion ; he had a controversy which caused some little stir at the time with one of the Editors of the *Transactions*, in which he certainly appears to have been rather unreasonable and even anxious to deal direct with the printers and leave the editor out altogether ! However this may be, he was an important figure in the actuarial circles of his day and did a great deal of work for the Faculty, particularly for the younger men. It was unfortunate that one who had served so faithfully should never have attained the Presidential Chair. Owing to the state of his health he found it necessary to retire from affairs at the early age of 55 in the year 1912. James Chatham died as recently as 1934.

Whatever may be said as regards the Victorian Era generally and particularly the later years of the nineteenth century, when people's minds were being upset by disturbing philosophies and tiresome scientific theories and discoveries, the phase of the Faculty's existence which I am attempting to describe in this chapter was an age of actuarial faith. A study of the period, more particularly of the earlier years, shows, it seems to me, a naive belief in the efficacy of figures ; upon the most meagre data it was not uncommon to build an astounding edifice of arithmetic. Everything was calculated in great detail and attention was paid to accuracy even in the third decimal place. The result of this was on occasion to give an air of verisimilitude to calculations based upon the slenderest statistical foundations, for the data were obliterated by a mass of figures so imposing as to banish all doubts ! But actuaries have always been practical statisticians and have ever had an eye to the financial uses to which the results of their work are to be applied ; they are statisticians, but also business men and, however nice might be the calculations, the men of that time did not forget to apply at the end an ample margin for contingencies when a contract was to be made ! In the early years of this century, I myself played a part (a very minor one, it is true) in performing these elaborate arithmetical feats and I can remember feeling a certain chagrin when my official superior would add a margin of 25 % or 33⅓%

(his two favourites) to the figure I had ascertained with infinite pains. It was the custom for a certain reversionary association to apply to the office in which I was employed for assistance in calculating the premiums required to cover the most complicated risks and I am proud to say that neither my blind use of formulae of approximate integration nor the light-hearted efforts of my immediate superior, whose duty it was to check my work (usually after an exhilarating lunch, for "food" was cheap in those days!) apparently did any harm to the company, which is flourishing to-day. I think that in those days there were many more complicated risks for the actuary to consider than arose in my everyday experience in later years; but, generally speaking, the actuaries were undaunted. I have heard, however, of one case where an actuary of that time confessed himself defeated. A person who wished to assure with his office, belonged to a religious sect in which the view was held that, as an alternative to the normal method of leaving this world, one might be "translated" to a higher sphere and he, not unnaturally, wanted his policy payable on "death or translation"; the actuary could not calculate the premium and handed the matter over to the Chairman (a wise old man) who solemnly assured the Board that he felt that the risk "was one they might reasonably undertake without extra charge."

The actuaries of those days did a great deal of work in connection with widows' funds, pension funds, friendly societies and the like, in addition to the duties they usually undertook in life offices. Hewat was a pioneer in constructing mortality and marriage tables from the statistics of the Scottish Banks and V. Marr (a very able man, whose early death was a serious loss to the profession in Scotland) extended his work in this connection. In time, Alexander Fraser, an important actuary of a rather later vintage, carried on this work and made the subject his own and the profession his debtor for the valuable information he gave regarding widows' funds and the tables he constructed from the Scottish Bankers' experience. McLauchlan did much pioneer work in regard to pension funds and his valuable papers upon that subject were studied by all actuarial students. These activities, in which practically all the senior actuaries in Edinburgh engaged, stimulated research and were, doubtless, greatly to the financial advantage of those concerned. But not invariably, for there is one piece of gossip from the old days which I must record for the benefit of my English friends. It appears that a well-placed Scottish actuary had completed a valuation of a friendly society or pension fund and, having collected his fee, felt under some obligation to the young Fellow who had assisted him. He discharged the obligation, I trust to his own satisfaction at least, by sending to his junior a really magnificent parcel of grapes !

Very early, it was decided to invite the Professors of Mathematics of the Scottish Universities to become Honorary Fellows of the Faculty. The first to be appointed was Professor Kelland of Edinburgh and shortly afterwards the Professors at St. Andrews, Glasgow and Aberdeen were received into the fold. Professor Kelland for a number of years advised the Council regarding the mathematical portions of the examinations and latterly set the questions himself. Unfortunately Professor Kelland died in 1879, and although the work for that year was carried out by his assistant, the practice lapsed. However, as will appear in the following chapter, the co-operation of the University of Edinburgh in connection with the examinations was revived many years later on a less personal but more permanent basis.

In the 1870's there was continual trouble about accommodation for the Faculty's meetings and even for Council meetings and examinations. The examinations were held in rooms provided by the life offices, and owing to the numbers involved the candidates were frequently spread over several buildings. On most occasions hospitality for the examinations was provided by the Scottish Widows', the Standard and the Scottish Provident ; but other meetings were for a long time held, under the influence of the Thomsons, in the offices of the Standard. The minutes show that in 1876 there was a proposal to obtain premises for the accommodation of the Faculty along with the Managers' Association and an Association connected with the Fire Offices and " it was agreed that, while the Faculty lay under great obligations to the Directors and Manager of the Standard Life Assurance Office for the use of their Board Room, steps should be taken to procure premises conjointly with these other bodies." A committee was appointed, but the meetings continued to be held in the Standard. In 1880, Sang, as Convener of a specially appointed Committee of the Society of Arts, requested that the Faculty send representatives to a conference of members of the educational and scientific societies with a view to securing premises in which all might be accommodated. This again fell through as did a proposal in 1886 from the accountants that the actuaries and bankers should join with them in finding rooms for a joint library. It was not until 1889 that premises

were finally secured at 24 York Place and a final
acknowledgement sent to the Standard "for the
great privileges the Faculty had enjoyed for upwards
of twenty-one years." The rent of the new rooms
was £75 per annum; £10 10s. was voted to Chatham
for arranging the correspondence and papers of the
Faculty; a dinner was held to celebrate the opening
of the new home; and on 17th February 1890 we
find a Council Meeting "held in the Hall of the
Faculty." There seems to have been some hesitation
in coming to the decision to accord a gratuity of £2 to
the housekeeper, for it is mentioned several times in
the minutes ! In 1894 it was discovered that there
had been some laxity in the supervision of the library
in the new rooms—there was much confusion and
the duty of making additions to the books seems to
have been neglected—and Meikle stepped into the
breach, as he was wont to do, and put matters in order.
He had in the previous year undertaken the task of
classifying for binding the multitude of pamphlets in
the library and one wonders where the Faculty would
have been at this period had it not been able to rely
upon his indefatigable energy and wholehearted
devotion to its interests.

The lease of these premises in York Place became
due to expire in 1896 and in 1895 we find the Standard
and the Scottish Equitable, both of which offices
were undertaking extensive rebuilding operations at
their respective headquarters, each offering to provide
in their new structures a permanent home for the
Faculty. The annual rental suggested was £100. In
1896 the Society of Accountants and the Institute of
Bankers offered a share of their premises at a rental
of £85, with other expenses estimated at £50. A
report giving the various proposals in full detail was

prepared ; but, after consideration, it was decided to renew the lease for the premises at York Place, belonging to the Sickness and Accident, for a further period of nine years at the old rental—the house-keeper's allowance being increased from £5 to £10. However, either the Faculty was restless or the premises not quite what was required, for in 1898 it was decided to lease for a period of twenty-five years from the Edinburgh at a rental of £150 premises at 24 George Street consisting of a hall, room etc. A platform was constructed in the hall for the accommodation of the President and Council at the Faculty's meetings and the decoration, bookshelves and electric lighting were each the subject of pains-taking discussion. These new premises were in a high degree satisfactory and Deuchar, then President, invited the Fellows to " cake and wine " to celebrate their acquisition.

" The best laid schemes o' mice and men gang aft agley " and in spite of the suitability of the George Street rooms, it was only seven years before the Faculty was on the move again. The Royal Society of Edinburgh wished to buy the building and the Edinburgh of which Hewat was then Manager, as well as being President of the Faculty, offered alternative accommodation in their new building, to be erected on the site adjoining that to be vacated, on what appeared to be very generous terms, which were tentatively agreed to by the Faculty. In the event, however, when the plans of the building became available, the arrangements provided for the Faculty were regarded as unsatisfactory—a trying situation for Hewat in his dual capacity. It was decided to look around again and nothing suitable immediately presenting itself, the ideas were canvassed of either asking the Scottish insurance companies to supply the funds to enable the Faculty to build a home for itself or of hiring a hall on the occasion of each meeting and seeking permanent offices only. Fortunately, towards the end of 1907, it became possible to arrange with the Scottish Education Department to lease a hall, reception room etc. at 14 Queen Street for £100 per annum. The hall was very much the same size as that which was being vacated and the lease was agreed to in March 1908. The decoration and furnishing was carried out under the advice of Sir Robert Lorimer and the cost of the removal in all its aspects came to some £350. Here at last a resting place had been found and it was not until more than twenty years had passed that a further change was found necessary.

In 1898 the Faculty presented to the National Portrait Gallery a statuette of Napier of Merchiston, who seems, one trusts justifiably, to have been regarded as our patron saint, and a similar statuette was placed in the Faculty Hall. Three years later a bust in marble of W. T. Thomson, referred to in the particular minute as the " Founder of the Faculty," was obtained. It was copied from one in the possession of the Standard by D. W. Stevenson, R.S.A. Finally, to complete the Faculty's statuary, it acquired a bust of Dr. T. B. Sprague, by Pittendrigh Macgillivray, R.S.A. and to this day and for a very long time into the future, one hopes and expects, these works of art will serve to remind successive generations of actuaries of a great mathematician and two great actuaries.

For many years the business of the Faculty was carried on by its honorary officials with a little part-time clerical assistance, but it soon became the practice to appoint one of the junior Fellows as Secretary and Librarian at a small remuneration and still with clerical assistance. Many of the Faculty's most distinguished sons held this position which persisted until new arrangements were made after the first World War. A small change in the appointments was made in 1905 when V. Marr retired from the post after very distinguished service as one gathers from a Council Minute of appreciation. It was then decided to increase the remuneration of the Secretary to 25 guineas to include the cost of clerical help and relieve him of certain duties by having a Librarian to be paid 10 guineas and to act of course under the Honorary Librarian. In connection with the payments the following remark is recorded in the minutes—" The emolument offered is to be looked upon more in the light of an honorarium than as the equivalent of the work involved in the duties of the offices ; and they, (the Council), trust that the younger members of the Faculty will be as ready in the future as in the past to undertake these appointments in view of the education and experience which can be obtained from the performance of these duties." A minute typical of the times and, it seems to me, a very sensible one ; there had been no lack of applicants for the appointments which gave some little cash and definite help in increasing the prospects of professional advancement.

However, in 1908, with increasing size and consequently business, it was found necessary to appoint a permanent official. The first idea was to obtain someone connected with the Faculty ; but this was found to be impracticable. Consequently Mr. John Forsyth was appointed Assistant Secretary and

Librarian at a salary of £80 which was later increased to £90 and to £100 in 1910, a few months before his services were dispensed with. The post was then advertised at £100 per annum, no fewer than 200 applications being received ! The appointment finally went to Mr. William McLachlan, F.E.I.S. whom I mentioned in an earlier chapter and who took up his duties in December 1910. Meanwhile, the office of Secretary was continued, with an emolument of 20 guineas, although the hope was entertained that in time the Assistant Secretary and Librarian would be able to take over most of the duties—a hope which in the long run was to be justified.

In 1873, Chisholm, Meikle and S. C. Thomson were appointed as a committee to consider the system of actuarial notation proposed by the Institute and in the following year the Council signified its agreement with the system, but suggested several alterations in the interpretation of the symbols. The notation was given a firm basis of authority when adopted generally at the first Actuarial Congress which was held in Brussels in 1895.

In 1883 the feeling which had been simmering for a good many years, in regard to the appointment of Fellows without examinations, boiled over. J. H. W Rolland of the Standard and W. A. Smith of the English and Scottish Law, who had been recommended as Fellows in virtue of holding appointments as Secretaries of insurance companies, were turned down at the General Meeting on 26th January. It was stated at the time that this was not a criticism of the individuals concerned, but of the rule admitting Secretaries, subject to election, to the Fellowship. As Dr. W. Smith, who sponsored his son, pointed out in a temperate and well-reasoned letter, it was quite indefensible to make individuals suffer for a defect in the rules. The two applicants were ultimately admitted and a modification was made in the rules to the effect that the Secretary, Actuary or Assistant Actuary of a Scottish office or a practising actuary who possessed qualifications which rendered his admission desirable might be nominated by a two-thirds majority of the Council at a special meeting of which ten clear days' notice had been given, the nomination, if adopted, to be submitted to the first General Meeting of the Faculty. To this day, of course, it is permissible to introduce to the Fellowship suitable persons possessing the required qualifications and several distinguished members of the Institute— G. J. Lidstone and Sir William Elderton, to mention only two—have been brought into the fold in this manner. In 1909 it was decided that in the published list of Fellows a mark should be placed against the names of those who had not passed the Faculty's examinations and this practice is still continued, although the danger which rendered the members apprehensive in 1883 is hardly present to the same extent in these times, when the professional qualifications which are necessarily antecedent to a nomination are so well-defined.

In 1900, during the Presidency of G. M. Low, it was decided that the Faculty itself should hold periodical meetings to discuss actuarial subjects and receive papers. At a meeting of a Joint Committee of the Faculty and the Actuarial Society held on 11th June, the Faculty was represented by the President (who took the chair), T. Wallace, Deuchar and S. C. Thomson and the Society by Meikle, J. M. Warden and W. A. Sim. It may have been a sad occasion for

Meikle, for the welfare and work of the Society seem to have been very near to his heart ; but however that may be, the following resolutions were adopted and their later acceptance sealed the fate of the Society :—

1. That the Actuarial Society of Edinburgh has rendered valuable services to its members and towards the advancement of actuarial knowledge.

2. That this has been largely due to the support and assistance given to the Society by the Faculty of Actuaries in Scotland.

3. That the original objects of the Society, in so far as these were of an educational character, are now largely met by modern facilities and methods of study.

4. That the functions now performed by the Society are largely of such a character as might suitably be undertaken by the Faculty of Actuaries as the representative body of the profession in Scotland.

5. That it is desirable that the Faculty should undertake those functions.

6. That upon this being done and sufficient provision being made for the rights and privileges of existing members, the Actuarial Society, as having fulfilled its purpose, may, without detriment to the interest of the profession or to its own members, cease to exist as a separate organisation.

7. That such provision should embrace the right on the part of members of the Society who are not also members of the Faculty to attend meetings where papers are read, to take part in discussions and to retain the privilege of access

to the Faculty Library, but not to take part in the business management of the Faculty.

8. That further details should be a matter of arrangement between the bodies.

In these resolutions one feels that one can surely perceive the working of Low's orderly mind and it is interesting that a class of " Library members " arising originally from the arrangements still exists. The change was bound to come in time and the whole matter appears to have been carried through with the utmost goodwill on both sides ; the young men would now require to summon up their courage and to brave the " awful presence of the Managers " ! The Faculty's sessional meetings were to be held as far as possible on the first Monday of each month from November to April and the Annual Meeting was transferred to June to avoid interference with the winter's activities.

The first Presidential Address to the Faculty was delivered consequently by G. M. Low on 4th November 1901 ; the event was an important one and the President rose to the occasion with a careful, interesting and dignified address upon " The History and Present Position of the Faculty of Actuaries in Scotland." The termination of the Society, after it was considered to have served its purpose, was perhaps justified by two points made by Low in his address. They are :—

1. That the Society was not of spontaneous origin among the junior members of the profession, but was originated by the Faculty in its desire to promote their studies and professional attainments ; and

2. That the objects the Faculty had in view were mainly of an educative character.

The President was of opinion that students had ceased to look to the Society for their early instruction ; the publications of the Institute of Actuaries and of the Society itself and the superlative achievement of the publication of the Institute Text Book in 1887, as well as the fact that in course of time " gentlemen were to be found who, having passed their examinations and been admitted to the Faculty, were willing *for the sake of revising their own studies* to give private instruction to their younger brethren " had left the Society mainly as a body for promoting research and discussion. The italics are mine, for it seems to me to be possible that tutors—drawn from a profession whose younger members were very poorly remunerated in those days—may have cherished other motives in the back of their minds ! Chatham had been the great tutor and there were others. His mantle rested on Henry Moir for a few years prior to his departure for the United States in the beginning of the century and in 1900 W. A. Robertson qualified and early followed in the footsteps of his distinguished predecessors, becoming famous as a teacher in his circle and conferring great benefits on many of the Faculty's students. With F. A. Ross, he published a book of students' notes under the title of " Actuarial Theory " which was read by all students of my vintage.

In this, the first Presidential Address, Low paid graceful tribute to Meikle, in connection particularly with his work for the now defunct Society, and to W. T. Thomson ; he congratulated the members upon the acquisition of the bust of Thomson as an excellent representation of one whom they should always delight to honour and upon that of T. B. Sprague, as a " fitting memorial of our distinguished Fellow."

The *Transactions* of the Faculty had now entered upon the stage, opening with the Address to which I have just referred. Whilst it is of course out of the question that this story should include a review of all that has appeared in the *Transactions*, it may be remarked that in Volume I, covering the period from 1901 to 1903, there are contributions from several well-known actuaries—Henry Moir from New York, A. E. Sprague, and James Chatham, to mention only a few. On the suggestion of Thomas Wallace, it was decided to include decisions of the Scottish Courts which might be considered of interest to the profession and William Harvey, Advocate, first undertook the task at a fee not to exceed £5 5s. Harvey became Sheriff-Substitute in Kirkwall in 1904 and was, consequently, unable to continue with this work, which was undertaken by John L. Wark, Advocate, who carried on for many years. Another suggestion by Wallace, that the resolutions of the Managers' Association should also be included, was very properly turned down. A committee, with Low as chairman, was appointed " to consider what rule should be adopted as to the interest of members in papers read by them " and its report, which is of interest, was adopted and is printed in Appendix VIII.

Although mortality investigations had been proposed and some executed prior to the foundation of the Faculty—in 1849 a Scottish member of the Institute suggested, with the blessing of the Managers' Association, a continuous collection of data, but nothing came of it—the first full scale enquiry of this nature, the HM experience, was discussed in 1862 by the Institute and on 29th May of that year a Committee consisting of McCandlish, Chisholm and Meikle was appointed by the Faculty to co-operate. The history of mortality investigations is a subject in itself and in this place only a passing reference is permissible. The Faculty adopted cards similar to those in use in England and by 1864 the work was making definite progress. The results were available in 1872 and the tables served the profession for many years. Meikle was, as has been remarked earlier, the mainspring of the Scottish end of the investigation and in an Address presented to him in a silver casket by his actuarial colleagues in Scotland shortly after his retirement the sentence occurs—" You also conducted an elaborate investigation of the Mortality Experience of the Scottish Life Assurance Offices up to 1863 " ; which seems to place a high proportion of the credit and responsibility upon the shoulders of this indefatigable individual. The idea of the next great investigation was promulgated in 1893 ; in the Council Minutes of the Faculty, Meikle is credited with suggesting it ; but it appears to have been discussed unofficially in England in 1892. The President of the time (A. H. Turnbull) with Meikle and Deuchar were originally appointed as a Committee to get in touch with the Institute and the Managers' Association. In this investigation there was the fullest co-operation with the Institute and a Joint Committee was required. The data to be collected, covering a period of thirty years, was very extensive and its collection was not unattended with disappointments and delays, although early in 1896 satisfactory progress in this regard was reported from Scotland. It is possible that never again shall we see an enquiry of this magnitude carried out with such meticulous attention to detail, and the important volume of " Principles and Methods " is a monument to the industry, ingenuity and actuarial accomplishment of those concerned. In 1905 the Committee were discharged and R. P. Hardy and T. G. Ackland of the Institute were appointed Honorary Fellows of the Faculty, in recognition of their great services. Gordon Douglas, Honorary Secretary of the Scottish Committee was presented with a " piece of plate." In my own study of the work of this enquiry, the O^M, the most intriguing part has always seemed to be the contribution by Sir George Hardy, who undertook graduations and effected them with unerring skill ; but it was not until 1914, in fact a few days only before his death, that Sir George became an Honorary Fellow of the Faculty.

In December 1911 L. P. Orr read a paper upon the subject of " Research in Life Assurance ", and since we are dealing with the statistical investigations undertaken by the Faculty this important event must be mentioned now. There is nothing of a deeply scientific nature in this paper, but the idea which it embodied was announced at the opportune moment and Orr's paper was the starting point of an important chain of events and is consequently itself important. In substance it was a plea for the establishment of a permanent bureau of research covering the whole area of the selection of lives for life assurance and the idea was that under the aegis of the Institute and Faculty such an organisation would be available to study mortality statistics in all aspects. The Faculty did not allow the grass to grow under its feet and in the same month in which the paper was read a Committee was appointed to set the matter going. Dr. Arthur Hunter in New York was asked for and furnished particulars of the " Medico-Actuarial " investigation which was being carried on in North America and a suggestion to the Institute, in t he early months of 1912, that they should co-operate drew a favourable response. The Institute agreed that the bureau should be of a permanent character and suggested that it be carried out on simple lines with due regard to economy and that the data should be accumulated from the start of the scheme—the collection of back data being regarded as expensive, laborious and of doubtful value. In fact the view had been expressed that the great O^M Investigation was out of date when it was published. It was felt that the great elaboration of that study had carried the disadvantage of delay in publication to far too great an extent. The Scottish offices gave a conditional agreement in 1912, and the English (with few exceptions) in 1913, but stated that they would be able to give only the details for an ordinary mortality investigation in respect of their existing business and that if a medico-actuarial series of studies were in contemplation, the data would require to be built up gradually from new business as it came along. Actually, the original idea was that the chief purpose of the bureau was the examination of specialised risks ; but, thus early, this was set aside and deferred as a possible future development. Amongst other joint decisions of the Institute and Faculty was one which tended to simplify matters—that the investigation should be on the basis of policies not lives—and this elicited " a lengthy letter " from G. M. Low in protest, for Low was nothing if not a purist. In the end the Committee adhered to its original view, after considering an actuarial note on the subject by F. W. Robertson with editorial comment thereon by Alexander Fraser, and Low withdrew his objections in a graceful letter. Although events did not permit of the immediate fruition of the scheme—quite

inevitably it was postponed until after the end of the
1914-1918 war—it was to have satisfactory and
practical results in the long run as we shall see when
in the next chapter we deal with a later period of the
Faculty's story.

Towards the latter part of the period under review
in this chapter there was increasing evidence of the
recognition of the Faculty's influence and importance ;
there were on a number of occasions consultations
with the Board of Trade about life assurance legislation
and as to safeguarding the position of the profession
by definition of " actuary " in bills before Parliament.
In 1900, representations were made to the Secretary
of State for Scotland and to the Local Government
Board in connection with the 1901 Census and it
seems that the suggestion of the establishment of a
permanent Census Department was put forward. The
National Insurance Act in 1911 naturally aroused the
interest of the Council and suggestions were made
about it ; in January 1912, it is reported that Gordon
Douglas, then President, had been appointed to the
Actuarial Advisory Committee set up in this connection. There was of course by this time active
participation in the various Actuarial Congresses and
the Faculty was officially represented at a number
of congresses of a kindred nature instituted by other
bodies.

In Edinburgh, the standing of the profession
received official recognition in 1903, when the
Sovereign's Lord High Commissioner intimated that
a deputation from the Faculty would be welcomed
at his Levée. The reigning Sovereign is represented
each spring in the Scottish Capital by a Lord High
Commissioner, who, for a period, is in residence at

the Palace of Holyroodhouse, the occasion being an ecclesiastical one—the General Assembly of the Church of Scotland; the City and particularly its once famous tea-shops are filled to overflowing with members of the clergy and their relatives—representatives from all parts of the kingdom, gathered together for their annual orgy of meetings, discussions and social occasions. During this period, the Commissioner, until fairly recent times, held a levée at which representatives of the law, the Royal Scottish Academy and the professions were received; the first deputation from the Faculty consisted of Low (President), Deuchar, Turnbull, G. C. Stenhouse, Chatham, Colin McCuaig and McLauchlan. In 1906, during his Presidency, Hewat, ever mindful of the dignity of the Faculty, presented a beautiful Badge of Office for the President—a medallion in gold to which I referred previously—and in 1912, he pointed out that at the Lord High Commissioner's levée the deputations from public bodies were, with the exception of the Faculty's representatives, suitably robed. A committee was appointed, upon which W. G. Walton—whose artistic qualifications were of a high order—was specially asked to serve, with a view to getting suitable robes. Eight robes were obtained made of " rifle green cloth, faced with green velvet and with velvet cap " and these same robes are in use to this day. They were first worn at the levée held on 22nd May 1912 by a deputation led by Gordon Douglas. Up to the second Great War, this was an annual occasion and I have myself been included on several occasions in the Faculty's deputation and have presented myself " suitably robed." I have been fortunate in being able to arrange for a photograph of a deputation in robes to

the Service at St. Giles Cathedral on the occasion of
the opening of the Edinburgh Festival in 1953 and
include it here, quite wrongly from a chronological
point of view it must be admitted, but since we are
on the subject of robes ! The Deputation in the
photograph was led by R. Ll. Gwilt, C.B.E., President
at the time. I am aware that at least one other photograph of a Fellow in his robe exists, but I have been
unable to obtain a copy for publication. During a
short leave from military service during the first
World War, an old friend of mine, but recently a
Fellow and no doubt acting under the exhilarating
influence of leave from the front line, had his photograph taken in one of the robes ; but he won't give
me a copy and insists upon anonymity.

In 1903, W. R. Macdonald, a Fellow of the Faculty
and one who took an interest in the abstruse subject
of heraldry, ascertained from the Lyon King of Arms
that the seal in use by the Faculty was open to serious
objection as bearing an unauthorised design, which
too closely resembled the Royal Arms. The matter
was remitted to James Watt, LL.D., W.S., a distinguished Fellow of the Faculty, who acted as its
legal adviser at this period. Dr. Watt upheld in his
opinion the view of the Lyon King and remarked
" that not being even a proper arms—heraldically—
a Society, the basis of the operations of which is
accuracy, may deem it inappropriate to continue to
use a device which is unauthorised and inaccurate."
The Lyon King did not intend to take action, but had
expressed his view since the matter had been brought
to his attention. However, the Council decided to
make a change, but decided upon a non-heraldic
design incorporating the Royal Arms of Scotland as
a decorative feature and although W. R. Macdonald,

Deputation wearing the Official Robes at the opening ceremony of
the Edinburgh Festival, 1953

Front row (l. to r.):—A. Bateman, R. Ll. Gwilt (President) and
A. R. Reid

Back row (l. to r.):—F. J. McGregor, D. A. B. Scrimgeour and
E. Waugh

Book Plate and Second Seal (1904)
in use until 1950

after consultation with the official, reported " that there was no really serious objections to their use as ornamentation," the future hardly bore out this view and the idea of not adopting a proper heraldic device duly approved and registered proved to be a mistake, as will appear in its place. I reproduce here the seal and corresponding book-plate to which reference is intended and which were in use for over forty years. It will be observed that there is a suggestion of astrology about the design—for we are not astrono-mers. Although no doubt the majority of mankind place reliance upon the science of astrology, it has been generally discredited in Scotland for some little time and ceased to be a compulsory subject of study at Continental universities as long ago as the sixteenth century. Perhaps the design was preferred as lending an air of mystery to our work and as suggesting that the first Scottish actuary was Michael Scot, the medieval mathematician, who was an astrologer of note and has been called a wizard !

Dr. James Watt, to whom I have just referred, was a man of outstanding character and achievements. I have been told by one who should know that when, as an apprentice to a firm of Writers to the Signet, he intimated his intention of sitting our examinations, an important official of the Faculty told the chief of his legal firm that it was " damned cheek " for a W.S. apprentice to do so ! This was a curious opinion, for several of the original members of the Faculty were Writers to the Signet and as it turned out, of course, to a man of Watt's ability the examinations were no great obstacle to overcome—he passed them in short order. Dr. Watt's services were required in the early years of the century when attempts were made from time to time by other bodies to appropriate to their own use the initials employed by the Faculty to distinguish its Fellows. This occurred on a number of occasions ; for instance in 1908, a body called the Faculty of Accountants wrote to ask if the Faculty would have any objections to their using the letters F.F.A. and A.F.A. Naturally this idea was unacceptable and the Secretary acting under the instructions of Hewat, then President, wrote to say that the Faculty would have the strongest objections and would be prepared to take all steps necessary to enforce them.

Watt was of course consulted when a movement was on foot to promote a bill to protect designations and distinctive letters used by incorporated professional bodies and was again in 1913 when an institution arising out of the National Insurance Act and called the Faculty of Insurance proposed to grant the degrees of A.F.I. and F.F.I. It seems that there is some legal difficulty in the way of preventing a new institution from poaching upon the preserves of even a chartered body ; there was an amusing example in 1948. One of the persons officially in attendance on the happy occasion of the birth of Prince Charles was described as " F.F.A., R.C.S." and, whilst of course greatly honoured, actuaries were not a little surprised that the scope of their professional activities had expanded to involve an occasion of this nature ! It transpired that the gentleman concerned was, however, not an actuary but an anaesthetist—a member of a recently formed offshoot of the Royal College of Surgeons. Unlike the case of the Faculty of Accountants, which I have mentioned, no previous approach had been made to the Faculty and when our Law Agents entered into correspondence with the officials of the new body, it was found that all they were willing to do, of their courtesy, was to drop the comma and use " F.F.A.R.C.S."—a nice distinction which, to an acute observer, might conceivably render confusion less—or slightly less—confounded ! There are quite a large number of combinations of three letters chosen from twenty-six—even if one of them must be A—and in any case, if they were not able to think up something original, why not " C.A." —Competent Anaesthetist—if that be a proper description ! However, since the activities of the two bodies are, and are likely to continue to be, poles apart, probably no great harm has been done, and a breach of good taste may not be considered a matter of prime importance in the middle of the twentieth century.

In November 1908, J. J. McLauchlan gave his Presidential Address and set an excellent example (which has not generally been followed) by giving a constructive paper on an actuarial theme ; his subject was " The Fundamental Principles of Pension Funds " and his paper formed an important milestone in his series of contributions to our literature on this subject. I have referred to McLauchlan at some length earlier in this chapter ; he was first and foremost an actuary and perhaps not so much a " business man " as some of his colleagues. He had occasion at a Council Meeting on 12th March 1909—fifty-three years after the founding of the Faculty—to refer in suitable terms to the death of James Howden " the last surviving original member of the Faculty."

Gordon Douglas followed McLauchlan as President and his term of office was a busy one. He had acted as Secretary to the Scottish Committee in connection with the 1863-93 mortality investigation and had served the Faculty with devotion prior to becoming

President. Although Douglas seems to have been at some pains to uphold the dignity of his position and was in a sense autocratic, he was credited with being approachable and having a keen sense of humour, which he could employ to advantage in discussion. He took great pride in his literary style, but, particularly for his period, his calligraphy was poor—his signature was considered a work of art; having sketched the outline, he went over it again and touched it up! He took a keen interest in golf, fishing and music and as a golfer was, it is said, an extremely pleasant companion. Although he took part in many discussions at the Faculty's meetings, his only original contribution to the *Transactions* was his Presidential Address, which dealt with "Life Assurance under the 1870 Act." W. Hutton, who succeeded Douglas as President, was interested more in the investment and financial than in the purely actuarial side of his work and was another whose only contribution to the *Transactions*, other than a few remarks in discussions, was his Presidential Address. In that paper, Hutton referred to the important work done by his predecessor (Douglas) whilst serving upon the Actuarial Advisory Committee in connection with the National Health Insurance Act and referred to the increasing importance of the actuary as the result of the growth of railway, bank, and other pension funds, the introduction of Workmen's Compensation Insurance and National Health Insurance. It is perhaps typical of the man and of the period that, referring to actuaries and the new health scheme, he should remark—" they were not the architects of the scheme, and have no share in responsibility for the effect, beneficial or otherwise, that may result from its introduction."

He went on to express apprehension of possible ill-effects of such schemes upon the national character—a fear that has been reiterated at a later date in regard to the more ambitious and far-reaching arrangements to which we now stand committed.

I have remarked earlier that the Faculty was true to the Scottish professional and academic tradition in supplying men who were willing to spread the gospel and serve overseas and Hutton remarks that at this time (November 1913) more than 40 per cent of the Fellows were carrying on their work outside Scotland. A proportion of these were in England of course and could hardly be said to be ploughing virgin soil; but others were in "India, each of the Colonies, the Straits Settlements, the United States and Central and South America." The term "Colonies" embraced a much wider range of territory in 1913 than it does to-day. In 1891, Charles Gordon, who became a Fellow in 1875, went to South Africa as actuary to the life office now known as the South African Mutual Life Assurance Society and held that post until he retired in 1917. About the turn of the century and particularly in the early 1900's several Fellows and Students settled in Cape Town or Johannesburg and made South Africa a stronghold of influence for the Faculty. G. C. McLaren arrived in 1902 as a student, passing his final examination there in 1905 and in the latter year Donald Macphail arrived, eventually becoming a consulting actuary in Johannesburg, where he was joined in partnership early in 1914 by D. Spence Fraser. To these Fellows of the Faculty—actuarial pioneers—the profession in South Africa owes much indeed. To the firm of Macphail and Fraser, the Union Government early turned for actuarial advice and to-day the firm is virtually carrying on the work of a Government Actuarial Department. There is a wide range of problems for the actuary in South Africa, for instance questions arising out of gold mining involving investigation as to the effects of phthisis and silicosis upon longevity. As a result of the important work of these pioneers, the Faculty made a notable impact upon the business life of the country, and although to-day the actuaries in South Africa are divided almost equally between Fellows of the Institute and Faculty, for a long period the influence and numbers of the Faculty predominated and to this day the majority of actuarial students there enter for our examinations.

It is said that in Australia, where there has been no great development of actuarial science (as distinct, of course, from practical life assurance), Faculty men have borne their share in affairs, although it would be correct to say that the predominant part there has been played by the Institute. Amongst the early Fellows of the Faculty who had an influence upon actuarial matters were W. R. Davey, who qualified in 1879, James Pullar, 1886 and A. M. Laughton, 1896. Laughton was Government Actuary in Victoria for many years. There are at present a number of younger members of the Faculty who are keeping the flag flying in this part of the world.

The spearhead of the Scottish actuarial invasion of the United States was a distinguished Fellow of the Faculty—Dr. Arthur Hunter—who went to New York in the early 1890's. He is one of only two Fellows who, in the history of the Faculty, so far as I can find, have been honoured by the University of Edinburgh for their actuarial attainments—the other was Lidstone. As has been remarked, he gave advice to the Scottish Committee on Research just prior to the 1914 War and this he was well qualified to do for he took an extremely active part in the medico-actuarial investigation in America and was for a time Chairman of the body in charge of the work. In the early years of the Actuarial Society of America, which was founded in 1889, Scottish actuaries played an important part in its affairs. Several, including of course Dr. Hunter and Henry Moir, took an active share in the preparation of the syllabus of examinations and in the education of students ; the first course of lectures for the Fellowship was given in New York under Dr. Hunter's leadership and Moir's " Primer of Life Assurance " was, in those early days, a great help to students. During the first twenty-five years of the Society's history there was only one Fellow of the Institute resident in the United States and there were quite a number of representatives of the Faculty, so that perhaps we may claim that Scotsmen had a very real influence upon early actuarial thought on the other side of the Atlantic. Many of our Fellows have filled positions of the highest importance there, and to this day we are represented both in the United States and in Canada by younger men who are worthily upholding our traditions. Dr. Hunter, a man of untiring energy, has done much to keep the Faculty in touch with actuarial progress in America by giving lectures on his periodical visits to this country and is one of whose varied activities and unremitting zeal our members may justly be proud. In the later chapters there will, of course, be references to Scottish actuaries overseas, but here it may, with due modesty, be remarked that our Fellows have been true to the pioneering traditions of Scotland

and that the services they have rendered in other lands have been important.

The Jubilee of the Faculty was celebrated by a dinner held on 19th January 1906 in the North British Station Hotel—where so many delightful actuarial dinners have been held since—and N. B. Gunn, then President, occupied the Chair. One hundred attended and the guests were representative of all the most important aspects of Scottish life—the church, the law and the Universities. The occasion is reported in detail in Volume 3 of the *Transactions* of the Faculty ; the speeches were very much what one would expect upon such an occasion and perhaps the most effective, from the point of view of one reading the record long after the event, was that of G. M. Low in proposing the toast of the Institute of Actuaries. The acknowledgment of this toast was made by the then President of the Institute—Henry Cockburn, a Scotsman, who, as Low pointed out, had become a Fellow of the Faculty by examination before going south in search of fortune, as so many of our people have done. Lord Ardwall proposed the toast of the Faculty and the President replied in a speech about its history and work. It is interesting to note that Gunn had received and read a cablegram from New York in the following terms :—" We greet our Alma Mater. Congratulations on past and best wishes for even increased prosperity in future from Cathles, Gibb, Hunter, Hutcheson, Moir, Webster and Young."

No doubt all present enjoyed this party, but it does not seem to have been a particularly mirthful one ; only twice has the reporter found himself able to interject " Laughter." The Lord Justice-Clerk

Cast of medal presented jointly by the Faculty and the Institute of Actuaries to George James Lidstone, LL.D.

(the Right Hon. Sir J. H. A. Macdonald) in responding to the toast of the College of Justice referred to a disappointed litigant, who, after losing his case, was marching down the High Street in a state of towering indignation and was heard to exclaim, " The College o' Justice ! It's ma opeenion they were a' the waur o' drink." The speaker's comment, " I am not quite sure whether the impeachment was true or not," called forth " renewed laughter " and this and one other titter is apparently the sum total of successful jesting for the evening !

In 1913, the late C. Keith Granger proposed the establishment of a branch library in Glasgow and R. Gordon-Smith agreed to supervise it. This small library has been maintained up to the present time for the convenience of our many students and Fellows in the West, and the Faculty is indebted to the courtesy of the Scottish Amicable, which has provided house-room for it from the beginning. In the same year, G. J. Lidstone was appointed a Fellow of the Faculty ; he was then a Vice-President of the Institute and the accession of this great actuarial figure was to prove of the first importance in the future.

It would not be correct to close this phase of the story without some reference to one or two of the other men who carried on the work in various official positions. One must record a particular debt to the Honorary Editors of the *Transactions*, and in the period under review mention should be made of J. M. Warden, J. R. Armstrong, J. A. Thomson and A. Fraser. Warden held the position from 1903 to 1906 and no doubt had an influence on the early issues ; but one gathers that he was a man of many hobbies or interests and that these may have involved a certain procrastination in dealing with the more immediate business of life. He is said to have been deeply interested in the study of prime numbers and in his own genealogy and to have been engaged upon the gigantic enterprise of translating the Bible into Esperanto. Armstrong was Editor from 1906 to 1908 when he was succeeded by J. A. Thomson who continued to hold the post until 1913, when Fraser started his long reign—until 1920. These three men are still Fellows of the Faculty*, although all of them have retired from active affairs, and it is doubtful to what extent it would be proper to write essays about them. They are each in his own way distinguished and have a common characteristic, so far as my observation goes, each displaying in his work a meticulous accuracy very proper in actuaries. Armstrong's main interest has been in the mathematical side of our work, Thomson's in its financial aspects and Fraser became an authority on widows' funds and laid the profession under a deep debt for his work in this subject. The early numbers of the *Transactions* stand as a monument to their self-sacrificing energy and devotion to the service of the Faculty. J. A. Thomson actually held the post of Secretary concurrently with the Honorary Editorship for one period. W. G. Walton was Honorary Treasurer for a period and afterwards Honorary Secretary and A. E. Sprague was Honorary Treasurer from 1911 to 1914. The proper place to dwell more fully upon their services to the Faculty is in the next chapter, however, for both became President in due course.

It has been said to me that the period immediately prior to the 1914-1918 War was not one of great activity or achievement in the Faculty, and of course

* Mr. Fraser died in June, 1955.

94

it is true that in every type of enterprise the tide of endeavour tends to ebb and flow. But we may feel that the period reviewed in this chapter was one of solid progress ; our institution had been built on a sound foundation and had become an important part of the life of Scotland. The influence of the Faculty was recognised—although, at this period, its functions were only vaguely understood outside the professional classes—and the authority of its members in their sphere had been endorsed by Act of Parliament ; our Fellows occupied positions of high responsibility both at home and overseas and the ever-increasing complication of our national life was continually suggesting new channels for the use of actuarial skill. But

> . . . " Man is hurled
> From change to change unceasingly,
> His Soul's wing never furled."

and a change, drastic indeed, occurred in the scene when, in 1914, " the lamps went out all over Europe." This chapter must close on a note of sadness, for at this point of time it is terribly evident that the years of slaughter, of unhappiness and of heroism brought no lasting benefit to Europe or to mankind. " It is not the lofty sails, but the unseen wind that moves the ship " and the wind was a hurricane ; the voyage of discovery was abandoned, but the ship of the Faculty remained ready to resume its work and, as will appear in the next phase of the story, there was a great resurgence of activity when the seas became more calm. The loss amongst the Fellows and students was grievous and their names are recorded with honour and gratitude along with others of a later and not more fortunate generation in the Memorial, which stands in our Hall—a tribute to their self-sacrifice and an acknowledgement of a debt which we can never repay.

CHAPTER VI

ACHIEVEMENT
1914 - 1939

" . . . , whatever may be alleged to the contrary by the
sceptic and the scorner, to each duty performed, there
is assigned a degree of mental peace and high con-
sciousness of honourable exertion, corresponding to
the difficulty of the task accomplished."
—" The Pirate," SCOTT.

IT is reported that the late Lord Keynes committed
himself to the statement in 1914, that he was quite
certain that the war could not last more than one
year and that the belligerent countries could not be
ruined by it. It was in such intelligent company that
a majority of the people of Britain under-estimated
the protracted nature of the struggle and indeed its
gravity; the idea that a catastrophe so atrocious
could overtake the world in the twentieth century was
unthinkable to the ordinary citizen of our land and
almost certainly had never occurred to him. It has
been said that " no great country except English-
speaking America has ever been so utterly civilian
in thought and practice as Victorian England " and
this is almost equally true of the first decade of the
twentieth century and of course of Scotland. For one
hundred years, the nation had been immune from
great wars—indeed from any grave national disaster
—and people were accustomed to feel that under the
protection of the Royal Navy they could pursue the
even tenor of their lives in peaceful security; there

were voices raised in the contrary sense before 1914, it is true, but they were crying in the wilderness and went largely unheeded. Bitter experience has taught us to look at matters in a different light ; inventions in the realm of scientific warfare have had the effect of rendering our island home more vulnerable, and in the middle of the twentieth century we find it necessary to maintain a conscript army and a powerful air force in addition to our great navy. But as we think back to what it may not be too much to call happier days—in this respect at all events—it is perhaps hardly surprising that, during the first few months of the War of 1914, there was a failure to appreciate the situation and that an effort was made to carry on ordinary civilian activities in the normal way.

The Council of the Faculty, naturally enough, went in step with the rest of the people ; there were four sessional meetings in the winter of 1914-1915 and examinations were held in the spring of 1915. But the fateful condition of the times was gradually brought home to everyone ; in January 1915 it was decided to postpone until the conclusion of hostilities the projected continuous mortality investigation and after G. M. Low, who had undertaken the duty of President for a second term, delivered another Inaugural Address on 8th October 1915, sessional meetings and examinations were suspended until the dawn of more settled times. But, looking forward to a period when activities would be resumed, those Fellows who, under Low's wise and experienced guidance, were responsible for the Faculty's affairs were not idle ; the Council and various committees met from time to time and plans were laid. The new syllabus of examinations, which had been under consideration for some time prior to the outbreak of

War, was finally prepared against the time when it could be put into operation and a further important step forward in the educational sphere was initiated in conjunction with the University of Edinburgh. In 1917 a Committee was formed, of which G. J. Lidstone was an influential and active member, to consider a suggestion, made in a letter from Sir Richard Lodge, that the University should institute a degree of B.Sc. in actuarial science. A memorandum was prepared on behalf of the Faculty by Dr. A. E. Sprague, W. G. Walton and W. Borland and informal discussions took place with Sir Edmund (then Professor) Whittaker. In 1918, after discussions between the Professor and the President of the Faculty, it was decided to proceed with the less ambitious plan of a University Diploma in actuarial mathematics. The plan was successfully adopted and carried out in post-war years; the Diploma of the University of Edinburgh in Actuarial Mathematics is still and will no doubt continue to be a feature of Scottish actuarial education. The Diploma exempts a student from Parts I and II of the Faculty's examinations and, having obtained it, he requires to sit Parts III and IV on the same terms as other students in order to qualify as an Associate of the Faculty. The matter is referred to further in the chapter on Education and here it will suffice to remark that the Faculty Committee which finally agreed the regulations with the Authorities of the University consisted of G. M. Low (President), G. J. Lidstone, A. E. Sprague, R. M. Hunter and W. Borland. Sir Edmund Whittaker was appointed an Honorary Fellow of the Faculty in the Spring of 1918 in recognition of his services—not by any means the last he has rendered to the Faculty and to actuarial science.

G. M. Low retired from the position of President in 1919; he had the distinction, which no one has so far shared, of being President on two occasions and, owing to the War, his second term of office was unusually protracted. He was followed in the Presidential Chair by Alfred Ernest Sprague, D.Sc. Low had placed the Faculty under a great debt on account of his devotion to its interests and the outstanding ability as an administrator which he brought to bear upon its affairs. The new President, son of T. B. Sprague, entered upon his duties at a moment critical indeed in the story of the Faculty; there was a great resurgence of activity and Sprague, being a very real and loyal friend to the younger men and to the students, was very much the right man for the time. One of his earliest duties was a sad one; after the conclusion of hostilities early consideration was naturally given to setting up a War Memorial which would give fitting expression to the feelings of respect and gratitude which the surviving members of the Faculty entertained towards those Fellows and Students who had given their lives for their country in the course of the great struggle. The dreadful toll which the war of 1914-1918 exacted from the young men of Britain is exemplified by the fact that forty-three from amongst the Fellows and Students (six of them Fellows) of such a small body as was the Faculty fell whilst on active service.

The President, Low and Walton were appointed as a Committee to consider the nature of the Memorial and the matter was completed by 1921 as is shown by the following extract from the Report by the Council to the Ordinary General Meeting of the Faculty held on 27th June of that year:—" A Memorial of the Members and Students of the

Faculty who fell in the War has been placed in position in the Hall. The Council felt that the Faculty would desire to perpetuate the memory of those men, and subscriptions for the purpose were invited from the Members and Students. The appeal met with a most gratifying response and contributions, amounting to over £260, have been received from all parts of the world. The Memorial, which was designed by Mr. John Kinross, R.S.A., takes the form of an enclosed case, containing an illuminated vellum scroll, ornamented with Scottish national emblems, and set in a rosewood frame, giving prominently the names of all who fell and also recording the names of those who served in the War. The framework of the case is of ebony and the doors of coromandel wood, with specially designed brass hinges and inlaid inscription in boxwood. The Memorial is of a very handsome and artistic character and is considered worthy of the object for which it is provided." An illustration is shown in Volume 9 of the *Transactions*. The Memorial was removed from the Hall in Queen Street and set up in the present Hall in St. Andrew Square; but it has since been replaced by a new Memorial, erected after the second World War, which records the names of the fallen in both conflicts. A description of this Memorial will be given in its place, when the point is reached for dealing with the second stretch of melancholy years.

During the War of 1914-1918, other losses fell upon the Faculty; Archibald Hewat and Andrew H. Turnbull, each of whom in his own way had given such memorable service to the Faculty, died—the former in 1915 and the latter in 1917. The Council minute regarding Hewat refers particularly to "the kindness of his disposition, infectious enthusiasm and

high sense of duty," whilst that relating to Turnbull
mentions his high attainments as a man of affairs
and his steadfast character and, from what I have
been able to glean from the past, those were in fact
the salient features of those two important figures in
our story. Two other civilian deaths during the period
robbed the Faculty of the services of younger men
who were full of promise and each of whom had
early shewn devotion to its interests—Walter Borland
and Vyvyan Marr. Walter Borland was a highly
successful tutor and, although his connection with the
Faculty was brief owing to his untimely death, he
had been energetic and had already rendered useful
service, more particularly in connection with the
negotiations with the University regarding the institution of the Actuarial Diploma. Marr, a man of
pushful and vigorous character, was also a distinguished tutor and he, along with Alexander Fraser,
did much work on widows' funds, originally under
the influence of Hewat. Marr and Fraser were both
enthusiastic mountaineers—as quite a few other
Fellows of the Faculty have been—and it has been
said of Fraser that in his climbing days he was as good
a mountaineer as he was an actuary—which is a
substantial tribute to his skill at the sport, for his
professional attainments, when actively engaged,
were high indeed. Since the name of Alexander
Fraser has come up again at this point, it may be
appropriate to mention now that, most unfortunately
from the point of view of the Faculty of which he
had already proved himself a devoted member, he
found it necessary, on account of his health, to retire
from active business in 1922, and although his
interest in actuarial matters continued—he contributed an important paper to the *Transactions* on the

" Scottish Bankers' Mortality and Marriage Experience " after his retirement—even his partial withdrawal from the scene was a very real loss to the profession.

It is a nice question whether it is wise for a brilliant father, who, in his day, has been an important figure and almost dominated a particular profession, to train up his son to follow in his footsteps ; the fame of S. C. Thomson does not rank with that of his father and it seems to me to be possible that the reputation of Alfred Ernest Sprague has suffered somewhat from the inevitable comparison with the triumphant figure of Thomas Bond Sprague. That the younger Sprague was a man of outstanding capacity, there is no room for doubt—his contributions to the *Transactions* bear eloquent tribute to his ability ; but it may fairly be doubted whether he possessed either the energy or the strength of character of his awe-inspiring parent. Although he attained to the highest honour which the Faculty has to offer and served with distinction, he appears, towards the latter part of his professional career, to have suffered from a sense of frustration, for he did not in fact reach that position in the business world which his attainments might lead him to expect and to which the compelling example of his father must have constrained him to aspire. Dr. A. E. Sprague was of rather an unconventional habit and I have been told that he was sometimes " difficult " ; but, however that may be, I am one of a generation of actuaries which lies deeply in his debt. He was always approachable and we all held him in high respect—it would not be too much to say, affection ; his unfailing willingness to hear, to advise and to help the younger men, added to what I recollect as his charm of manner and kindness were an inspiration to us all. He was never too occupied to accord an interview to one who was anxious to improve his professional attainments and to try to do something for the Faculty. Sprague was an enthusiastic and practical yachtsman; he built a new yacht in his own dining-room—a window was removed from his house to accommodate it.

During the War, the question of the admission of women to the Faculty was raised; but it was not until towards the end of 1919 that the decisive step was taken. Dr. Watt had been consulted and the Sex Disqualification (Removal) Act smoothed the way for the momentous occasion. At the time it must have appeared to be a momentous, indeed a revolutionary, move; but in the event it must be admitted that the revolution, so far as the Faculty is concerned, has not proved to be of a particularly formidable character. So far only three women have become Fellows and I am afraid it must be admitted that we have yet to hear of a Scottish lady actuary who has laid claim to high office either in the Faculty or in practical actuarial affairs. Mr. Gradgrind remarked " In this life we want nothing but facts, Sir; nothing but facts " and it may be that in actuarial life, at the least, the severely statistical and practical approach to our problems leaves little room for those flashes of intuition with which the fair sex are generally supposed to cope with life's little difficulties. In any case, the gruelling course of study for the actuarial degree, concurrent as it is with a busy official life, requires a degree of physical endurance and of singleness of purpose, which, without the least disrespect, may be considered as unlikely to appeal to the average young woman. The Institute of

Actuaries opened its doors to women about the same time and in doing so quoted " the example of their sister institution, the Faculty of Actuaries in Scotland, which had already passed a resolution in terms similar to the one before the meeting."

I have already referred to the time-honoured jest that Scotsmen go South to seek their fortune ; but in the actuarial sphere at all events, the traffic is not " one-way." Several Fellows of the Institute came to Edinburgh before the War and three of them reached the goal of the Presidential Chair of the Faculty— T. B. Sprague, G. J. Lidstone and S. E. Macnaghten, who was appointed a Fellow of the Faculty in 1918. At the instigation of the last of these, another Institute man—A. E. King—arrived from London during the War and, elected to the Fellowship of the Faculty in 1920, King, who was an untiring worker, repaid the honour which the Faculty had done him by energetic devotion to its interests. The first fruits of his efforts appeared shortly after the resumption of peaceful activities. The Institute of Actuaries Students' Society has, as Simmonds puts it, " contributed much to the life of the Institute since the year 1910 " and, before the War, King had been an enthusiastic member. I write from intimate personal knowledge of the circumstances of the formation of the Faculty Students' Society (I had the honour to be chosen as its first " Chairman of Committee ") when I say that King was a zealous advocate of the idea of following the English example and forming a Students' Society in Scotland. Although still a young man, his perseverance and ever-ready help had much to do with getting the Society started and helping it along in its early, difficult years. A project of this sort also received, as a matter of course, the fullest support from A. E. Sprague, who was most opportunely President at the time and whose interest in the students and younger members never flagged. The Society was inaugurated at a meeting held in the Hall in Queen Street on 26th January 1920, at which the first office-bearers and Committee were appointed and, although it is not for me to write the history of this off-shoot of the Faculty—no doubt in time one of its members will take up the task—I give their names here, for the venture is an important milestone in our story :—

Hon. Secretary	-	R. Calder.
Hon. Treasurer	-	A. B. Johnstone.
Committee -	-	A. R. Davidson (Chairman), S. Burrows, D. S. Fraser, R. Ll. Gwilt, A. E. King, G. W. Melville, C. S. Penn, W. C. Reid and W. L. Swan.
Hon. Auditors	-	J. Barnett, C.A., & H. M. Ferguson.

It was a graceful and appropriate gesture on the part of the Committee to appoint, at its first meeting on 30th January, Wm. McLachlan, the Assistant Secretary of the Faculty, as an honorary member of Committee, for he had put himself to a great deal of trouble to help us, particularly in connection with the preliminary arrangements. McLachlan's connection with the Society was, however, destined to be brief, for he died in the summer of 1920 and was succeeded in his office of Assistant Secretary by D. G. Cochrane. The appointment to the Committee of the Students' Society did not of course extend to Mr. Cochrane ; the step had been taken entirely as a personal tribute to Mr. McLachlan, as a respected, popular and very helpful employee of the Faculty.

The President entertained the Officials of the Faculty and of the new Society to dinner after the meeting of 20th January and I, and no doubt others, have the pleasantest recollections of the occasion and of the geniality of our host. Dr. Sprague was Faculty Representative on the Society's Committee for the first three years and in 1927 he was elected a Life Member of the Society.

At the first sessional meeting, which was held on 16th February, 1920, W. C. Reid gave a paper on the " Net Premium Method of Valuation," and A. E. King presided. King was a regular attender at the early meetings and was a member of Committee for several years, being its second Chairman. At the first meeting there were only 26 present, but by May 1920 the membership had reached 60 and to-day it approaches 150. The Society was successful from the beginning and, over the years, the Students and younger Fellows have derived the greatest help and encouragement as the result of the activities carried on in its name. Some little time after the Society had passed its thirtieth birthday, Mr. J. F. T. England of Johannesburg generously provided the means to set up a fund—the England Fund—from which the annual income of £10 10s. was to be used to encourage the active interest of members of the Society in any matter pertaining to actuarial work. In the meantime, the income is being employed to offer a prize each year to the member of the Society whose paper, read before the Society during the Session, best merits the award.

Since we are on the subject of students' organisations, it may be appropriate to mention here that the Glasgow Actuarial Students' Society was established in 1931, largely due to the initiative and energy of G. F. Menzies and C. Rattray, and has had a highly successful existence, greatly to the benefit of our students and junior members in the west. The Society was inaugurated at a meeting held in October 1931 at which the Chair was occupied by C. L. Stoodley, who delivered a paper to the Society at its first sessional meeting. Stoodley, a young actuary of promise, was unfortunately cut off in his prime as the result of an air accident.

The year 1920 saw the passing within a few weeks of each other of two more of the old guard of the Faculty—T. B. Sprague and J. J. McLauchlan, who had worked together in the same office for many years. No tribute was too high for the elder Sprague who, as the Council minute has it, " was regarded as the most distinguished actuary of his time " and, referring to McLauchlan, a minute mentions his " keenness and accuracy of intellect, soundness of judgment and unswerving integrity." About the same time G. M. Low was appointed an Honorary Fellow ; but, in December 1922, the Council had the melancholy duty of recording his death also—" It would be difficult to exaggerate the services which Mr. Low rendered to the Faculty "—and so an important triumvirate, all of whom served the Scottish Equitable, leave the stage, but will ever, one dare hope, be gratefully remembered by successive generations of Scottish actuaries.

Lewis Potter Orr followed A. E. Sprague as President, but his term of office was curtailed ; he found it necessary to resign after only one year, owing, it is said, to increasing deafness—although his disability never became a real handicap to him in business or private life. Orr was of a dignified presence—very much in our Victorian tradition of Presidents—and had considerable strength of mind ; he was thoughtful of others and could unbend on occasion. His courtesy to the junior men with whom he came in contact was genuine, although it would be going too far to say that he identified himself with the interests of the younger generation in the manner, for instance, of his immediate predecessor. It has been said of him by one who knew him well that he entertained strong likes and dislikes and that anything in the way of " sloppiness " was anathema to him; in coming to an important decision, he would consider the matter with care and, having reached his conclusion stick to it although the heavens fell! Prior to the 1914 War it had been the practice for a number of years for successive Presidents to invite to dinner at their homes all the Fellows within reach, in groups of some twenty at a time. This must have been quite an undertaking even in those days and may conceivably have induced one or two, after it became an established practice, to decline the honour of the Presidential Chair. After the War, it was quite out of the question to maintain the usage, however, both on account of the increasing numbers and because of the changing times. Orr, whilst no doubt realising that it was impracticable to follow the precedent set by his pre-war fore-runners, yet did something to revive the old custom; he held a large and very successful reception, which I remember well for I attended it with my wife. This was the last occasion, and will in all reasonable probability remain so, of a President undertaking on his own account the whole-sale entertainment of the Fellows of the Faculty.

Orr, without being in any sense outstanding from a strictly actuarial point of view, attained to an important position in business life and he had a contribution to make in the service of the Faculty. In the preceding chapter, mention was made of his paper on " Research in Life Assurance " and of the project to which it gave rise ; he followed this with two papers on the " Selection of Lives ", one in 1919 and the other in 1930—painstaking studies of medico-actuarial questions. In this connection, it is interesting to record here that in 1954, one of Orr's successors as Chief Officer of the Scottish Life, C. S. Penn—an ex-President of the Faculty—took up the banner and carried on the good work by contributing, in colla-boration with Dr. Fergus Hewat, whom I have already mentioned as the son of the ex-President of that name, a further very valuable and up-to-date paper on the same subject. Orr's original idea of the " Bureau of Research " was, as I indicated previously, that the investigations to be undertaken should aim at assisting the Life Offices in the selection of lives for assurance and should be of a medico-actuarial nature ; this is clear from the original suggestion and also from the fact that Dr. Arthur Hunter was asked for advice as to the lines adopted for the medico-actuarial investigations being carried on in North America. It has always appeared to me, in spite of the obvious difficulties of conducting such inquiries and the fact that broad assumptions may have to be made, that the procedure might well help not only the life offices, but the medical profession itself ; unless we have statistical information anent the effect of various conditions of personal history and present health, of family history and occupation upon longevity, we have no information at all. For the opinion of the Medical Officer and of the Actuary of a Company, who meet in daily conclave to decide the fate of aspirants for assurance, must be based upon their experience, or the experience of others, of similar cases and in so far as this cannot be expressed

statistically, it may not, with every respect, be based
on more than vague impressions—which are hardly
satisfactory. Mere ambiguously supported personal
opinion must be subject to whims and idiosyncrasies
and to the state of well-being for the moment of the
referee; should the M.O. have been informed by his
" ever-loving wife " (to quote the late Mr. Runyon)
at the breakfast table, of the imminence of a two-
months' visit from her mother, he may well, unless
restrained by the stern influence of statistics, treat the
morning's proposers for assurance more harshly than
he need! The British life assurance institutions have
been eminently successful, there is no doubt, in their
selection of lives up to date. But they have been on
a good wicket; the steady and still-continuing
improvement in the vitality of the people of Britain
has been in their favour and may have obscured the
effect of defects, if one may be permitted to use the
word, in their methods of selection. It is the case
that a member of the Institute of Actuaries has stated
that in his opinion a full medico-actuarial investigation
is rendered futile by the difficulties in the way; but
difficulties are there to be overcome—this aspect of
actuarial statistics is still in its infancy and it is said
that when, long ago now, the news of the invention
of the telephone was reported to Professor Tait of
Edinburgh, he said " It is all humbug, for such a
discovery is physically impossible." It is pleasing
to note that, as I write, the advisability of instituting
such studies as Orr had in mind is being thoroughly
scrutinised and surely the combined intellectual
resources of the Institute and Faculty will yield
enough of ingenuity, energy and imagination to wrest
the secrets from the vast volume of statistics at their
disposal and so to confound those who, like Professor

Tait, consider the enterprise to be impossible of execution. It is true therefore that up to the date at which I am writing the plan of research has not followed the original conception, and it is probably fair to say that the first direct result of Orr's initiative was the arrangement made in 1921 to set on foot a continuous investigation into the mortality of annuitants. In November 1920, Lidstone had pointed out that a new annuitants' investigation was required and a Committee was formed, in the first instance by the Institute. A Faculty Committee was also formed, but in the early days liaison was not satisfactory, although arrangements were jointly concluded for the continuous observation of the mortality of annuitants. In 1924, the work was extended to cover the mortality of healthy assured lives and as we shall see it has been carried on to the present time.

On Orr's premature resignation, William Gandy Walton succeeded to the Presidential Chair; but he accepted the honour with reluctance. Walton was approaching three score and ten years of age when he was invited to undertake the duties of President and it was only after a great deal of pressure that he agreed to do so. It is doubtful whether his friends were wise, either from his own point of view or that of the Faculty, in urging him to shoulder this burden at his advanced age. In the session 1878-9, he delivered a paper to the Actuarial Society and he gave several more during its existence; but, after the birth of the *Transactions* of the Faculty in 1901, he made no further original contributions, although he took part in discussions on a number of occasions. In his younger days Walton had done his share of research and he had filled the posts of Honorary Treasurer and Honorary Secretary; but the highest honour came

Cast of medal presented jointly by the Faculty and the Institute of Actuaries to Sir William Palin Elderton, K.B.E.

too late for him and there is no doubt that he found the work irksome and worrying. As a young man he seems to have been a keen and competent actuary and it is a pity indeed that the Presidency, if he was to have it, should not have fallen to him at an earlier period. Walton came of a well-known artistic family and was invariably called upon by the Council on the comparatively rare occasions when questions of an artistic nature arose. In these matters his taste was generally regarded as impeccable, but as an assurance journalist, a side-line which he followed to some extent in earlier days, he occasionally allowed himself to be lively, to put it nicely, and he gave offence to one President of the Faculty, creating a breach between the two men which was never healed. This, when I first heard it, left me quite amazed, for I knew Walton well when he was President and he struck me as one of the gentlest and most courteous of men. It is not surprising, in all the circumstances, that Walton is singular amongst our Presidents as being the only one who did not find himself able to give an Address.

Walton's reign was not, however, in any way a period of lassitude for the Faculty; the post-war actuarial enthusiasm was getting thoroughly under weigh. The first report upon the mortality of annuitants was placed before the Faculty and here it is necessary to lay stress upon the debt which the profession owes to Sir William Palin Elderton, K.B.E., F.I.A., for his work in this connection and generally in actuarial and statistical science. For many years Sir William was the guiding spirit in the Continuous Mortality Investigations, and in 1931 the Faculty very properly acknowledged its obligation to him by electing him a Fellow.

There was at this time much activity in connection with tuition and examinations, which will be mentioned in more detail in the chapter on education. It will suffice to say, in the meantime, that arising partly from representations made by the Students' Society in 1922, a full course of instruction for the examinations, both oral and correspondence, was set up for Faculty students and was maintained in an eminently satisfactory manner until in course of time the work was taken over by the Actuarial Tuition Service of the Institute and Faculty. A further arrangement was made in holding examinations at half-yearly instead of yearly intervals with a view to assisting students to make up for time lost in the war years and to help them through the difficult period of resettlement. That this plan of holding half-yearly examinations was a boon to students there is no doubt; but it may be that on occasion it had the effect of inducing certain of their number to " have a shot " in October, having failed in April and without devoting themselves exclusively to study during the period of our delightful Scottish summer! This may possibly be, in part at least, an explanation of the fact that in one of the examinations in October 1923 some twenty candidates presented themselves and all failed. The incident created quite a furore and greatly upset the President, as I am well able to recollect, for at the time I was Secretary of the then newly-started Board of Examiners. There was, and still continued to be, an Examination Committee; but the examiners under the new arrangement constituted a Board which reported to the Committee. There were a few letters in the " Scotsman " on the subject of the examinations and, repeatedly, I was called to wait upon Walton, who was, not unnaturally, considerably agitated, both by the letters and by a noticeable feeling of dissatisfaction amongst the students themselves. One letter particularly bothered him ; it was *ex facie* a well-reasoned letter and was signed " Anxious Parent." Actually the Faculty was doing, very rightly of course, more than ever before to help the students and neither I nor any of the other examiners of the time felt that there was the smallest ground for complaint. In time the storm, such as it was, blew itself out and, a good number of years afterwards, I was informed of the identity of " Anxious Parent." The writer was one of the students ; he has since, I am informed, had a successful, but not an actuarial, career.

To actuaries, one might say of our next President, George James Lidstone, in the words of Wren's Epitaph in St. Paul's—*Si monumentum requiris, circumspice* ; for the *Journal* of the Institute and the *Transactions* of the Faculty are lavishly adorned by his many brilliant contributions. His original works built a fitting memorial for him and ensure that he will always be remembered amongst those of his profession. In an earlier chapter, I included his name as being, in my view, one of the four outstanding men in the history of the Faculty ; all were great actuaries, each one in his own manner, and all brought unusual gifts to the service of the profession. It is unnecessary, and in any case it would be difficult, to draw distinctions as to the relative influence upon our Institution of these four—W. T. Thomson, J. Meikle, T. B. Sprague and G. J. Lidstone. Thomson founded it and nursed it through the perils of infancy ; Meikle laboured unwearying in its service and was its early mainstay in research ; Sprague was an ornament to it and enriched it by his uncommon ability ; but

Lidstone's authority and enthusiasm inflamed a fresh spirit of research and intellectual curiosity and gave it a new orientation and scientific integrity.

Lidstone became President in 1924 and died as recently as 12th May 1952 in his eighty-second year. In Volume 21 of the *Transactions* there is an admirable essay upon the man and his career written by R. Ll. Gwilt, than whom no one was in a better position to understand his subject—particularly regarding the later period, with which we are chiefly concerned here. It was at the age of 42, in 1913, that Lidstone came to Edinburgh to take up the position of Manager and Actuary of the Scottish Widows' Fund and shortly after his arrival he was elected a Fellow of the Faculty. One of his earlier contacts in our City was with Professor Whittaker and the result was a lasting friendship between these two talented people, which had highly beneficial results for the Faculty. Lidstone's professional reputation was established before he came north, for he had already made what were perhaps his most important original contributions to our subject, and he had attained an influential position in the business world; but it may be that his professional interest was given an added mathematical bias as the result of his intimate friendship with the Professor. Too often it happens that the more successful members of the actuarial profession find themselves so engrossed in business in middle and later life that they cease to take an active interest in the theoretical, mathematical and statistical aspects of their subject; but this was far from being the case with our distinguished President. He attained to a position of the first professional eminence and of high responsibility; but he did not allow the inevitable preoccupation with matters of finance which his position entailed to tarnish his keen and effective interest in the subject that had made him what he was. Even after his retirement, which took place in 1929 on medical advice, he continued to contribute to the *Journal* and to the *Transactions*—his later work being frequently concerned with interpolation and finite integration. In spite of failing eyesight and the ultimate tragedy of blindness, his interest in his subject did not fade and, with what must have been great determination and effort, he contrived for long to keep abreast of actuarial affairs. Amongst my more cherished possessions is a characteristically kind letter of congratulation from Lidstone, which he sent to me after I had delivered my Inaugural Address as President of the Faculty in November 1948. The paper had of course been read to him; but it was clear from the discussion in the letter that it was no mere cursory interest he had taken in it—and he was then approaching his 78th birthday and was completely blind.

For a time at least, Lidstone was misunderstood by some of his contemporaries in Scotland; his manner had perhaps a superficial aloofness or austerity, no doubt due to his intense shyness, which tended to leave a chill upon those who did not know him well. But I can write from personal knowledge of his infectious enthusiasm and his courteous helpfulness to a very junior member of the profession; I found him approachable and always he gave me the feeling that he was pleased to discuss with me those aspects of actuarial work in which I was especially interested. His sincerity was to me his outstanding character; there was nothing pompous or bogus about Lidstone. It is probably true to say, however, that his very conscientious thoroughness and desire to examine all sides of a question made it difficult for him to make up his mind and perhaps his colleagues may sometimes have felt like asking, in the words of Elijah, " How long halt ye between two opinions ? " It seems to me that he would have liked best to be remembered as a mathematician and I know that he had pondered the question whether he would not have found more satisfaction in an academic career rather than that which he chose—or which fate chose for him, for he set out at a very young age. He was well above the normal actuarial standard of competence in the mathematical field ; but one, well qualified to judge, long ago expressed to me the view that Lidstone's extraordinary mind was more suited to a forensic career than to a strictly mathematical one. During his term of office as President, his eminence was recognised when, in 1925, the University of Edinburgh, conferred upon him the honorary degree of LL.D.

I have indicated that Lidstone altered the character of the Faculty. There is a tendency for a body such as ours to reflect in its activities the preoccupation of a majority of its members with practical affairs to the detriment of work in the purely theoretical and scientific fields, upon which all progress must ultimately depend ; in the Faculty Lidstone's compelling influence arrested this tendency and imparted a new outlook to many of our members. I believe that he did far more than any other in the last forty years to guide and stimulate the development of the Faculty on the scientific side and that, primarily due to his influence, our *Transactions* have attained a respectable reputation as a repository of studies in the more theoretical aspects of actuarial work. It is not too much to say that without Lidstone the climate of the Faculty would have been vastly different. As

Gwilt says, Lidstone "played a leading part in forging and strengthening that close link between the Faculty of Actuaries and the University of Edinburgh which has been so greatly valued by the Faculty and which has not been without advantage to the University." As I have indicated earlier he was active, if not indeed the main influence, in connection with the introduction of the University Diploma in actuarial mathematics. It was at his suggestion that Professor Whittaker made his first contribution to the *Transactions*; a paper, now well-known, "On some disputed Questions of Probability." The number in which this important and interesting contribution was included was a very special one; Lidstone's determination, so characteristic of him, to spare no pains in probing a problem to its very foundations was the inspiration. Correspondence between Sir George Hardy and a reviewer, which had appeared in the Insurance Record in 1889, was reprinted; it dealt with the question of the applicability of the well-known Bayes-Laplace formula to mortality rates. There was also a note by Lidstone himself on the " General Case of the Bayes-Laplace Formula for Inductive or *a posteriori* Probabilities." And a paper by John Govan presented to the Actuarial Society in 1893 which had special reference to the lecture delivered to the same Society by Professor Chrystal some two years previously was printed for the first time and included in the number. It was an intellectual feast indeed, dealing as the number did with a question which may conceivably lie at the root of actuarial work and constitute its basis. I have used a cautious phrase here, because, as I said in a previous chapter, the difficulties are not entirely resolved to this day and I personally have the temerity to entertain doubts as to its fundamental importance even in the face of the eminent authorities who have interested themselves in a subject so intriguing, but who have not, so far as I can ascertain, yet arrived at any clear-cut and obvious unanimity. Professor Aitken, Sir Edmund Whittaker's successor, who was elected to an Honorary Fellowship of the Faculty in 1946, followed in the footsteps of his two illustrious predecessors by giving a paper in 1949 on " Theories of Probability." With such humility as I have at command, I venture to suggest that it is still a question whether there is such a thing as ' Probability ' outside the rarified atmosphere of the mathematician's study ; but ' *Paris vaut bien une messe* ' and Probability is well worth a discussion, which always proves stimulating and exciting. Ultimately I suppose we shall all be at one on the subject, but present indications seem to me to suggest that this dull and enervating state of acquiescence may not arrive in all its deadly finality—

> " Till the sun grows cold,
> And the stars are old,
> And the leaves of the Judgment Book unfold."

The *Transactions* entered upon a period of prosperity following this number and research was in the air. Dr. James Buchanan made important contributions ; he was a painstaking and accomplished theorist and when Steuart Macnaghten gave his Presidential Address in 1930 he referred particularly to Buchanan's work—much of it ingenious and erudite. There were several papers and notes regarding Whittaker's method of Graduation and specifically a discussion of the subject by Dr. Aitken (as he then was) entitled " The Accurate Solution of The Difference Equations involved in Whittaker's Method of Graduation and its Practical Application." Papers dealing with the theory of the construction of mortality tables were given and Dr. W. F. Sheppard delivered an address on " The Relation between Probability and Statistics." In spite of the new and ample blossom appearing on the theoretical branch of our particular Tree of Knowledge, more immediately practical affairs were not neglected. Two scholarly papers on certain aspects of finance were presented around this time by C. M. Douglas ; his work reached an extremely high standard and it is sad indeed that, as I shall require to mention again later, one so gifted and so assiduous in his labours for the Faculty—latterly carried on in spite of distressing ill-health—should have been cut off before his work was done and before he had reached the position of honour in the profession to which his distinguished ability must surely have brought him.

Fortunately for Lidstone, as I think, the Honorary Secretary during his Presidency was his loyal colleague J. A. Thomson ; for there was an immense amount of work to be done—and with this particular combination at the head of our affairs, it was done—in connection with proposed amendments to the Assurance Companies Act 1909. Lidstone had been chosen to represent the whole British actuarial profession on the Departmental Committee established to consider what changes were desirable, but was unable to accept since of course the meetings were to be held in London. However, in due course, he gave evidence before the Committee on behalf of the Faculty and was assisted by Steuart Macnaghten. Everything was considered and reconsidered in the utmost detail and with painstaking diligence—the mass of correspondence and memoranda in the files leaves no doubt of the magnitude of the task—but nothing has come out of it so far, although no doubt some day the work will bear fruit, when Parliament can afford time for a quiet session on the important subject of insurance legislation.

In his Presidential Address, delivered after he had been eleven years in Edinburgh, Lidstone referred to the fact that Low had mentioned the possibility of a union with the Institute. He said : " It is indeed permissible to doubt whether a profession which probably will always be small in numbers, in spite of the great and widespread financial interests for which it is responsible, can for all time afford the luxury of two independent representative bodies. But as Mr. Low himself indicated, there are reasons, national, historical and geographical, which will probably for some time to come, if not permanently, prevent the serious consideration of such an important step." He went on to refer to the possible advantages of combining the examinations, and even the trans-actions, of the two bodies and the idea of joint examinations was considered fully and, one hopes, finally in the next few years. I have mentioned the subjects of union with the Institute and of joint examinations when they arose in an earlier chapter and I have there indicated the arguments involved. The question of a union was not considered, and when Lidstone's attention was drawn to the manner in which, with the best will in the world, joint examinations must inevitably undermine the indepen-dence of the smaller body, he saw the force of the argument and at a Council Meeting of the Faculty held during the Presidency of Charles Guthrie, he agreed that the idea should be abandoned. This was the last occasion upon which the question was officially considered.

The so distinguished services which Lidstone had rendered were recognised both by the Institute and by the Faculty shortly after his retirement from business in 1929 ; the two bodies decided jointly to present him with a gold medal " in recognition of his unique services to actuarial science." Although the busts of W. T. Thomson and T. B. Sprague stood as a tribute to their memory in the Hall of the Faculty and although the Institute had presented a gold medal in 1927 to George King, this was the first occasion upon which the two institutions representative of actuarial science in the United Kingdom had combined to honour an outstanding member of the profession. The presentation was made on 28th October, 1929 in Staple Inn Hall, a number of members of the Faculty being present, and Charles Guthrie, then President, gave an appreciation of Lidstone on behalf of the Faculty.

Lidstone was of course a difficult man to follow in the Presidential Chair and it fell to the lot of Ralph Hill Stewart to carry out this task. Stewart delivered his Address on 8th December, 1926 and paid eloquent tribute to his predecessor ; the speech dealt chiefly with matters which had been considered by the Committee on insurance legislation and this was to be expected from the author, who was a business man chiefly. Prior to becoming President, he had not taken an active part in the affairs of the Faculty and it may be that he achieved this signal honour, not for any particular actuarial accomplishments, but in virtue of the position of importance which he attained in the business world—he was latterly General Manager of the Caledonian. For whatever reason, he kept himself very much aloof and was not well known either to his colleagues in his Office or to actuaries in general. For this reason it has proved a little difficult to get an insight into his character, but on the few occasions upon which I met him I found him a pleasant conversationalist. A distinguished member of the Faculty, who has since reached a position of pre-eminence in his profession, started out upon his career as an apprentice in the Caledonian during Stewart's term of office as General Manager. There were two apprentices—he was the junior—and an irksome but not unusual part of their duty was to despatch the letters each evening. On one occasion Stewart was taking longer to sign his letters than suited the convenience of Mr. X, the senior apprentice, who wished to play golf, so he instructed his junior to tell the General Manager to hurry up, as he wished to go away. Mistaking in his innocence a hasty jest for a serious instruction, the future ornament of the actuarial profession did just that and Stewart's reaction was merely a mild request to inform Mr. X that the office was not run for his convenience. Of course, this could only have occurred in a Scottish office ; but it is an interesting, if not anomalous, fact, that the message was carried by an Englishman !

The Eighth Actuarial Congress was held in London in June, 1927, during Stewart's term of office and he acted with acceptance as host, when meetings of a social nature in connection with this event were held in Scotland. S. F. M. Cumming acted as Congress Correspondent for Scotland on this occasion and everything was carried through with great success and smoothness. Cumming, who has served the Faculty in many ways—he became Vice-President in 1942—took a keen interest in and did much work in connection with the Actuarial Congresses, which is definitely one of the more thankless tasks. At the various international meetings the position of the Faculty was for a long time quite unsatisfactory; in 1903, N. B. Gunn, then President, reported unfavourably as to the position in which the Faculty was placed at the Congress in New York and Archibald Hewat, who followed him as President, made strenuous efforts to rectify matters. However, in Holland in 1912 and again in Rome in 1934 it seems that Continental actuaries did not appreciate that the Institute and Faculty were entirely separate bodies, although the President of the Institute on the latter occasion went out of his way to clarify the situation. The confusion arose quite naturally in the minds of our overseas friends, for Scotland was not separately represented on the Permanent Committee until quite recent times. That everything is now satisfactory in this respect I can certify from personal experience at Paris in 1949, when, along with R. Ll. Gwilt and James Davie, I attended the celebrations in connection with the Jubilee of the Institut des Actuaires Français. This is not the place to tell the story of the actuarial congresses and celebrations in various parts of the world, although, of course, the Faculty has always played an active part in them. On numerous occasions we have made presentations to actuarial bodies to mark an occasion, but perhaps for us in Scotland the meeting in Paris was rather a special one as typifying the "Auld Alliance" and as illustrating the fact that by 1949 at least the independent status and the seniority of the Faculty had received full recognition on the Continent. The present we gave took the form of an ivory gavel and the unusual feature of the gift was that the box holding it was, to translate the inscription engraved upon it, " made from wood taken from a room in Edinburgh Castle, where Mary, Queen of Scots and formerly Queen of François II of France, 1559-1560, gave birth in 1566 to the Prince who was later James VI of Scotland and I of England." As regards the status and seniority of the Faculty, a place of honour on the platform had been reserved for our President (myself, as it happened) and I was the second speaker called upon, following of course the President of the Institute. I made my speech in English, for had I spoken in French, the famous warning of the Great Englishman—" Prenez garde ! Je vais parler français ! "—would have been doubly—nay trebly—necessary.

Ralph Hill Stewart died early in 1928, whilst still President, and was followed by Charles Guthrie. Guthrie, who died on 27th May 1953 at the age of eighty-four, had a long connection with the Faculty ; he became a Fellow in 1895. I think it would be fair to describe him as a kindly and wise man ; but he was not one who took a noticeably active part in strictly actuarial affairs. The only positions, apart from membership of the Council, which he occupied in the Faculty were the important ones of President and Vice-President and, although in the Session 1898-9 he contributed a paper to the old Actuarial Society on one aspect of life office organisation, it does not appear that he made any contribution to the *Transactions* other than his Presidential Address. His term of office as President was, however, an active and successful one ; I was Honorary Secretary at the time and I found him approachable and easy to deal with. Essentially a business man of conservative outlook, his career as a man of affairs was outstanding, and as a President his advice in connection with the subject of insurance legislation, which was still very much to the fore, and regarding the necessity of obtaining new and permanent accommodation for the Faculty, was highly valued. He was an active member of the Episcopal Church in Scotland, of the Council of which he was a member for no less than thirty-five years. His sense of humour was of a characteristically gentle nature.

Guthrie was interested, as of course his position in the business world required, in the subject of finance and early in his term of office a Committee of the Faculty—consisting of C. M. Douglas, A. E. King, A. C. Murray, J. A. Thomson, R. S. Caverhill and J. Dunlop—was appointed to examine the question of investment research. Later a joint meeting with members appointed by the Institute was held and, in May 1930, whilst Guthrie was still President, the Actuaries' Investment Index was first published. This service to the financial community has been successfully maintained in spite of troublous times and under the aegis of both actuarial bodies is still published at regular intervals.

There was much activity at this time in connection with the Insurance Undertakings Bill; there were joint meetings with the Associated Scottish Life Offices and Steuart Macnaghten represented the Faculty at a meeting with Government officials in London. A tremendous amount of detailed work was done, but, so far, as I mentioned earlier, legislation has not resulted.

The lease of the Faculty's premises in Queen Street ran out and was renewed on a temporary basis; but the question of a more permanent home was under constant consideration. When the Scottish banks decided to build a new clearing house, the opportunity was taken in 1929 to approach them with the suggestion that an upper storey should be added to their building and leased to the Faculty. Under the expert guidance of the late Mr. Lindsay Auldjo Jamieson, the Faculty's architect, the negotiations went on and in 1932, during the Presidency of Steuart Macnaghten, who followed Charles Guthrie, a lease of the new rooms for twenty-one years from 15th May 1932 was executed. The lease was renewed for ten years from 15th May 1953 at the original rental (£298 10s.). It was agreed that the Faculty should pay the appropriate proportion of owner's rates and the original cost (exclusive of occupier's rates) was some £350—owing to increases in rates the cost has by now risen above that figure by about £20. The Scottish life offices owe, of course, a great deal to the Faculty; its Fellows have supplied the technical skill essential to their prosperity. It was none the less a generous action on their part when in 1930, through the Associated Scottish Life Offices, they agreed to pay an annual sum of £350 to the Faculty. The first payment was made in November 1931 and payments have been made annually since. The Committee Room is at the disposal of the Association for their meetings and in fact, under an arrangement which will be described later, the Faculty's premises are now, and have been for a long time, the offices and meeting rooms of the Association, so that the offices now receive value for their contribution in a concrete and direct form. The arrangement has been satisfactory to both bodies and has stood the test of time.

The new building includes a main Hall, where sessional meetings are held and where the Students' Society meets and classes and facilities for study are provided. The walls are lined with book-cases and

The present Hall, showing the new War Memorial, the platform and the clock presented (1933) by members of the Council of the Institute of Actuaries

The present Council Chamber, showing Adam fireplace

the War Memorial is built into the wall on the left side facing the platform. On the platform are the busts of W. T. Thomson and T. B. Sprague, whilst behind the platform are plaster casts of the gold medals presented by the Institute and the Faculty to G. J. Lidstone and Sir W. P. Elderton—the presentation of the latter medal will be referred to later—and the statuette of Napier of Merchiston, the inventor of logarithms, stands above the book-cases at the same end of the Hall. On the wall above the platform is a very lovely clock, the gift of the members of the Council of the Institute of Actuaries. This clock is of course visible to the audience during a meeting, but is so placed as to be behind the Chairman and speakers on the platform. After the death of W. A. Robertson, President 1938-1940, Mrs. Gray, his daughter, intimated that it had been Mr. Robertson's wish to provide a clock to be placed at the other end of the Hall so as to be visible from the platform, and Mrs. Gray in 1940 presented a clock which remains a tangible memorial of the devotion of her father to the Faculty. The Council Chamber, which is a very convenient room with a certain dignity, is entered from the Hall by a door on the right of the platform. There are several smaller rooms which are used as offices by the staff of the Faculty and one of which houses the library of the Insurance Society of Edinburgh.

Photographs of the main Hall and Council Chamber appeared in Volume 16 of the *Transactions*, that of the Hall shewing the old War Memorial in its place. For the purpose of this history new photographs have been taken and in one of them the present War Memorial is shown. Further reference to the War Memorial will be made later.

Steuart Macnaghten, a Fellow of the Institute, came as others have done to seek fortune in Scotland; he was elected to the Fellowship of the Faculty in 1918 and became President in 1930. Owing to his health, he abandoned the Army career for which he originally trained and became in London a qualified accountant and actuary. He came to Edinburgh in 1912 with a considerable actuarial reputation on the theoretical side—he had been a successful tutor—and with some name as a mathematician. He acted as examiner for a time in connection with the Diploma of the University in actuarial mathematics; but he did not contribute original work to the *Transactions* with the exception of his Presidential Address. His capacity for probing a problem to its foundation was remarkable; he was not easily persuaded that a particular solution was the best one or that suited to his purpose and had the habit of persistently worrying at a question which frequently gave amazing results. He had quiet charm of manner and an outstanding insight into business questions. There is little doubt that he could have made a greater name than he did in the purely actuarial field; but he became, as do so many, immersed in affairs. On the other hand, he did good service for the Faculty in many ways and particularly in connection with the Insurance Undertakings Bill, to which he referred in his Address. On that occasion he dealt also with some questions regarding mortality and particularly referred to the need for the examination of extra mortality due to occupational and climatic risks.

Research was still very much in the air in 1930 and 1931. James Davie and R. Ll. Gwilt prepared a report upon " the Effect of Withdrawals upon the apparent duration of Selection " for the Mortality

Committee and, although in the Council Minutes of October 1930 there is mention of a complaint about delay in furnishing the Faculty Committee with information regarding the investigation, the joint studies of normal mortality by the Institute and Faculty were soon working smoothly. In fact a Joint Committee was set up in 1931, the first representatives of the Faculty being the President, A. E. King, C. S. Penn, and R. Ll. Gwilt, and research into normal mortality has been successfully carried on upon this basis ever since. The first Chairman was Sir William Palin Elderton, who held this arduous post for many years with great benefit to the profession and who was succeeded fairly recently by R. Ll. Gwilt, the present Chairman. Meantime, two investigations of a specialised nature were set on foot : the first, to which three life offices and the Royal Infirmary of Edinburgh were to contribute data, was in connection with pulse rates and the second, for which data was to be obtained from the Scottish life offices, was on the subject of height and weight in healthy men and women.

There was evidence of imagination and enterprise, if nothing else, in the establishment of two Mortality Sub-Committees by the Faculty at this time ; the first was to deal with the matters referred to in Macnaghten's Address—occupational and climatic extra mortality—and the second, arising out of Orr's later paper upon the " Selection of Lives," was to prepare plans for a medico-actuarial investigation, which it was hoped could be placed upon a permanent basis, with the collaboration of the Institute. It may be true that " to travel hopefully is a better thing than to arrive, and the true success is to labour " ; but in statistical investigation the result is the thing. Probably the plans laid were over-ambitious for the number of helpers available ; in any case nothing much came directly from these undertakings at the time, although important investigations were then and later made by individual members of the Faculty on the lines contemplated. In time something definite and permanent may arise, for, as I said earlier, there are now stirrings in the Joint Mortality Committee and the indications are that the members will do all in their power to venture into new realms. Actuaries must conquer this ground and make it their own, or it may happen that others, perhaps less well qualified to weigh the evidence, may ejaculate—

"Infirm of purpose !
Give me the daggers"

and leave us in the humiliating position of merely destructive critics. There are not wanting signs that this may occur. The effects of various diseases upon longevity, the correlation between habits or particular items of personal or family history and the occurrence of certain disorders and many kindred fields of investigation can yield information of prime importance not only to the life assurance offices, which so many actuaries serve, but to the community at large ; the data which are available or could be rendered available to actuaries from the records of life assurance and the unrivalled opportunities which they have of collaboration with many of the most distinguished members of the medical profession, combined with their elaborate training as practical statisticians, render the members of our profession peculiarly fitted to undertake important studies which might well prove of great value to humanity. Much work on these lines has been done by actuaries in the United

States (and several members of the Faculty—notably Dr. Arthur Hunter—have taken an active part) and whilst the methods, assumptions and so on may be the subjects of differences of opinion, the only effective and helpful criticism is for the actuaries of Great Britain, using gratefully the experience of their brothers on the other side of the Atlantic, to produce if they can something better, with such improvements in technique as they may be able to devise.

The plan upon which I have endeavoured to work in writing this story has been to describe—so far as I have been able—the men who have been prominent in the affairs of our institution and to allow the facts to emerge as occasion offered. Now that I have reached a point at which I shall be dealing with persons still alive, some of whom still actively pursue their calling, good taste seems to require a rather less rigid application of the original design; but it will still be necessary, with due circumspection, to write of the outstanding personalities—for the men make the Faculty, moulding its destiny and varying its activities in the light of their own characters and views. It will be apparent that the Presidents have by no means invariably been those who have done most for the profession, for actuarial science or indeed for the Faculty itself. Alexander Fraser, A. E. King and C. M. Douglas, for instance, are names which must appear in our record and be accorded a position of honour for devotion and services rendered, before those of several of our Presidents. We were too early deprived of the services of these men and there are others—S. F. M. Cumming, A. G. R. Brown and A. C. Murray are amongst the number—who have rendered long and valuable service to the Faculty and who, for personal reasons, do not appear as Presidents.

The next Presidents in order, up to the outbreak of the Second World War, were Randolph Gordon-Smith, Hugh Wylie Brown, Alexander Graham Donald and William Alexander Robertson. Gordon-Smith did much valuable work in connection with the various actuarial congresses and reported specifically, whilst holding the office of President, upon that in Rome in 1934. He referred suitably in his Address to the death of George King—" one of the greatest actuaries of his day and generation, whom we were proud to claim as one of our members "—and dealt also with the subjects of Industrial and Unemployment Assurance. William Hutton died in 1933, and in his Presidential Address Hugh Brown intimated that Mrs. Hutton had presented the sum of £500 to form the William Hutton Memorial Fund in memory of her husband. The wish was expressed that the income from the Fund should be devoted to the advancement of actuarial education by the encouragement of research and study amongst the younger members of the Faculty and accordingly the Council made the following regulations for the purpose :—

The income from the Fund is to be applied :—

(i) in providing and awarding a medal, to be known as " The William Hutton Medal," for specially meritorious original work ; or

(ii) in granting a prize, to be known as " The William Hutton Prize," for the best essay on a subject prescribed by the Council and subject to such regulations as it may prescribe ; or

(iii) in making grants towards cost of investigation and/or preparing Papers in matters of original research ; or

(iv) in providing for delivery and publication of special lectures for the benefit of the younger members of the Faculty, to be known as " The William Hutton Memorial Lectures," on subjects and by persons selected by the Council ; or

(v) in making grants to the Students' Society in the furtherance of its general work or for any special matter approved by the Council ; or

(vi) for such other purposes as the Council may decide in accordance with the expressed wish of Mrs. Hutton.

The excellent intentions expressed in these rules have hardly been matched in action in the years which have intervened since the presentation was made ; some small awards have been made however and recently—as I write—the Council have made plans for a more vigorous effort to make use of the benefits of this Fund and of the Lidstone Endowment Fund, which I shall refer to in its place.

Hugh Brown, who was unassuming and gentle of disposition, was a frequent contributor to the *Transactions* ; he gave several papers of sound practical value on life assurance matters and took part in many discussions. His Presidential Address dealt with those subjects which were agitating the life assurance world at the time—the Insurance Undertakings Bill (still very much to the fore, but destined to be stillborn), Unemployment Assurance and Workmen's Compensation. About this time, C. L. Stoodley, to whom I referred earlier, contributed to the *Transactions*, which were definitely flourishing, with such contributors as Dr. A. C. Aitken, G. J. Lidstone, A. E. King, A. R. Reid, W. A. Robertson, and later A.C. Murray and A. W. Joseph. Several of the papers were of importance and the scientific and theoretical contributions were of a high order.

Graham Donald's Address was very much on practical lines, dealing with contemporary insurance problems, with some remarks upon Census and Population, and in the course of it he gave interesting figures. The number of petitioners named in the Charter of the Faculty in 1868 was 52, the number of Fellows and Associates in 1910 was 206, which rose to 225 in 1914, fell to 209 in 1919 and at the time of the speech (1936) was 260. Donald gave delightful dinner parties from time to time at his home of which many actuaries will have pleasant memories, and was prominent in the Scottish Actuaries' Club. It was during his term of office that the Institute and the Faculty combined to present a gold medal to Sir William Palin Elderton, " in recognition of his distinguished services to actuarial science "—a plaster cast of which adorns the Faculty Hall. Sir William Elderton, who had been elected to the Fellowship of the Faculty in 1931, has for long now been a familiar and welcome figure at those Faculty meetings which he is able to attend—for of course he lives in the South —and his great services to the profession have always received the high appreciation they deserve from the members of the Faculty. He has frequently addressed the meetings in Edinburgh, but a particularly delightful evening which he gave us was his sketch of the life of William Morgan—the Father of the Profession— which appears in Volume 14 of the *Transactions*.

During 1937, there was a proposal to hold an " Actuarial Conference " in the United States in 1938 and Dr. Arthur Hunter was compiling a list of members of the Faculty to be invited; but dire circumstances intervened to prevent the occurrence of this happy occasion.

In 1930, the Council set up a Students' Registry for the assistance of employers who required the services of an actuary or actuarial student; it did not however function as was expected or hoped—little publicity was given to it. In 1938 the Registry was abandoned and the present Appointments Board constituted " for the benefit of Members of the Faculty and of those who wish to employ actuaries in a permanent capacity." This body has carried on its work satisfactorily and is still given prominence in the Faculty's Year Book, greatly to the convenience of our younger members. In this year (1938) also a step of the highest importance in the domestic arrangements of the Faculty took place. Mr. D. G. Cochrane, the Assistant Secretary, had been retired on pension some time previously and after considerable deliberation a long-cherished project of the authorities of the Faculty was put into execution—one of the Fellows was appointed to a full-time position on the permanent staff. It was the close liaison of the Faculty with the Associated Scottish Life Offices that rendered the arrangement feasible and made it possible to create a post worthy of a man of the calibre of Mr. Edward Waugh, who was appointed Assistant Secretary of both bodies and very shortly afterwards promoted to be Secretary. Since his appointment Mr. Waugh has, through the busy years, demonstrated the wisdom of the arrangement and with his staff has dealt with admirable efficiency and versatility with the routine work and the many widely-differing matters that have come before the two organisations.

The useful and happy idea of producing a Year Book arose at this time and the first issue was published in the Spring of 1939. A. E. King, James Davie and K. K. Weatherhead were responsible for the first issue and were specially thanked by the Council. In spite of unavoidable delays in publication due to war and post-war conditions, which were naturally extremely frustrating, the publication has served its purpose admirably and latterly the responsibility for the subject matter has rested mainly, if not entirely, upon Mr. Waugh.

W. A. Robertson, in his Address, mentioned the death of his " old friend and tutor," Henry Moir, and referred to the distinguished services which Moir had rendered to the Faculty in his early days as a contributor to the *Transactions* and as an able tutor, as well as to his work for life assurance both here and in the United States, where he spent the last thirty-six years of his life. It was only to be expected that Robertson, when inaugurating his reign as President, should deal with questions of interest to the younger men ; he felt that the profession held opportunities for youth and that insufficient numbers were availing themselves of them. Robertson was probably the most popular man of his time in the profession ; he was an enthusiast and, whatever his years, he was always young. His outlook was full of vigour to the end of his life—he died in harness and whilst still President. The clock, which I have mentioned, on the wall of the Hall opposite the platform, presented by his daughter, is a memorial to an untiring servant of the Faculty and one of our most successful tutors. He was one of the earliest and principal authorities on sickness and disability insurance. He would give his time and advice unsparingly to help the students and junior Fellows, although he had a passion for business and could ill spare a moment of his long working day for a merely social visit from one of his friends and contemporaries. He was a distinguished referee at Rugby football and has, so far as I have been able to ascertain, the distinction of being the only President to refer to the game in his Address. Of course we should all have been astounded had he not done so—we were waiting for it! To watch Robertson at his favourite pastime of refereeing a schoolboys' game was to receive a lesson in how to promote the highest spirit of sportsmanship with the greatest degree of enthusiasm and " rigour of the game."

The jubilee of the Actuarial Society of America was celebrated early in 1939; a gavel was presented to celebrate the occasion and the Faculty was represented by L. M. Cathles, a Fellow long resident in the United States, who has had a distinguished career in that ample field.

But once again the happy career of the Faculty with its growing momentum and broadening spirit of scientific and professional enterprise was to be arrested; the lamps went out again and this time both literally and metaphorically. The important, simple and enduring things of life were hustled into the wings and heroism and beastliness, selfless devotion and meanness, gallantry and brutality were to hold the stage for six terrible years.

CHAPTER VII

MODERN TIMES
1939-1956

> "There is therefore hope that in the end man
> may use his new powers to make his life
> fuller and happier than of old, if some day
> an escape is found from totalitarian war and
> violence."
> — TREVELYAN.

MY previous chapter began with " the War to end
war " and this begins with " the Unnecessary War " ;
once again the ship sought refuge in harbour—and
an uneasy berth it proved to be. Once again the
peaceful voyage was rudely interrupted ; but once
again it was resumed after the years of affliction and
that with a renewal of the vigour and enterprise
which had characterised its earliest years and which
were strongly in evidence in the years succeeding the
conflict of 1914-1918. The very necessity to start
afresh after years of comparative inactivity (from a
strictly professional point of view) has seemed to
call forth all that was best from the members of the
Faculty—its recent years have proved to be not the
least fruitful in its history. As I write, there are heavy
and dark clouds upon the political horizon ; surely
the arts of peace do not require the dreadful stimulus
of these dire interruptions. Perhaps we may find
some comfort in the words which the eminent
historian has allowed himself to use and which I
have quoted at the head of this chapter, and preserve
our faith in the destiny of man. In the year 1650, the

people of Norwich petitioned Parliament to grant to them the land and fabric of " that vast and altogether useless Cathedral of Norwich " to enable them to build a workhouse ; in these grim times, when it is so obvious that humanitarian materialism is not enough, we may find some solace in the reflection that Norwich Cathedral still stands in all its beauty, to proclaim its message of hope.

On the outbreak of war in 1939, those questions which had arisen twenty-five years before were again pressing ; but this time the men in charge of the Faculty's affairs had experience to call upon—the situation was not so unfamiliar as it had been in 1914 and many decisions had been taken out of the hands of individuals by the Government. Questions about the position of actuaries *vis-a-vis* national service and the status of those in the service of the Government in a professional capacity arose at once, as did the subject of allowing the younger members to volunteer for service in any form. On all these matters, the President represented the Faculty upon the Actuaries and Statisticians Committee of the Central Registry Advisory Council. The examination in Part I due to take place in the autumn of 1939 was held in spite of war and the general question of holding examinations was considered. On 29th September, the Council decided not to hold examinations in 1940 ; but, less than a month later—on 20th October—the decision was reversed and the 1940 examinations were in fact carried out over the whole range of the syllabus. After full and repeated consideration, it was decided to conduct only Parts I and II in April 1941 and to abandon the examinations in Parts III and IV for the duration of the War. Later on it was agreed to drop Part II also, so that only Part I examinations were held each year from 1942 until April 1946, when examinations covering the full syllabus were resumed. The idea underlying the continuation of the earlier Parts of the examinations was to enable those students who were below military age to prosecute their studies until called up for service. There can be no room for doubt that the arrangement helped to sustain the interest of the younger students and to secure them for the profession when they returned to civilian life ; for, having passed some of the examinations, they had set their feet on the ladder and it was the most natural thing for them to continue the climb when opportunity offered. An air-raid shelter was provided for the Faculty's staff at the commencement of the War and regulations were devised about air-raid warnings during examinations and for the transmission of question papers to, and answers from, overseas examination centres—the answers of the Australian candidates in the April 1942 examinations were lost in transit, but photographic copies arrived safely later. The matter of holding meetings in the Hall arose out of the official ban on congregations of persons ; but this very largely and naturally settled itself, for everyone was quite properly far too preoccupied and busy to write actuarial treatises. During 1942, it was decided to suspend publication of the Year Book and, during this period, the work of the Actuarial Tuition Service was maintained, not without difficulty, to the limited extent required by the restricted scope of the examinations.

Just after the outbreak of war, A. E. King resigned from his activities in the Faculty owing to a breakdown of health and in 1942 he succumbed to an illness which he had borne with courage and patience. As mentioned in the last chapter, W. A. Robertson

also passed from the scene. Robertson had served
the Faculty much longer than had King and had
reached the Presidential Chair ; but the two men were
alike to the extent that they had unbounded enthusiasm
for their profession and regarded it, so far as one
might judge, as one of the highest and most satisfying
forms of human activity—it would never have
occurred to either to wish that he had adopted another
field of endeavour. There is of course a delightful
variety available for one who enters with zeal into the
actuarial life ; it has its scientific, mathematical and
academic side, with endless scope for research and
statistical enquiry ; and it has its business side, rich
in human contacts and in the practical problems of
administration and finance. The very variety of
opportunity might be expected to lead to a certain
dissipation of effort in the different fields ; but its
dual aspect has in fact tended, particularly in the case
of the more financially successful members of the
profession, to concentration upon business—for there
the tangible prizes are to be won—to the exclusion of
almost all else. This is, of course, unfortunate and
could, by drawing the best brains into absorbing
business interests, stultify research and scientific
progress ; but there have always been exceptional
men (T. B. Sprague and Lidstone, for instance) who
were not unmindful of the debt they owed to their
profession and of the fascination of original research.
There are signs, as I think will appear in this narrative,
that in recent years even the most successful modern
actuaries do not allow themselves to become absorbed
in business to the detriment of their interest in the
scientific aspect of their work. The rigorous course
of training which the present actuaries have had to
undergo has implanted in them a spirit of professional

integrity upon which we may rely. Robertson and King were examples of men, who, throughout their professional lives, maintained a wide and whole-hearted interest in many phases of the actuary's work, and the Faculty was greatly the poorer for their loss. They had each a certain boyishness to the end of their lives—although in King's case this was hidden from all but those who knew him well by a shyness and superficial severity of manner. In outward appearance the two men could hardly have been more unlike—Robertson was short and exuberant ; King was tall and restrained. Robertson received the recognition that was his due when he became President ; but King was not so fortunate. When C. S. Penn delivered his Presidential Address, he said of King, " I feel certain that had he survived, he would have been in my place to-day," and went on to pay tribute to King's exceptional services to the Faculty in the years between the wars.

William Bannatyne succeeded Robertson as President and read his address on 16th December 1940, under the shadow of war. He had taken over the office at a time of great difficulty and anxiety ; his attention was inevitably largely confined to the numerous and troublesome war-time questions of administration which arose and, whilst I do not suppose that he regards himself as in any sense an actuarial innovator, greatly no doubt he regretted that circumstances so severely limited his activities. It was a worrying time and it was unfortunate from his point of view that the opportunity for leadership, which falls to the head of the profession, should have come to him when it did ; he is a man of wide cultural interests and had a successful professional career, attaining to an important position in the business world.

Actuaries overseas demonstrated in a practical way their feeling of kinship with those of Britain. In 1940 the actuaries of North America offered accommodation to the children of members of the Faculty or Institute who might wish to send their families overseas for the period of the War. The offer was a particularly generous one for it included the payment of all the expenses of upkeep of the children in the United States and, in spite of the fact that no families were sent across the Atlantic under the arrangement, it was received here with deep gratitude. Later, a similar proposal came from Australia, and from Cape Town an offer of hospitality to those members or students of the Faculty who might be passing through South Africa as members of the Forces. When the United States became an active partner in the hostilities and large numbers of their service men arrived in Britain, the Institute and Faculty communicated to the actuarial bodies in the United States the wish of British actuaries to show hospitality and render any assistance in their power to any of their members who were stationed in or passing through this country.

Finlay James Cameron, James Gray Kyd, Colin Strathern Penn, and I were the next four Presidents and for the first two the state of war very much limited their activities. Finlay Cameron, one of the most agreeable of men and with a lively sense of humour, began his actuarial career in Edinburgh ; but shortly after he qualified, he left for Bradford and later transferred to London. It was not until 1928 that he returned to the Scottish Capital to take up the post of General Manager of the Caledonian, so that for a long period he was unable to take that intimate part in the affairs of the Faculty which fell to his lot in his later years. Cameron was greatly concerned with the welfare of the younger members and at his instigation a Committee was appointed in June 1943 to consider examinations in the post-war era; once again, plans were being laid during war for a vigorous resumption of activities when the conditions should become favourable. The Committee met frequently and had always in view the provision for students of such facilities as would help them, so far as might be possible, to make up for lost time and to resettle themselves in professional life. As after the 1914-1918 War, it was recommended that the examinations be held half-yearly instead of yearly and now a notable innovation was the suggestion of a plan of day-time study for students employed by life offices which was actually put into operation after the war and which proved a great boon to those concerned. The President referred at length in his Address, delivered on 30th November 1942, to the subject of the post-war training of students and took a keen and practical interest in the subject. After his retirement, Cameron was the victim of a severe illness and it was with great sorrow that his many friends heard of his death on 9th April 1954 at the age of 74.

J. G. Kyd, who followed Cameron as President, was Registrar-General for Scotland—the first professional actuary to hold this post. His predecessor in that important position, Dr. J. C. Dunlop, had been an Honorary Fellow of the Faculty and was a familiar and welcome figure at those meetings which dealt with subjects in which he was interested. Kyd exerted himself to maintain the activity of the Faculty and to prepare the ground for the post-war period. There was, about this time, a tentative stirring of actuarial interest in spite of war; Alexander Fraser contributed to the *Transactions* from his retirement in

August 1943 on his own particular subject of widows' funds—the paper was published, but in the circumstances, it was not read at a meeting—and in the early months of 1945 J. Murray Laing and D. A. Porteous submitted papers. The President arranged for a lecture to be given to the Faculty by Professor Crew of Edinburgh University on the subject of " The Role of Statistics in the Furtherance of Medical Research " and another lecture was given by Sir Alexander Carr-Saunders, the eminent authority on population. There had been a suggestion for a statistical enquiry into the subject of war deaths by the Institute and the Faculty, but there were actuarial and other difficulties in the way and it fell to the ground, as did an idea promulgated in 1944 for a study of the mortality under assurance policies of large amounts. The interest in research was maintained, however, and Kyd was the author of a scheme to promote the use of the services of members of the Faculty, in their capacity of practical statisticians, by members of the medical and other professions who might be engaged in scientific investigations. In his Address, which he delivered on 25th October 1945, the President referred to the vast untilled field of research in which actuaries by their training were peculiarly fitted to serve and the Scottish Statistical Research Bureau was established at his instigation for the purpose of giving practical expression to his views. A small committee was formed and was received in turn by the Universities of St. Andrews, Glasgow, Edinburgh and Aberdeen for preliminary discussion. I was myself a member of the deputation which attended at the Universities and have a lively recollection of the meetings, which were not without their amusing side. We were of course received with the greatest courtesy, but inevitably it was pointed out to us that the subject of statistics was taught by the Universities themselves (a fact with which we were, naturally, familiar) and some stress was laid upon the depth and thoroughness of the treatment it received. It proved to be difficult, if not impossible, to persuade those concerned that there was a place which could be filled by the Bureau and it is possible that we might have had more success had we been interviewing the authorities of the various medical schools, whose pride would hardly have been touched, rather than the mathematicians. No one doubted for a moment that there were in each University members of the staff who were versed in the subject of statistics and more particularly in its theoretical aspects ; but I for one still adhere to the view that there should be ample scope for the collaboration we suggested. Actuaries are very practical statisticians with their feet firmly planted on the ground, who, in their every-day occupation, are dealing with statistical problems involving large sums of money and who are therefore accustomed and trained to a very real sense of responsibility ; the conclusions they draw from the statistics before them are generally speaking those of efficient and reliable men who are dealing with these things every day of their lives. There was no suggestion by us of competition between the University statisticians and the actuaries ; rather, what we were trying to put forward was the idea that in the face of an almost unlimited field of research, there was room for collaboration between research workers in all their various provinces and a group of persons whose professional life was spent, more or less, in coping with practical statistical questions. The Bureau was started and some few cases were dealt with, but it

The Members of
he Actuarial Society of America
and of
The American Institute of Actuaries
in joint meeting assembled November 8, 1945, hereby

Resolve, that fraternal greetings and congratulations upon the victorious conclusion of the war be extended to the members of The Institute of Actuaries and of The Faculty of Actuaries in Scotland;

That, in so doing, the members of both American societies express to the actuaries of Great Britain their gratitude for and their admiration of the immeasurable contribution to freedom and civilization made by Great Britain throughout the war, but particularly in "their finest hour" when the British held the line alone while the fate of the free nations of the world hung in the balance; and

That, they rejoice in the increasingly friendly relations between British, American and Canadian actuaries and express the firm belief that the dangers which have been faced together and the sacrifices made in the common cause will cement and further extend these friendly relations and result in still greater cooperation in matters of common interest among actuaries on both sides of the Atlantic.

The Actuarial Society of America	The American Institute of Actuaries
President *Tw. Marshall*	President *[signature]*
Secretary *Wilmer A Jenkins*	Secretary *W B Mac Kinnon*

AMERICAN ACTUARIAL BODIES

Resolution of fraternal greetings to the Faculty and the Institute of Actuaries (8th Nov., 1945)

seems now to have fallen into disuse. One can only hope that this admirable idea, brought forward in a practical way by Kyd, will in course of time fulfil the hopes we entertained for it and assist in purveying the benefits of research to the people of Scotland. The Bureau, although meantime, it must be admitted, moribund, is still in existence and its services are available on application to the Secretary of the Faculty. Our Year Book says—" It is expected that the Bureau will prove useful in small investigations where, for example, a doctor with medical statistics may wish an actuary to collaborate with him, as a practical statistician, in getting at the facts behind the rough data, but the Committee (of the Bureau) is also ready to consider arranging collaboration on a larger scale."

By the end of Kyd's Presidency, arrangements had been completed for the return of students to professional life. The insurance offices had agreed to the system of supervised day-time study, and this was not done without difficulty in the busy period of reconstruction after the War; representatives were appointed by the Actuarial Tuition Service at various centres throughout the country to advise students in regard to their work; an abridged course of reading was prepared and recommended; and the syllabus was revised.

On 8th November 1945, a resolution of fraternal greetings and congratulations was unanimously adopted at a joint meeting of the Actuarial Society of America and the American Institute of Actuaries. This resolution, which was addressed to the Institute and Faculty and an engrossed copy of which is reproduced here, was gratefully received and Kyd, as President of the Faculty, in the course of his letter acknowledging receipt of the copy of the resolution, wrote :—

> "I was instructed to convey to you our thanks not only for the resolution itself, but for the spirit of friendliness which prompted it and for the graceful tribute it contains to the steadfastness of the people of Great Britain during the recent War. This I gladly and proudly do.
>
> "The fight is over but much of the turmoil remains and the period of that turmoil can only be determined by common sense, comradeship and good-will between men of all nations. We therefore welcome the friendly gesture of your resolution. We endorse your belief that the common dangers which have been faced and conquered by the United States and the British Commonwealth of Nations will result in even more friendly relations and co-operation between the members of our profession on both sides of the Atlantic, and trust that that spirit will pervade the peoples of our two nations so that the freedom we have together so dearly won may be enduring."

One of the casualties of the War, which was especially grievous to actuaries in Britain, was the destruction of Staple Inn—the home of the Institute of Actuaries. The sympathy of all actuaries must have gone out to the Institute on the loss of this historic and beautiful old building ; many messages of condolence were received by the Institute and a facsimile of that sent by their closest friends (one may presume thus to describe the members of the Faculty) was reproduced in Vol. 72 of the *Journal* of the Institute. Although some relics were preserved from the ruin, the destruction of an historic building has a character of finality. It gave profound satisfaction to all British actuaries to see the Institute established in a new home on the old site ; but it is sad indeed that, however beautiful and worthy of a great institution, it must be a *new* home. Another casualty was the actuarial library of the University of Louvain and the Institute and the Faculty agreed to assist in its reconstruction by supplying such books as were available.

When C. S. Penn succeeded to the Presidency in 1946, there had not yet been sufficient time for a resumption of the full activity of the Faculty, particularly as regards sessional meetings, which require of course the preparation of actuarial treatises for submission and discussion; but it was then decided to restart the annual issue of the Year Book which had for some years been suspended. The President delivered his inaugural Address on 9th December and, whilst he referred therein to a variety of subjects, it was to be expected that, in view of his own personal interest in the subject, he should deal more particularly with the kindred matters of the selection of lives and research in life assurance and refer to the papers given by L. P. Orr. He, along with Dr. Fergus Hewat, has since placed the profession in his debt by the most valuable and exhaustive study of medical selection which I mentioned in an earlier chapter. He has of course done much other valuable work for the Faculty, particularly in the educational sphere—for long he was a most painstaking examiner and became Chairman of the Board of Examiners.

The question of the position of actuarial students in relation to compulsory national service arose in the autumn of 1946 and after protracted negotiations and discussion, eminently satisfactory arrangements were concluded with the authorities, so that, with suitable safeguards, deferment of calling up could be obtained for a reasonable period to allow of the completion of the course of study. Similar arrangements apply of course to other professional students and, needless to say, involve no neglect of their responsibilities as citizens. An early interruption of a student's work raises the question whether it will be resumed when the period of service is concluded, for the prospect of a long course of study may well be a formidable deterrent to one who, during his period in the forces, has felt some natural diminution in his interest in and enthusiasm for the subject.

S. F. M. Cumming after a long and valuable period of service retired at this time from the Permanent Committee on Actuarial Congresses, leaving R. Gordon-Smith and J. G. Wallace as our representatives. In 1949, during my own Presidency, the representation of the Faculty at international Congresses arose for consideration. Up to this time there had been only one national correspondent for Great Britain and he a Fellow of the Institute; this, as I indicated earlier, led upon occasion to misunderstanding of the completely independent nature of the Institute and Faculty and was generally unsatisfactory. We were fortunate in having in J. G. Wallace one who, on the grounds both of his accomplishments and interest in the subject, was admirably fitted to be national correspondent for Scotland. Happily we were able to arrange for two national correspondents in future for Great Britain and, also happily, Wallace found it possible to accept this somewhat arduous post. Since then, the new arrangement has proved highly satisfactory and has removed a long-standing source of occasional dissatisfaction. In 1951, R. Gordon-Smith found it necessary to retire from the Permanent Committee, where for so long he had rendered great service to the profession in Scotland, and his place was taken by A. C. Murray. J. G. Wallace remains a member of the Committee in addition to holding the post of national correspondent.

In 1948, the celebration of the centenary of the Institute was the outstanding actuarial event and Penn, as President, presented on behalf of the Faculty a silver inkstand to mark the occasion. This was the first actuarial centenary and the arrangements were worthy of a great event in the history of our profession. The President made a suitable speech of congratulation to the Institute and by his dignity and quiet charm of manner was a worthy representative of the Scottish actuaries and indeed in his own person illustrated the friendly bonds which unite the two old actuarial bodies.

One of the first duties that fell to my lot as President was the melancholy one of paying tribute to Charles Douglas to whom I have already referred and whose death was reported to the Council at their meeting on 22nd July 1948—the first meeting over which I presided. In my presidential address on 15th November 1948 I spoke of Douglas in these words :—

> "There is no need for me to dwell upon his service to the Faculty; his record of solid constructive work is well known to be one which few of our members can have equalled, and this in the face of distressing ill-health long-continued. There is no man whom I should rather have seen occupying this chair; he combined real modesty with great personal charm and with a scholarship and ability of which we were not to see the full fruits."

There was no sham or humbug about Douglas; if he allowed himself to express views on a subject, one could rely upon the fact that they rested upon no superficial acquaintance with it, but were the result of genuine and painstaking study. His greatest single work for the Faculty was in the establishment and operation of the Actuarial Tuition Service; he was Chairman of the Edinburgh section of the Committee for many years.

During my period of office, we were fortunate in having a highly satisfactory supply of contributions to the *Transactions*; in the first winter there were four sessional meetings and in the second there were five, including the delightful evening provided by Professor Aitken's paper on " Theories of Probability " of which I made mention in an earlier chapter. Time had now elapsed and the ideas of members had had opportunity to develop and fructify; in fact the spate of sessional meetings in the following years, with the consequent increase in size and expense of the *Transactions* caused some anxiety to successive Honorary Treasurers and was no doubt important amongst the causes which led to increases in the subscriptions of the various classes of members.

I mentioned at its appropriate point in my story that in 1904 the Lord Lyon King of Arms in Scotland gave it as his opinion that the design in use for the Seal of the Faculty was open to serious objection in that it closely resembled the Royal Arms and that a new, but not a heraldic, design was then adopted. A little before the time of which I am now writing, on one of the numerous civic occasions which take place in the Scottish Capital, the Faculty was represented in the procession by the then President (Cameron) and the Secretary and were accorded very proper (as I would like to think) precedence—in fact our deputation were placed in the forefront; this precedence gave rise to some comment amongst persons delegated by other older, larger and, in their opinion, more important bodies and the matter came to the attention of the Lord Lyon King of Arms.

On looking into it, he came to the conclusion that our right of any precedence whatever was gravely prejudiced by the fact that we had received no grant of Arms and that in any case in our Seal we were using two symbols, the Scottish Lion and the Crown, without right or authority. Accordingly in the autumn of 1948 discussions were undertaken with the Lord Lyon, who could not have been more helpful, to arrange that the Faculty should receive a grant of Arms appropriate to its position and dignity. The Faculty was represented by its architect, Mr. G. Lindsay Auldjo Jamieson, and I, as President, had the pleasure of attending one or two of the meetings with the Lord Lyon and seeing something at first hand of the work of an authority on the ancient science of heraldry. By Letters Patent dated 6th July 1950, the Court of the Lord Lyon granted Arms to the Faculty and a reproduction of the Letters Patent from Vol. 20 of the *Transactions* is given here along with the new Seal. Naturally there were quite a few preliminary drawings and ideas for the Arms and we received valuable assistance and suggestions from Alexander Bateman, Honorary Secretary of the Faculty at the time the grant was made. It was he who suggested the hourglass held by the owl " in its sinister claw," as lending a proper actuarial atmosphere of mortality to the design. In the Letters Patent there is no mention of the mathematical emblems included—the background of integral signs and the sine curve (except for the word " wavy ")— but no doubt such, comparatively speaking, modern mathematical frivolities have not yet achieved recognition by the authorities on heraldry. The result seems to me worthy of the Faculty and in every way fitting. It was necessary to have the design engraved afresh upon the President's Badge of Office and the generous offer of Dr. Fergus Hewat to bear the expense of this (the badge having been originally presented by his father as noted in Chapter V) was gratefully accepted.

An event of great importance in the actuarial world took place in 1949, when the Actuarial Society of America and the American Institute of Actuaries combined to form the Society of Actuaries. It was not found possible to arrange for a delegation from the Faculty to visit the United States for the occasion, but Sir George Maddex, then President of the Institute, conveyed the greetings of all actuaries of Great Britain when he attended. J. B. Maclean, who has been President of the Actuarial Society of America, a distinguished Fellow of the Faculty resident in the United States and a member of Council at the time, made a presentation of a specially-bound set of the *Transactions* from the Faculty to mark the occasion and reported to the Council upon the celebrations. He is now a Vice-President of the Faculty—the first Fellow resident overseas to hold that office.

Towards the end of 1949, the Council decided that the War Memorial in the Hall which commemorated those who gave their lives and those who served in the 1914-1918 War should be re-designed to include only the names of those who lost their lives in that War and to incorporate the names of those who fell in the 1939-1945 War. A Committee was appointed to consider how best to give effect to this decision and in 1952 the new War Memorial was erected. A photograph of the new Memorial in colour is reproduced here from Volume 21 of the *Transactions*.

The design was arranged by the Committee in collaboration with our architect, Mr. Jamieson, who upon this, as upon another occasion, earned the gratitude of our members. His skilful and sympathetic treatment of the subject has given general satisfaction, as has the manner in which the work was carried out by Messrs. Scott Morton Ltd., of Edinburgh. The panel of the Memorial is of Scots oak, with the names carved in " sunk-raised " channels ; the panel is surmounted by the Faculty Arms (duplicated) and various emblems, the thistle (duplicated), the poppy and the lily. The new Memorial occupies the site in the Hall formerly used for the old one, and the ebony framework which surrounded the first Memorial has again been used for this purpose. The doors which enclosed the first Memorial have been dispensed with so that the present one is always visible.

When I relinquished the Presidency, I was followed in succession by John Muirhead Ross, Richard Lloyd Gwilt and the reigning President, Kenneth Kilpatrick Weatherhead. All these men had taken a very active part in the Faculty's affairs and had borne their share in the educational work—as of course, had many of their predecessors in the Chair. In this respect Weatherhead may perhaps be singled out as specially distinguished, for he served for no less than thirteen years as Chairman of the Board of Examiners, having previously been Secretary of that Board for five years. It is customary on the occasion of the Annual Meeting at which a President retires for one of the Past-Presidents to thank him for the work he has done ; in the cases both of Ross and Gwilt this pleasant duty fell to me and I was able to pay sincere tribute to these two of my friends who had each completed a distinguished term of office.

When J. M. Ross was President important subjects of a practical nature arose in which the life offices and actuaries were closely interested and it was to be expected that the President would deal with these in his address. This he did on 30th October 1950, when he delivered a speech full of wise and well-considered comment upon current affairs. A committee was set up to consider the question of the treatment of provisions for retirement from the point of view of taxation and, after making a close study of the subject, sent forward evidence to the official body appointed by the Government to look into the matter. In January 1952 the Councils of the Faculty and Institute, having in mind the widespread feeling that the growth of pension commitments in relation to the national income had become a matter of major public policy, decided to appoint a small research group to prepare a study of the subject. The group of three, amongst whom M. D. W. Elphinstone was the Faculty representative, submitted their report to the Faculty on 13th April 1954, when interest in the subject had become general, and an important discussion took place, as also when the report was placed before the Institute. Some eighteen months after the study group had been appointed, the Chancellor of the Exchequer set up a Committee under the Chairmanship of Sir Thomas Phillips on the " Economic and Financial Problems of the provision for Old Age " and joint evidence was submitted by the Faculty and Institute. The foresight which had convened the research group so well in advance made it possible to use this very valuable study in the preparation of the evidence ; with the increasing average age of the population of Britain this subject has become so important and pressing that no perfunctory or hurried consideration of it could possibly have sufficed to form the basis of the evidence of the Faculty and Institute—bodies of which the evidence on a matter such as this was authoritative and deserving of the highest respect.

In August 1950, G. J. Lidstone presented the sum of £500 to the Faculty " in token of his great interest in the Faculty's welfare and as a mark of his gratitude to the members for their kindness since his election as a Fellow in 1913." The gift was to be used for any purpose of the Faculty and has in fact been placed in a fund to be called the " Lidstone Endowment Fund " and, in the meantime at least, the income from the invested fund is to be employed in a manner similar to that from the William Hutton Memorial Fund. Lidstone and his close friend Steuart Macnaghten both passed from the actuarial scene in 1952 to the great loss of the profession in Scotland.

R. Ll. Gwilt's Presidential Address, delivered on 19th October 1953, was a model of what such things should be ; an acknowledged authority upon mortality investigations, he dealt with the history of that subject and a most instructive and delightful evening he gave us. He has done much work for the Faculty in a variety of fields, but in none has his contribution been more successful and important than in that of research into rates of mortality. For long he has served upon the Joint Mortality Committee of the Faculty and Institute and, as I have already said, is now its Chairman. It is my wish, as it must be of many actuaries whose interest lies in that direction, that he will continue to guide these important investigations for a long time to come.

It fell to Gwilt to represent the Faculty in Westminster Abbey on the occasion of Her Majesty's

Coronation and at a Council Meeting held on 5th
June 1953, J. M. Ross addressed the President in
these words :—

> " Mr. President : Before we commence this meeting,
> may I be allowed to offer to you the congratulations
> of the Council—indeed the congratulations of all the
> members of the Faculty—on the honour which Her
> Majesty has just conferred upon you by creating you
> a Commander of the Order of the British Empire.
> The Faculty is proud of this recognition in the
> Coronation Honours List, and we are specially glad
> that you personally should have been the recipient.
> By your high example and keen enthusiasm you have
> most worthily earned the gratitude and warm affection
> of all the members of our profession and with very
> real pleasure we extend to you our sincere congrat-
> ulations and every good wish for the future."

These words are echoed by all of us. Ross (a highly
competent golfer) did not mention one of Gwilt's
more important accomplishments—he casts a pretty
fly. In earlier days Gwilt himself was a creditable
performer on the links ; but the years brought
wisdom and he saw the light.

I have referred in a previous chapter to the close
link which the Faculty has maintained with South
Africa and at a Meeting of Council in March 1953
it was reported that Messrs. Macphail & Fraser, the
important consulting actuaries there, had made the
handsome present of 300 guineas to the Faculty.
This gift, from a firm whose members have individually been loyal and helpful Fellows of the Faculty,
was received with gratitude ; in the meantime the
amount has been placed to Suspense Account pending
a decision as to the best method of putting it to use
and, almost certainly before this book is published, the
donors will have the satisfaction of knowing that their
generosity has benefited the Faculty in a practical way.

KENNETH KILPATRICK WEATHERHEAD, M.A.
President, 1954-56

The present Seal (1950)

At the same Council Meeting it was reported that a new lease for ten years from Whitsunday 1953 for the Faculty's premises had been arranged, so that so far as the period of the history with which I am to deal is concerned there will be no more upsetting removals to record. In fact, the Hall, Council Room and other premises are so satisfactory—so dignified and so convenient—that it must be the wish of all concerned that circumstances will permit of the indefinite postponement of any change. It would be pleasant to think that we might remain where we are for many years and grow old with our home, so that the Hall might become imbued with tradition and, as Staple Inn would so beautifully have done for the Institute, whisper to succeeding generations of actuaries of past days and past men.

The *Transactions* during this period continued to reflect the energy and enterprise of our comparatively small body of members and there has been—right up to the date at which I am writing—no lack of subjects for sessional meetings. Many years ago an undertaking was set on foot to issue, in a series, summaries of the World's Great Books and great ingenuity, scholarship and skill was shewn by the Editors—a Mr. Hammerton and a Mr. Mee, if my memory serves. A wit wrote some verses about the enterprise and, assuming these two gentlemen faced with the necessity of compressing " Bradshaw "—the railway guide—into a few pages, imagined the remarks :—

> " It can't be done, said Hammerton ;
> It must be done, said Mee " !

For reasons hardly less pressing, I have not attempted to epitomize the contents of the *Transactions* and have permitted myself no more than passing references to them; this is not to depreciate their importance or the significance of their contribution to the sum of our actuarial knowledge, for there has been over the years a happy blend of the theoretical and the practical. I believe that a high standard of professional integrity has been maintained; there is little that is shoddy or pretentious in the work that has been published. The *Transactions* contain a rich and ever-growing vein of actuarial learning and original research and will prove to be a source of inspiration and reference so long as our science is a living force in the world and that should be for a very long time indeed—unless some upstart Caesar or self-styled " intellectual " contrives to engulf us in another spell of the Dark Ages.

K. K. Weatherhead is now President and his portrait is included here, for he will have the honour and privilege of presiding over our Centenary Celebrations. He delivered his Address on 18th October 1954 and since, as he remarks there, his first contact with the profession was through the late L. P. Orr, it was natural (as with Penn who had come under the same influence) for him to be interested in Orr's original proposal for research in life assurance and to devote a part of the time at his disposal to a discussion of that subject. He expressed the hope that it might be found possible before too long to undertake an investigation under the aegis of the Joint Mortality Committee into the mortality of substandard lives, which was of course the end which Orr had in view when he made his first appeal for research upon a permanent basis. He dealt also at some length with practical problems of finance and he referred to questions about the education and recruitment of young men for the profession, which was not surprising in one who had played such an outstanding part over a long period of years in the instruction and examination of our students.

Weatherhead was the first of a group of young men introduced to the profession by Sir Edmund Whittaker, when he occupied the Chair of Mathematics at the University of Edinburgh; we in Scotland lie under a deep debt to Sir Edmund and to his successor Professor Aitken, for already that group of men (not all so very young now) has exerted a powerful and invigorating influence upon the Faculty.

The President in his Address expressed himself as being disturbed " to find that out of our six students who completed their examinations at home centres this year (1954), five were University graduates " and mentioned that the number of young men who become students of the Faculty straight from school seems to be falling off. Should this state of affairs show signs of continuing, a problem of some difficulty will arise for the consideration of the Faculty and conceivably some readjustment of our methods of training may in time become advisable.

Shortly before assuming the office of President, Weatherhead was appointed to the Population Investigation Committee—an independent research body under the Chairmanship of Sir Alexander Carr-Saunders. There can be no doubt that he must derive great pleasure and satisfaction from serving upon a Committee presided over by such a distinguished authority upon his subject.

And now, I must close my chapter about Modern Times, although I write some months before the end of the first hundred years; this book is to be in the hands of those concerned in time to enable them to read it, should they feel disposed to do so, before leaving home to attend the celebration of our Centenary—a surprising number will be coming from very far afield indeed—and the publisher and the printer have their work to do. The period I have been endeavouring to review in this chapter has been one characterised by renewed vigour and achievement and in the concluding chapter (X) I shall try to give a very brief indication of my reasons for viewing the future of the Faculty with full confidence that it will continue to serve Scotland—and in a degree a greatly wider field—in a manner worthy of the tradition that the years have raised.

CHAPTER VIII

EDUCATIONAL ACTIVITIES

HE YT THOLIS OVERCUMMIS
(He that tholes (endures) overcomes.)
—Legend over ancient doorway in West Bow, Edinburgh.

ONE of the first things to which those who instituted the Faculty directed their attention was the education of young actuaries ; and they did it with great energy. On the occasion of the secession from the Institute, the Council of that body had minuted the hope that the new Faculty would be the means of " raising up in Scotland an efficient school of professional study " ; there was no doubt of the need for this, but it could never have existed except through an independent professional institution. Almost at once, the system of examinations was arranged—an examination in general education for admission to the class of matriculated student and two subsequent examinations for the Associateship. An Associate might apply for admission to the class of Fellow after a period of one year and was appointed, subject to election, without further examination. At the present time there is no waiting period laid down and Associates (provided they have attained age 23) may and normally do become Fellows within a few weeks of passing their final examination. No doubt the original idea was to ensure that those carrying the full qualifications of the Faculty should have had the necessary practical experience ; but since the course of study now extends over a long period of years during which the student is, apart from his study, usually occupied with practical professional work, the delay is no longer considered necessary. A point of some importance occurs here. The fact that there are no examinations between the two types of membership has always meant that there are seldom any members who remain Associates and consequently the letters A.F.A. are rarely if ever seen. Proposals have been before the Council from time to time as to granting a degree of A.F.A. after certain, but not all, of the examinations have been passed as does the Institute of Actuaries, which allows its members the use of the letters A.I.A. before completion of the full course for the Fellowship ; but, rightly or wrongly, the view has been taken that it would be a mistake for the Faculty to give countenance to a qualification that falls short of the full training of an actuary, to let loose upon the world a number of " qualified actuaries " who are not in fact properly qualified. It has been thought that those unfamiliar with the full circumstances might misinterpret the letters A.F.A., if they were authorised before completion of the full course ; but no doubt there are two sides to the question, although my own view is that the Faculty's attitude is logical. To grant such a degree of A.F.A. would be like awarding 2nd XV colours to boys at school ; it is often done, but frequently serves no purpose other than to advertise the fact that the poor lad did not achieve his ambition ! At one time there was a suggestion that Associates should be required to write a thesis before being admitted to the Fellowship and this would of course have permitted the present A.F.A. qualification, as all the examinations would have been passed ; but for good or ill the idea did not reach fruition.

Probably the most effective way in which to give a general view of the process of development of the syllabus of examinations to its present state is to show specimens selected at various significant dates. W. T. Thomson and Edward Sang were those who took the major part in arranging the original examinations. Professor Kelland, who occupied the Chair of Mathematics at Edinburgh, was also helpful. He became an Honorary Fellow in 1868 and until his death in 1879 actually set the questions for the mathematical papers.

The examinations began with a matriculation examination and two others, as I have already said. Later the syllabus comprised three regular professional examinations and after the first World War the number was increased to four and, later, before admission as a student, an applicant was required to show certificates of education up to University entrance standard. In Appendix IX the syllabus in force is given for each of the years 1885, 1899, 1915 (used after 1914/18 War), 1923 and that in present use and, from this series, the gradual evolution of the existing qualification may be traced. Records prior to 1885 are fragmentary on this subject and in any case there was of course a period of trial and error until a satisfactory basis was achieved.

Along with the growth of the examination system, the tutorial arrangements also developed; but these were much more haphazard right up to the 1914-1918 War and for a year or two after. Mention has been made of the subject of tuition in those chapters which deal with the general history of the Faculty. Edward Sang was appointed an official lecturer at the beginning and from time to time members of the legal profession gave lectures upon those sections of their subject which might be supposed to bear upon the work of an actuary. Generally speaking, and except for spasmodic efforts when the Council invited an individual Fellow to give lectures and remunerated him, tuition was left to private enterprise during the nineteenth and early part of the twentieth century, although attempts were repeatedly made to start regular classes and indeed the subject was discussed with the University of Edinburgh very soon after the Faculty was instituted. In those days, whatever may be the case to-day, the remuneration of the younger qualified men was very small and it is not surprising that the desire to keep body and soul together, added to the urge for professional advancement, should have contributed to maintain a more or less adequate supply of private tutors. The system was, however, not satisfactory and, to give due credit to those in charge of the Faculty's affairs at the time, they never pretended that it was nor abandoned the discussion of ways and means to reach better arrangements. There was no feeling that, having set examinations, the Council's duty was ended; the duty to set up and maintain when it became possible a system of tuition and assistance to students was recognised from the beginning. It was only when numbers had grown that it was found feasible to do so, however, and a regular scheme of official Faculty classes was first set up in the winter 1922-1923, after Dr. A. E. Sprague at the Annual Meeting of 1921 had referred to the unsatisfactory nature of the available tuition and had promised that it would receive the attention of the Council. Classes were then set up covering the whole range of the syllabus and a prospectus of the classes is given in Volume 9 p. 293 of the *Transactions* and is reprinted in Appendix

X. Mainly the classes were oral and consequently largely restricted to students resident in Edinburgh ; but some tutors under the system did in fact conduct correspondence courses also, although the clerical work involved was a matter of real difficulty as I know, since I was one who did so.

Of course it is right to lay stress upon the fact, as I have endeavoured to do in the main narrative, that before the establishment of a full official course of tuition, there had been brilliant and successful private tutors—Chatham, Moir, W. A. Robertson and the rest—so that students were not left entirely to their own reading ; on the other hand from time to time, as is unavoidable in a system of that kind when applied to a relatively small professional body, there was a distinct lack of good tutors and students had to make do with what they could get. The new system was a great improvement and, with official backing, a sound body of tutors was maintained until, with the session 1937-1938, the Actuarial Tuition Service, provided by the Institute and Faculty, was started.

As I mentioned elsewhere, the University of Edinburgh introduced, just after the 1914-1918 War, a Diploma in Actuarial Mathematics and certain of the classes for the Diploma and those for the Faculty examinations were conducted by the same tutors. Lecturers under the University scheme for actuarial classes (as distinct from purely mathematical ones, for which the University naturally had its own lecturers) included A. E. Sprague, W. A. Robertson, G. O. Gunn, R. Ll. Gwilt, A. R. Reid, J. B. Dow, H. A. Fraser, D. W. A. Donald and J. S. Hume.

The Faculty tutors under the first official scheme formed themselves at the request of the Council into a Board of Tutors in 1925. It will be seen from the records that, amongst others who became Chairman of that Board, the name of our President, K. K. Weatherhead, appears. In the late 1920's, this Board of Tutors noticed a marked falling off in the number of students and this was apparently due to the competition of correspondence courses emanating from Birmingham and run as a private venture. In the event these courses were taken over by the Actuarial Tuition Service when it was instituted in 1937.

The existing arrangement run jointly by the Institute and Faculty is one of which I think both bodies may be proud and for which their students may be grateful. At the Annual General Meeting of the Faculty in 1937 R. C. Simmonds of the Institute and C. M. Douglas of the Faculty were specially thanked for their work in starting the Actuarial Tuition Service and, in view of the difficulty of inaugurating a matter of this kind and maintaining it for a long period of specially difficult years, it is fair to say that actuarial students in Britain stand deeply in the debt of these two accomplished and tireless men. R. C. Simmonds was Chairman of the London Section of the Committee from 1937 to 1944 and C. M. Douglas of the Edinburgh Section from 1937 to 1945. Douglas was followed in the Chair by J. B. Dow and Dow in his turn by D. G. Kellock. It is difficult, and would prolong this chapter unduly, to attempt to do credit to all the men who helped the Faculty in the educational sphere between the wars and up to the present time ; I can only trust that I have not omitted to mention anyone who stood in the forefront—for many have given generously of their time and work, and that not to the detriment of research, as the *Transactions* show.

Brief mention should be made of another side of

our educational work—the publication of textbooks. Past generations of actuarial students had good reason to be grateful to Hardy, George King, Todhunter, Spurgeon and the others for providing the tools of their trade. With the exception of *Actuarial Theory*, which was published privately by W. A. Robertson and F. A. Ross, these were Institute publications. One of the principal activities of the Actuarial Tuition Service has been the joint production by the Institute and Faculty of textbooks covering the greater part of the syllabus. The first of these—*The Construction and Graduation of Mortality Tables*—was planned just before the outbreak of war in 1939 and was published in two volumes in 1947, in the second of which the Faculty can claim some share since it was written by J. L. Anderson (who, though an Institute man by qualification was a Faculty man by adoption and later by admission as Fellow) and J. B. Dow. Towards the end of the War, when the syllabuses of both the Institute and Faculty had been revised, a Committee of both bodies met under the energetic Chairmanship of A. T. Haynes to arrange for the production of further volumes of which two were written by Faculty men, *Principles of Finance and Investments* by L. G. Whyte and *Compound Interest and Annuities-Certain* by D. W. A. Donald.

There is one matter, and that of the first importance, which remains to be mentioned. With the widening scope of the profession, the increasing complexity of actuarial science itself and the variety of its modern applications, the ground to be covered in the examinations so as to ensure a due standard of general competence has become much greater than even in the early years of this century and may well go on expanding. One estimate of the average time taken to qualify by successful finalists in the years 1934-1940 is just over 7 years and for those of the period 1946-1952 the corresponding figure is over 9 years, after making allowance for war years. Even remembering the fact that the second figure has (after all allowances) probably been affected adversely by the effects of war, the period does seem a long one—even for part-time students, for the majority of our men engage in practical work during the day and must look largely to evening study to cover most of their work. At the time of the celebration of the Centenary of the Institute of Actuaries one quite independent writer described the actuarial qualification as involving a stiffer test than that applied by any other comparable professional body ; but this is not necessarily a matter in which to take pride. It is well and in fact necessary to maintain a high standard of professional competence ; but everything should be done to render the obstacles to Fellowship no greater than is strictly implied by that aim. The Council of the Faculty has had this subject before it on a number of occasions and under the advice of the Board of Examiners and of the Tutors has done what it could and will no doubt persevere in endeavouring to ameliorate the lot of our students ; but if the trend in the future is similar to that of the recent past (and for the good of the profession generally one hopes that its influence and interests will continue to expand), then some more drastic step may well require to be taken. On several occasions, the question of permitting speciali-sation in the final examinations has been considered— a system, which, whilst requiring a general competence over the whole range, would call for a fuller and more comprehensive practical acquaintance with certain aspects of the actuary's work at the choice of the

student, according to the particular line of activity
he proposes to follow. The idea has not yet found
favour with the Council, but it appears to me to be
possible that some day a solution involving a change
of policy no less radical may require to be sought.

CHAPTER IX

THE LIGHTER SIDE

English Girl (with great distinctness, addressing chef-de-gare) :
" Pardon, monsieur ! Voulez-vous chercher pour moi l'homme
avec le mot ' Cuisinier ' autour de la couronne de son chapeau."
—PUNCH 1908.

" The older one grows, the more does one understand that the
drinking of fine wine and the luring of large trout are among
the few physical pleasures that do not decline with the years."
—MORAY MCLAREN.

As the perspicacious will have divined from the
quotations at the head of this Chapter, I consider
that there are two quite distinct spheres in each of
which the members of the Faculty permit themselves
to unbend—one at actuarial congresses and celebrations overseas and the other in the genial
atmosphere of the dining clubs. I should not wish it
to be thought that I deride or wish to minimise in
any way the business which has been transacted at
the various actuarial congresses ; much valuable
work has been done and many important contributions
have been made to the literature of our subject. But
it is not for me to write the history of these achievements and this volume is not the place to record
them. On the other hand, it would be less than frank,
and even churlish, were I to fail to mention when
writing of the lighter side of actuarial life the
unbounded hospitality and good fellowship which
Scottish actuaries have experienced from those of
other countries.

Those who have attended meetings on the Continent or across the Atlantic all invariably return inspired with enthusiasm for the country they have visited. They have made new friends ; they have tasted new foods and drunk new wines ; and they have seen new scenes. Some of the energetic, if misguided, ones may even feel that they have learned a new language ; but of these last, I do not approve. The people of foreign nations are, in my experience, extremely clever at languages and are rather proud of it ; and I feel that it is more courteous in me as their guest to allow them to take what liberties they will with my tongue rather than that I should murder theirs. But I am of course a lazy man and a duffer at languages anyway. However that may be it is true to say that the overseas visits, in addition to their more serious purpose, have contributed a most important lighter side to actuarial life from their social aspect and that many Scottish actuaries and their womenfolk have the happiest memories of these occasions and have made many friendships as a result of them.

The more local and continuous lighter side is provided by the dining clubs. Of course, dining is not the main occupation of Scotsmen or of Scottish actuaries ; but evidently they must dine occasionally and hang the expense ! Everyone likes a good dinner, although opinions differ as to the ideal ingredients ; the cannibal, for instance, has his own views on the subject, but is like the rest of mankind since he enjoys over-eating occasionally. Charles Lamb remarked of the copybook maxim " that enough is as good as a feast " that there is " not a man, woman or child in ten miles round Guildhall who really believes this saying." It seems that Sydney Smith did not like the suppers he had in Edinburgh at the beginning of the nineteenth century; but he liked the company and as Dick Swiveller put it, in a moment of eloquence, " What is the odds so long as the fire of soul is kindled at the taper of conviviality and the wing of friendship never moults a feather ! " I suspect, by the way, that the suppers of which Smith spoke so slightingly would not have come amiss to the people of Edinburgh and their guests for a few years in the middle of the twentieth century; and I am sure that the stupid aversion which young people of to-day entertain towards the writings of Charles Dickens is due to an envious irritation at the meals he describes. The most forlorn of his creatures pops out to buy a steak for twopence, that now the greatest in the land will hardly get for love or money (if he has any money) !

In earlier chapters I have mentioned convivial occasions; the Managers' Association (when it was so called) discussed affairs after dinner and there were other parties from time to time. I have mentioned in an earlier chapter that for a time it became the practice for the President to entertain to dinner those Fellows of the Faculty who lived within easy reach of Edinburgh. Even in the early days two or three dinners were required in view of the numbers involved and those provided by Archibald Hewat are still remembered. But with still increasing numbers as the Faculty grew, the practice became difficult and one of the minor effects of the 1914-1918 War was to render it impossible. As I wrote when discussing his Presidency, L. P. Orr, President from 1922 to 1924, carried on the tradition as far as possible or desirable by giving a large and successful reception. And Dr. A. E. Sprague, during his term of office,

Menu

⸰⸰⸰

HORS D'ŒUVRE VARIÉS CRISE

⸰

PETITE MARMITE DÉPRÉCIATION
OU
CONSOMMÉ DEFAUT

•

FILET DE SOLE AMORTISSEMENT

•

POULET DE GRAIN CHEZ SOI

HARICOTS VERTS FINS

POMMES PERSILLÉES
ET TOUS CEUXCI SANS
TRANSFORMATION DE LA
BASE D'ÉVALUATION

•

POIRE BÉNÉFICE RÉSERVE
MAGNARDISES CARENCE

•

CAFÉ OPTIMISME

The "Dining Club"
Menu of the final dinner (19th February, 1932)

In Memoriam

⁂

THIS Card is the only Official Documentary Evidence of the existence of what, for want of a better name, may be called " The Dining Club," which successfully carried out its function for four years, had No Official Name, No President, Secretary nor Other Officials, No Minutes nor Other Records, and No Subscriptions. All Members were Fellows of the Faculty of Actuaries, but the Qualifications for Membership, although they existed, never appeared, and never will appear, in print. The Club voluntarily disbanded in view of a proposal to form an Official Actuaries Club in Scotland, and the last Act of its Members was to appoint a Committee charged with the duty of offering every assistance in its power in connection with the new formation. Having No Fund and No Debts the financial position of The Dining Club has been at all times entirely satisfactory.

The "Dining Club"
Page of Menu Card of the final dinner

gave a delightful dinner to inaugurate the Students'
Society. That Society still has an annual dinner;
but the Faculty has not made a regular practice of
giving official banquets and this may very well be
sound policy, for such affairs may become a shade
pompous and an occasion for boring speeches,
replete with statistics and self-congratulation.

During the period between the great Wars,
although taxes had risen and although it was a time
of queer fads regarding food—all who lived through
it will remember the exhortations to stave off eternal
bliss as far as possible, with the aid of whole-meal
bread and oranges—it was quite possible to have an
excellent dinner! In the clubs of Edinburgh and in
the restaurants and hotels one might dine as well as
before the first World War; but until the year 1928
there was no regular meeting of Scottish Actuaries
over the dinner table. In that year nine of the younger
actuaries in Edinburgh formed themselves into a
Dining Club and had many an enjoyable evening
together. They entertained on occasion guests from
the south—H. J. P. Oakley attending on one occasion,
before he became President of the Institute, and on
another G. S. W. Epps, the then Government Actuary.
The former was exuberant and induced us to engage
in some form of horseplay, and the latter praised the
brandy! To A. C. Murray goes the credit of starting
this little Club and indeed for running it and no one
could have done it more efficiently or pleasantly, for
all its meetings were quite delightful. Since Murray
began "The Dining Club" and since it was, to a
large extent, the forerunner of the Scottish Actuaries'
Club, he should also be regarded as "the onelie
begetter" of the latter, of which he was the first
Secretary when it started in 1932 and of which he was

Chairman in 1944. The Dining Club held its last dinner in 1932 and I am fortunate in being able (by the courtesy of Murray) to reproduce here a photograph of the menu. When sending me the menu, Murray remarked in his letter referring to the page headed " In Memoriam," " I think this page is a very satisfactory and complete account of the Club's history ; also the menu clearly indicates the problems of 1932 ! In saying this however, I am quite sure I am prejudiced, because I wrote both ! " In order to save the eyes of my readers, I reprint here the page headed " In Memoriam " as it may well turn out to be on the small side for reading in the photograph:—

" This card is the only official documentary evidence of the existence of what, for want of a better name, may be called ' The Dining Club ', which successfully carried out its functions for four years, had No Official Name, No President, Secretary nor Other Officials, No Minutes, nor Other Records, and No Subscriptions. All Members were Fellows of the Faculty of Actuaries, but the Qualifications for Membership, although they existed, never appeared, and never will appear in print. The Club voluntarily disbanded in view of a proposal to form an official Actuaries' Club in Scotland, and the last Act of its Members was to appoint a Committee charged with the duty of offering every assistance in its power in connection with the new formation. Having No Fund and No Debts the financial position of the Dining Club has been at all times entirely satisfactory."

At a meeting held in the Faculty's Hall on 21st March 1932 it was decided to form The Scottish Actuaries' Club ; Charles Guthrie was the first Chairman and Steuart Macnaghten Vice-Chairman, and the Committee consisted of J. Davie, A. E. King, C. S. Penn, R. M. M. Roddick, and A. C. Murray (Hon. Secretary).

The Scottish Actuaries' Club is a dining club of which an actuary may become a member by invitation, and the practice has generally been followed of meeting after each of the Sessional Meetings of the

Faculty. Gradually a tradition has been built up and many pleasant dinners have been held. In 1956, the year in which the Faculty completes the first hundred years of its existence, the Club will be almost twenty-four years old and, there is every reason to suppose, " going strong." Many distinguished guests have been entertained and throughout one might say that there has been indeed a high standard of after-dinner speaking. There has been no pomposity and little boredom (no club can avoid the odd uninspired speaker !); but the pervading influence has been a kindly wit and a pleasant humour. At the Club no one stands on his dignity (real or assumed) and all follow the spirit of the maxim of Wilson's Shepherd " — everybody kens ye're a man o' genius, without your pretending to be melancholy ! " How many lovely evenings I have spent at these dinners ; how many friendships I have renewed ! There has been the least possible formality and no order of precedence ; one sits amongst the friends of one's choice, enjoying the wine, the companionship and the speeches and nothing could be more delightful—

" As bees flee hame wi' lades o' treasure
The minutes winged their way wi' pleasure."

The first dinner was held in the Caledonian Hotel and Guthrie was in the Chair ; there were thirty-six members present and seven guests. The President of the Institute (Sir William Elderton) and Geoffrey Marks and H. M. Trouncer, Past Presidents, were there, as were the Chairmen of the Actuaries' Club and of the Gallio Club. R. C. Simmonds, then Secretary of the Gallio Club, was also of the number. The Chairmen of the two London Clubs each presented a handsome snuff box to the new body and these are still treasured possessions which appear at all dinners.

Gradually the Club got into its stride and the members learned to look forward with lively anticipation to its meetings, which have been carried on in steady sequence, except of course for a period during the Second Great War, when there were few meetings either of the Faculty or of the Club. It soon became a tradition of the club, after Grace and the Loyal Toast, to propose the Club Toast—" The Point." The Point is the decimal point and many witty speeches have been made about it ; now and for a good many years, since the subject is one which, if brought up too frequently might well result in unhappy speeches and a forced humour, although the toast is honoured at all meetings, there is only one speech, I think, in each session. Although not a regular feature of the Club's activities, one or two Ladies' Nights have been held with every success and another enterprise, of recent origin, has been a series of golf meetings, held at a point studiously selected as being half-way between Edinburgh and Glasgow.

On 24th November 1939 it was decided to hold no meetings of the Club for the time, but on 8th July 1940 an informal dinner was held in the Caledonian Hotel. At this meeting, the late A. Graham Donald presented to the Club a beautiful gavel. It is proper that this beautiful gift should be described in Graham Donald's own words :—

" The intrusions of Herr Hitler among other lamentable results have curtailed the activities of the Scottish Actuaries' Club. I thought this gavel had been safely deposited in the vaults of the Club, along with our snuff boxes, but its Committee has thought it well to use the gathering of the Faculty to-day at its only meeting since the beginning of the war as an occasion when the gavel might be formally handed over, and it has been suggested that something be said about the origin of this hammer, mallet, mell or gavel.

" Last year the Faculty was invited to nominate a representative to the celebration in May of the jubilee of the Actuarial Society of America. Our Council wished to give a clock in token of its goodwill but found that, as the Society has no permanent rooms, this would not be suitable. The Society, however, expressed its willingness to accept a gavel and as time was short this was bought from Tiffany in New York instead of being sent out from here. The incident, however, suggested that an instrument for keeping order at the meetings of the Club might be obtained and an association gavel was naturally thought of. It was not considered that it would be easy to obtain anything associated with Dr. Alexander Webster* or W. T. Thomson or other of the pioneer actuaries of Scotland, but seeing that the foundations of Actuarial Science were well and truly laid when logarithms were invented, something associated with Napier seemed to fill the bill. Through the kindness of Mr. E. J. Macrae, the City Architect, a log of oak was obtained from Merchiston Castle during some alterations there. As it was a sufficiently dirty piece of wood it was an agreeable surprise to find that in the sculptor's hands it showed a pleasing rich colour. The next step was to settle the form of the instrument. Auctioneers often use an ivory hammer but the shape did not seem particularly attractive. Stone masons use mallets or mells. As I am not a freemason I enquired of the Most Worthy Grand Master Mason, but he was not able to tell me anything special about the form which mallets take in the lodges. I found that the Victoria and Albert Museum had only one dirty hammer, knew nothing about the subject and said there appeared to be no literature. The Fitzwilliam Museum at Cambridge was drawn entirely blank.

" By now, the war had begun and the Royal Scottish Museum was closed. I badgered most people I met those days for information about gavels but practically the only thing different from the normal round mell which I came across was a replica of one presented by Dr. Wm. Maxwell of R. & R. Clark to the Double Crown Club, a printers' organisation in London. This takes the form of a compositor's hammer. On the suggestion of a daughter of one of the members of this Club (Professor Whittaker) who confirmed that there was no available literature, I got in touch with Mr. N. J. Forrest, Sculptor, and together we evolved the result you see. The head shows the curve $y = \log_e x$. You

---

* Dr. Alexander Webster can hardly be described as an actuary; he was chiefly distinguished for conducting the first census of Scotland.

remember the story about someone telling Landseer how much he admired the lions at the base of the Nelson Monument in Trafalgar Square. Landseer replied : " There is only one lion four times repeated." The head of the gavel has one curve eight times repeated. Similarly the shaft has the curve $y = e^x$ repeated four times. On the top of the head is a little hollow where sticks up a point of silver to represent the Point—a frequent toast of the Scottish Actuaries' Club. The gavel produced by Tiffany, as you will see from the photograph, is enclosed in a box, but on Mr. Forrest's suggestion this one has been put into a sheath, two sides of which are decorated with curves representing $y = \sin x$.

" It was thought that the sheath might be enriched by the Napier Arms, and one remembered that the volume issued in 1914 in connection with the tercentenary of the publication of the logarithms had a reproduction of a portrait of Napier showing the arms of the family at the beginning of the 17th century. The book stated that the portrait was reproduced by permission of the University of Edinburgh. On enquiry the portrait could not at first be traced but was soon found to have been lent to the Scottish National Portrait Gallery. This also had been closed for the war, and the portraits distributed to places of safety. The Secretary, however, very kindly got into touch with the person in charge in a country home and obtained information facilitating the reproduction in correct tinctures. A deceased Fellow of the Faculty, Mr. W. R. Macdonald, translated Napier's Wonderful Canon of Logarithms and was an authority on heraldry. One of our old students became Lyon Clerk and I thought he might " vet " the reproduction of the Coat of Arms, but he had gone to the war. However, the Lord Lyon King of Arms himself kindly examined it, made no objection, and gave me to understand that he would not sue the Club to pay for a Licence on armorial bearings ! The motto is *Sans Tache*. Another motto is engraved on the sheath—*In Prudentia et Simplicitate*—as it appears on the portrait of Napier referred to, but is it not known whose maxim this is. On the opposite side of the sheath is the Motto of the Faculty—*Ad Finem Fidelis*.

" The blazoning of the Arms is—Argent, a saltire engrailed, between four roses, gules, the roses barbed vert.

" The inscription on the base of the sheath—

Scottish Actuaries' Club
Gavel and sheath of oak from Merchiston
Castle, Edinburgh, the place of birth,

1550 and death 4th April 1617 of John
Napier inventor of logarithms.
" The curves represented are
$$y = \log_e x$$
$$y = e^x$$
$$y = \sin x$$
" A.G.D. Chairman 1935-36."

A list of the Chairmen, Vice-Chairmen and Honorary Secretaries of the Scottish Actuaries' Club is given in Appendix XI.

There is another Dining Club connected with the Faculty—The Faculty of Actuaries' (England) Club—which was founded on 31st October 1933 and of which my two old friends, J. W. More and G. H. Recknell were the first two Chairmen. Both had gone to London from Edinburgh, Recknell immediately after the first War and More some years later, after an interlude in South America. More tutored Recknell and myself for the second of the Faculty's examinations and managed to get us through; his early death was a sad loss to his friends and to the profession. Membership of the Club is open to all Fellows of the Faculty resident in England and normally two dinners are held each year. All Presidents of the Faculty are invited and each of them has, since the foundation of the Club, been able to attend at least once during his term of office. I have myself enjoyed the hospitality of the Club and have pleasant memories indeed of the occasions. A list of office-bearers is given in Appendix XI and there are five Honorary Members—A. R. Davidson, A. T. Haynes, J. M. Ross, R. Ll. Gwilt and K. K. Weatherhead.

CHAPTER X

CONCLUSION

Ad finem fidelis

In a recent number of the *Transactions* several Fellows
of the Faculty gave accounts of their activities during
the late War and a reading of these yields a vivid
impression of the very many and varied directions in
which an actuarial training may prove useful, for all
the contributors laid some stress upon the fact that
their professional equipment proved of the utmost
value in what were to them unaccustomed fields of
labour. I have remarked in an early chapter that
there are signs, not alone or even mainly in this
country, of the ever-widening scope of the profession
and particularly that actuaries are now to be found in
the employment of important commercial and industrial concerns. Originally our members were engaged
in the control or in the service of life assurance offices
and kindred bodies, but the scope of the profession
has widened, and, if, as we all hope and believe, the
Faculty is to go on and prosper with the years, there
must be no standing still ; the tendency for the range
of actuarial influence to broaden must be earnestly
fostered and no opportunity lost to show to the
public in general the value of an actuarial training
in all its facets. The Council of the Faculty has, in
an effective way, recognised this and a Committee
is in existence charged with this duty. H. G. Wells
is said to have written " statistical thinking will one

day be as necessary for efficient citizenship as the ability to read and write " ; but there are many and varied pitfalls for those unversed in the subject and it seems to me that the realm of figures is one to which an efficient and a trustworthy guide will always be required. Disraeli said, " There are three kinds of lies : lies, damned lies, and statistics " and it is unfortunately only too true that the manipulation of figures has very frequently been used by the unscrupulous to mislead the unwary and that even perfectly conscientious, but untrained, and sometimes stupid, persons have drawn entirely unjustifiable inferences from figures and have based a course of action upon these to their own discomfiture and that of others.

There is the " vast untilled field of research," which should provide unlimited scope for actuaries and, I trust, a growing influence for the Scottish Statistical Research Bureau, which I referred to in its place as one of the Faculty's activities ; but there is also the immense, increasing, and to many terrifying, flood of figures issued annually by Government Departments, by political organisations, by scientific and commercial institutions as well as others which threatens to stupefy the public, and which requires, not less than expert preparation, expert, conscientious and, so far as may be possible, objective interpretation. No large business organisation can in these days dispense with statistics and nothing can be more misleading and dangerous in unskilful and untrained hands ; here again there is an opportunity for actuaries to find a greater outlet either in a consultative capacity or as regularly employed statisticians. The opportunities for professional enterprise by actuaries are unbounded.

It is to the younger members of the Faculty that we, who are no longer young, look to build upon the foundation—" not without the taint and reproach incidental to all human work, but constructed on the whole with pure and splendid purpose "—which has come down to them; and I, for one, do so with unstinted confidence. I believe that the present generation are better actuaries than their predecessors — better trained, better equipped and, generally speaking, better educated. Let them, with their skill, their youth and strength join an ambition that the Faculty, which has been handed to them full of years, and rich in enterprise and vigour, will go down to their posterity greater, more influential and no less vigorous than they found it.

The young, it is said, tend to despise the older men who have gone before them and we may speak to them as did the late Sir James Barrie to Rhodes Scholars. " If to despise us helps you in your enthusiasms, then, gentlemen, continue. Far worse than your scorning us beyond reason would be your not having a cheery belief that you can do better." I pray they will do better—much better; but I hope that in these pages I have given them the feeling, which I have myself derived from a study of the records, that their predecessors have on the whole done their duty according to their lights and opportunities and have left them in the Faculty an institution which they may regard with proper pride and even affection, and which is worthy of all the effort they may expend in its support, and in repaying the debt which, as professional men, they owe to it.

I wonder, if William Thomas Thomson were looking over my shoulder as I write these last words of my story, would he murmur the well-known lines :—

> " There the workman saw his labour taking form
>   and bearing fruit
> Like a tree with splendid branches rising
>   from a humble root."

Being a Victorian and not afraid of sentiment, I think he very well might.

APPENDICES

APPENDIX I

PRESIDENTS (from the inception of the Office).
Prior to 1887 either a "Chairman of Council" was elected for one year or the Senior Member of Council present took the Chair.

1887-1890	JOHN MACGREGOR MCCANDLISH, F.R.S.E.
1890-1892	SPENCER CAMPBELL THOMSON, B.A., F.I.A., F.R.S.E.
1892-1894	ANDREW HUGH TURNBULL, F.I.A., F.R.S.E.
1894-1896	THOMAS BOND SPRAGUE, M.A., LL.D., F.I.A., F.S.S., F.R.S.E.
1896-1898	JAMES MEIKLE.
1898-1900	DAVID DEUCHAR, F.I.A., F.R.S.E.
1900-1903	GEORGE MACRITCHIE LOW, F.I.A., F.R.S.E.
1903-1906	NIEL BALLINGAL GUNN, F.I.A.
1906-1908	ARCHIBALD HEWAT, F.I.A., F.S.S.
1908-1910	JAMES JOHN MCLAUCHLAN.
1910-1913	GORDON DOUGLAS, F.I.A.
1913-1915	WILLIAM HUTTON, F.I.A.
1915-1919	GEORGE MACRITCHIE LOW, F.I.A., F.R.S.E.
1919-1921	ALFRED ERNEST SPRAGUE, M.A., D.SC., F.I.A.
1921-1922	LEWIS POTTER ORR, F.R.S.E.
1922-1924	WILLIAM GANDY WALTON.
1924-1926	GEORGE JAMES LIDSTONE, LL.D., F.I.A., F.R.S.E.
1926-1928	RALPH HILL STEWART.
1928-1930	CHARLES GUTHRIE.
1930-1932	STEUART MACNAGHTEN, A.C.A., F.I.A.
1932-1934	RANDOLPH GORDON-SMITH, F.I.A.
1934-1936	HUGH WYLIE BROWN, F.I.A., F.R.S.E.
1936-1938	ALEXANDER GRAHAM DONALD, M.A., F.R.S.E.
1938-1940	WILLIAM ALEXANDER ROBERTSON, F.R.S.E.
1940-1942	WILLIAM BANNATYNE.
1942-1944	FINLAY JAMES CAMERON, F.I.A., F.R.S.E.
1944-1946	JAMES GRAY KYD, C.B.E., F.R.S.E.

1946-1948   COLIN STRATHERN PENN, M.C., F.I.A.
1948-1950   ANDREW RUTHERFORD DAVIDSON, F.I.A., F.S.S.
1950-1952   JOHN MUIRHEAD ROSS, F.R.S.E.
1952-1954   RICHARD LLOYD GWILT, C.B.E., F.I.A., F.R.S.E.
1954-1956   KENNETH KILPATRICK WEATHERHEAD, M.A.

APPENDIX II

(a) VICE-PRESIDENTS (from the inception of the Office).

1887/89	A. H. TURNBULL.
1890/91	J. M. McCANDLISH.
1892/93	S. C. THOMSON.
1894/95	A. H. TURNBULL.
1896/97	T. B. SPRAGUE.
1898/99	J. MEIKLE.
1900/01	D. DEUCHAR.
1902	D. DEUCHAR.
	A. H. TURNBULL.
	J. MEIKLE.
1903/05	G. M. LOW.
	D. DEUCHAR.
	A. H. TURNBULL.
1905/06	G. M. LOW.
	A. H. TURNBULL.
1906/08	N. B. GUNN.
	G. M. LOW.
	A. H. TURNBULL.
1908/10	A. HEWAT.
	N. B. GUNN.
	G. M. LOW.
1910/13	J. J. McLAUCHLAN.
	A. HEWAT.
	N. B. GUNN.
1913/15	G. DOUGLAS.
	J. J. McLAUCHLAN.
	A. HEWAT.
1915/18	W. HUTTON.
	G. DOUGLAS.
	J. J. McLAUCHLAN.

1918/19 ...	...	W. HUTTON.
		G. DOUGLAS.
		G. J. LIDSTONE.
1919/21 ...	...	G. DOUGLAS.
		G. J. LIDSTONE.
		G. M. LOW.
1921/22 ...	...	G. DOUGLAS.
		G. J. LIDSTONE.
		A. E. SPRAGUE.
1922/23 ...	...	G. J. LIDSTONE.
		A. E. SPRAGUE.
		L. P. ORR.
1923/24 ...	...	G. J. LIDSTONE.
		L. P. ORR.
1924/26 ...	...	W. G. WALTON.
		C. GUTHRIE.
		R. M. M. RODDICK.
1926/28 ...	...	C. GUTHRIE.
		R. M. M. RODDICK.
		G. J. LIDSTONE.
1928/30 ...	...	R. M. M. RODDICK.
		S. E. MACNAGHTEN.
		G. J. LIDSTONE.
1930/32 ...	...	R. M. RODDICK.
		G. J. LIDSTONE.
		C. GUTHRIE.
1932/34 ...	...	R. M. RODDICK.
		G. J. LIDSTONE.
		C. GUTHRIE.
		S. E. MACNAGHTEN.
1934/36 ...	...	R. M. RODDICK.
		C. GUTHRIE.
		S. E. MACNAGHTEN.
		R. GORDON-SMITH.
1936/38 ...	...	R. M. RODDICK.
		S. E. MACNAGHTEN.
		R. GORDON-SMITH.
		H. W. BROWN.

1938/41	S. E. MACNAGHTEN. R. GORDON-SMITH. H. W. BROWN. A. GRAHAM DONALD.
1941/42	R. GORDON-SMITH. H. W. BROWN. A. GRAHAM DONALD. F. J. CAMERON.
1942/43	R. GORDON-SMITH. H. W. BROWN. S. F. M. CUMMING. W. BANNATYNE.
1943/44	H. W. BROWN. S. F. M. CUMMING. W. BANNATYNE. J. G. KYD.
1944/45	H. W. BROWN. S. F. M. CUMMING. W. BANNATYNE. F. J. CAMERON.
1945/46	S. F. M. CUMMING. W. BANNATYNE. F. J. CAMERON. C. S. PENN.
1946/47	S. F. M. CUMMING. W. BANNATYNE. F. J. CAMERON. J. G. KYD.
1947/48	W. BANNATYNE. F. J. CAMERON. J. G. KYD. A. C. MURRAY.
1948/49	F. J. CAMERON. J. G. KYD. A. G. R. BROWN. C. S. PENN.
1949/50	J. K. KYD. A. G. R. BROWN.

1949/50 (contd.)		C. S. PENN.
		J. M. ROSS.
1950/51 ...	...	A. G. R. BROWN.
		C. S. PENN.
		G. H. RECKNELL.
		A. R. DAVIDSON.
1951/52 ...	...	C. S. PENN.
		G. H. RECKNELL.
		A. R. DAVIDSON.
		A. C. MURRAY.
1952/53 ...	...	G. H. RECKNELL.
		A. R. DAVIDSON.
		A. C. MURRAY.
		J. M. ROSS.
1953/54 ...	...	A. R. DAVIDSON.
		A. C. MURRAY.
		J. M. ROSS.
		K. K. WEATHERHEAD.
1954/55 ...	...	A. C. MURRAY.
		J. M. ROSS.
		J. B. MACLEAN.
		R. LL. GWILT.
1955/56 ...	...	J. M. ROSS.
		J. B. MACLEAN.
		R. LL. GWILT.
		F. J. McGREGOR.

(b) HONORARY SECRETARIES (from the outset)

1856/63 ...	...	R. BALFOUR.
		J. M. McCANDLISH.
1863/78 ...	...	J. M. McCANDLISH.
1878/85 ...	...	A. H. TURNBULL.
1885/88 ...	...	S. C. THOMSON.
1888/92 ...	...	D. DEUCHAR.
1892/96 ...	...	J. MEIKLE.
1896/02 ...	...	T. WALLACE.
1902/06 ...	...	J. J. McLAUCHLAN.

1906/08	G. DOUGLAS.
1908/11	W. G. WALTON.
1911/14	G. C. STENHOUSE.
1914/19	A. E. SPRAGUE.
1919/21	J. FENTON.
1921/24	A. GRAHAM DONALD.
1924/26	J. A. THOMSON.
1926/29	G. O. GUNN.
1929/31	A. R. DAVIDSON.
1931/32	A. R. DAVIDSON.
	W. C. REID.
1932/33	W. C. REID.
	C. M. DOUGLAS.
1933/35	C. M. DOUGLAS.
	J. EDGAR.
1935/37	J. EDGAR.
	J. DAVIE.
1937/39	J. DAVIE.
	F. W. ROBERTSON.
1939/42	F. W. ROBERTSON.
	D. A. B. SCRIMGEOUR.
1942/45	D. A. B. SCRIMGEOUR.
	F. J. McGREGOR.
1945/47	J. D. WILLIAMS.
1947/48	N. M. LAW.
1948/50	N. M. LAW.
	K. K. WEATHERHEAD.
1950/52	K. K. WEATHERHEAD.
	A. BATEMAN.
1952/54	A. BATEMAN.
	A. T. HAYNES.
1954/56	A. T. HAYNES.
	J. B. DOW.

(c) HONORARY TREASURERS (from the outset)

1856/78	G. A. ESSON.
1878/85	W. WOOD.
1885/88	H. BLAIR.

1888/92 ...	...	J. Turnbull Smith.
1892/95 ...	...	D. Pearson.
1895/99 ...	...	J. A. Robertson.
1899/1903	...	C. McCuaig.
1903/06 ...	...	W. G. Walton.
1906/08 ...	...	J. Chatham.
1908/11 ...	...	G. C. Stenhouse.
1911/14 ...	...	A. E. Sprague.
1914/19 ...	...	L. P. Orr.
1919/23 ...	...	S. F. M. Cumming.
1923/24 ...	...	S. E. Macnaghten.
1924/25 ...	...	W. A. Robertson.
1925/27 ...	...	A. Fraser.
1927/30 ...	...	A. Graham Donald.
1930/32 ...	...	H. G. Sharp.
1932/35 ...	...	A. E. King.
1935/40 ...	...	A. G. R. Brown.
1940/47 ...	...	A. C. Murray.
1947/52 ...	...	R. Ll. Gwilt.
1952/56 ...	...	A. R. Reid.

(d) HONORARY EDITORS of the *Transactions* (from the inception of the Office)

1903/06 ...	...	J. M. Warden.
1906/08 ...	...	J. R. Armstrong.
1908/13 ...	...	J. A. Thomson.
1913/20 ...	...	A. Fraser.
1920/23 ...	...	A. M'Intosh.
1923/28 ...	...	C. S. Penn.
1928/30 ...	...	C. M. Douglas.
1930/35 ...	...	J. Davie.
1935/45 ...	...	K. K. Weatherhead.
1945/50 ...	...	F. J. McGregor.
1950/51 ...	...	A. R. Reid.
		D. W. A. Donald.
1951/54 ...	...	D. A. B. Scrimgeour.
1954/56 ...	...	H. A. Fraser.

APPENDIX III

HONORARY FELLOWS

1914   HARDY, SIR GEORGE F., K.C.B., F.I.A.

1918   ‡WHITTAKER, EDMUND TAYLOR, M.A., F.R.S., SC.D., LL.D., Professor of Mathematics, University of Edinburgh.

1925   DUNLOP, JAMES CRAUFURD, M.D., Registrar-General for Scotland.

1927   †SPRAGUE, ALFRED ERNEST, M.A.(CANTAB.), F.I.A., D.SC.

1946   AITKEN, ALEXANDER CRAIG, M.A., D.SC., F.R.S., F.R.S.E., HON. F.R.S.N.Z., Professor of Mathematics, University of Edinburgh.

* Formerly an ordinary member ; was also an original member.

† Formerly an ordinary member.

‡ Now Sir Edmund Whittaker.

APPENDIX IV (*a*)

REPORT OF PROCEEDINGS
AT
TWO GENERAL MEETINGS
OF THE
MEMBERS OF THE INSTITUTE OF ACTUARIES
RESIDENT IN SCOTLAND,
Held at Edinburgh on 16th Nov. 1853, and 16th Feb. 1854.

THE Meeting held on 16th November 1853, was convened by the following

REQUISITION.

EDINBURGH,
7th November, 1853.

SIR,—You are requested to attend a Meeting of the Members of the INSTITUTE OF ACTUARIES resident in Scotland, to be held within Messrs. Cay and Black's Rooms, No. 45, George Street, Edinburgh, on Wednesday the 16th of November current, at Four o'clock, afternoon, with reference to certain alterations recently made in the Laws of the Institute, and to consider generally the position of the Scotch Members, and whether any steps should be taken for promoting the interests of the profession in Scotland.—We are, Sir, your obedient Servants,

JAS. BORTHWICK.	H. D. DICKIE.
GILB. L. FINLAY.	WILL. THOS. THOMSON.
GEORGE RAMSAY.	ARCH. BORTHWICK.
ROBT. CHRISTIE.	JAMES WATSON.
HOLMES IVORY.	D. LINDSAY.
WILLIAM WOOD.	ROBERT BALFOUR.
GEORGE A. ESSON.	JOHN M. M'CANDLISH.
WILLIAM SPENS.	

199

At the Meeting, which was numerously attended by Members of the Institute, JAMES BORTHWICK, Esq., in the Chair, the following Resolutions were proposed by H. D. DICKIE, Esq., and seconded by GILBERT L. FINLAY, Esq., and having been put *seriatim* to the Meeting, were unanimously agreed to:—

RESOLUTIONS.

That the Meeting, considering that the Members of the Institute resident in Scotland, and connected with Scottish Assurance Offices, form more than one-third of the whole body, are of opinion, that in order to extend to the Scotch Members some of the advantages enjoyed by those resident in London, and to secure a continuance of their cordial support, some alterations on the present arrangements are indispensably necessary ; and that in the following particulars ; namely,—

1. That the Members resident in Scotland should have the right of voting by proxy at the Meetings of the Institute, (such proxies to be held only by a Member or Members,) and that due intimation should be given of all questions of importance which are to be brought before the Meetings.

2. That some improved regulations should be made for the examination and admission of Candidates resident in Scotland, through the medium of an examining Committee of Scotch Members, without requiring the attendance of Candidates in London.

3. That the increased contribution lately called for from the Non-resident Members, is inequitable and inexpedient, and if continued, a certain proportion of the Funds of the Institute should be applied in Scotland to carrying out the objects of the Institute among Members resident there.

4. That the Members resident in Scotland should form a Scotch Section of the Institute, and should have the right of electing annually from among themselves one of the Vice-Presidents, and a certain proportion of the general Council, and that the Vice-President and Councillors so

elected, should form the Council of the Institute for Scotland.

That it be remitted to a Committee to intimate the foregoing Resolutions to the Council of the Institute, with power to hold further communications with them regarding the same, and to take such further steps as may be required to carry out the views of this Meeting, and to summon another Meeting of the Scotch Members when they shall deem it necessary. That the Committee shall consist of the following Members of the Institute.

Messrs.	*Messrs.*
ROBT. BALFOUR.	G. L. FINLAY.
ARCHD. BORTHWICK.	DONALD LINDSAY.
JAMES BORTHWICK.	JOHN M. M'CANDLISH.
ROBERT CHRISTIE.	SAMUEL RALEIGH.
H. D. DICKIE.	W. T. THOMSON.
G. A. ESSON.	WILLIAM WOOD.

A copy of the foregoing Resolutions having been transmitted to the Council of the Institute, the same were remitted by them to a Committee, and thereafter, on 7th February 1854, the following extracts from the proceedings of the Council were received by the Committee in Edinburgh :—

EXTRACT FROM MINUTES OF COUNCIL,
Dated 2d February 1854.

The Committee upon the Constitution and Laws brought up their Report. Resolved that it be adopted and entered on the Minutes.

REPORT BY THE COMMITTEE UPON THE CONSTITUTION AND LAWS.

" The Committee having taken into consideration that portion of the matter referred to them which relates to certain Resolutions passed at a meeting of the Members resident in Scotland, recommend,—

" That the requisitionists from Edinburgh be informed that the Council has given its most careful consideration to all the suggestions made by them in reference to certain proposed alterations in the Constitution and Laws of the Institute.

" That a Committee of the Council is at this present time in communication with the Government to ascertain how far they would give their sanction to the Incorporation of the Institute, or to the formation of an incorporated body of Actuaries generally.

" That in the event of a Charter being obtained by the Institute, alterations and modifications in the Laws and Constitution will be required.

" That the Council will bear in recollection the suggestions of the Scottish Members, and will be prepared to recommend to the General Meeting, which will be called for the purpose of amending the Laws, or to the next Annual General Meeting, the following alteration :—

" That, as it is desirable that every Member of the Institute should have the opportunity of recording his opinion on any proposed changes in the Laws, &c., vote by proxy, under certain regulations hereafter to be made, should be allowed to all Members having the power of voting on the particular question to be raised, who reside beyond twenty miles from London, or who on the day of Meeting shall be at that distance.

" And further, that the Council will be disposed to adopt the following suggestions :—

" (1.) That in consideration of the large number of Members of the Institute resident in Scotland, such Members shall, yearly, at least two months before the Annual General Meeting, forward to the Council the names of six qualified Fellows, recommending one as a Vice-President, and the remaining five as Members of the Council ; and on the receipt thereof, the Council will include their names in the ballot-list as Fellows so recommended.

" (2.) That for the future, the third and final examination for certificates of competency of candidates resident in Scotland, may take place in Edinburgh, but that in order to secure uniformity, the plan of examination shall be agreed on by the Council in London.

(Signed) " PETER HARDY,

" <i>Chairman of the Committee.</i>"

" LONDON, THURSDAY, 19<i>th January</i> 1854."

At a second Meeting of the Members resident in Scotland, called by circular, held at Edinburgh, on 16th February 1854, H. D. DICKIE, Esq., in the Chair, the following Report of the Committee appointed at the previous Meeting was read :—

REPORT OF COMMITTEE.

The Committee were appointed with the following instructions, viz.:—To intimate the Resolutions, agreed upon at the Meeting, to the Council of the Institute, with power to hold further communications with them regarding the same, and to take such further steps as might be required to carry out the views of the Meeting, and to summon another Meeting of the Scotch Members when they should deem it necessary.

In terms of these instructions, the Committee lost no time in forwarding to the Council a copy of the Resolutions, and they were informed in reply that these had been laid before the Council, and by them had been referred to a Committee.

A further communication has now been received from the Council, dated the 3d curt., from which it appears that the Council have adopted and entered on their Minutes, the following Report by the Committee to whom the subject had been referred.

(<i>Here follows the Report already quoted</i>).

The Committee having anxiously deliberated on this communication, have summoned the present Meeting of the Scotch Members, in order to lay it before them, and in doing so they desire to make the following observations :—

It will be seen that the Council are prepared in certain important particulars to meet the views of the Scotch Members. If their recommendations are adopted by the Institute, all non-resident Members will have the right of voting by proxy at the Meeting of the Institute. Candidates from Scotland for admission as Fellows will pass the whole of their examinations in Edinburgh, without incurring the expense and inconvenience of one or more journeys to London, and a considerable proportion of the Office-bearers of the Institute will be nominated by the Scotch Members from among themselves, and will be thereupon proposed by the Council for election.

These alterations when adjusted in detail and carried into effect will virtually exhaust all that was applied for by the Resolutions adopted at the late General Meeting, with the exception, *1st*, That it does not appear to be proposed that the Scotch Members should be recognised by the Institute as a separate Section ; and, *2d*, That it is not proposed to apply any part of the funds of the Institute towards promoting its objects in Scotland.

With regard to the first of these points, the Committee are of opinion, that it will be better not to press it further on the Council in London. Their proposal recognises at least one Annual Meeting of the Scotch Members, with a specific subject of business to be transacted ; and if the arrangements are carried out, a certain number of the Office-bearers of the Institute will be resident in Scotland. This secures the commencement of an organization here, and it may probably be better to have it completed gradually by the Scotch members themselves, (which appears to the Committee to be quite practicable,) rather than to have it adjusted by the Council in London.

With regard to the second point, the Committee have to report that it has received their most careful consideration. They have been assured by members of the Council, that the revenue of the Institute does not admit at present of any reduction in the rates, or of a sum being set aside as a grant for Scotland ; and this being the case, the Committee are very unwilling to cripple its resources, or to make such a grant an indispensable part of the arrangements at this time, provided these are in other respects satisfactory. By the proposed alterations, the Scottish members will share in almost all the advantages of the Institute, and have a voice in its management, while the contributions, at least those of the Fellows and Official Associates, even at the increased rates lately adopted, are lower than those of the corresponding classes of members in London. Should the Institute succeed in obtaining a Royal Charter, the right of membership will become of greater value and importance than it is now ; and in the prospect of this result, and of the advantages that will thence arise to the Members from their organization as a recognised profession, and from whatever privileges this may confer upon them, it appears to the Committee that it would be inexpedient for those resident in Scotland, either to give up their own connexion with the Institute, or to impede its operations at this moment by withdrawing any part of its funds. Independent also of any personal advantages accruing to the Members, the Institute, if its regulations are fairly adjusted, is entitled to their support for its promotion of the science of Life Assurance, and especially as furnishing the machinery for friendly communication and co-operation among all persons in England and Scotland, and abroad also, who are interested in the subject.

On the other hand, the Committee are sensible that if the efficiency of the Institute is to be promoted in Scotland, some practical operations must speedily be commenced here, for which funds will be necessary. It has been suggested, that a separate fund for Scotland might perhaps be provided without requiring increased contributions from the individual Members, and the Committee recommend that, in the meantime, at all events, the Scotch Members should not press their claim for a grant from the funds of the Institute. The Committee would therefore suggest, that the Meeting, if they approve generally of the propositions of the Council, should remit the subject either back to the present Committee, or to such other Committee as may be named,—to see the recommendations of the Council adjusted and given effect to, and to consider generally what steps should be taken for promoting the efficiency of the Institute in Scotland, and how the necessary funds for this purpose are to be provided, and thereafter to report to a future Meeting of the Scotch Members.

In name of the Committee,

JAS. BORTHWICK, C.

13th February 1854.

The Meeting having heard the above Report, it was, on the motion of CHARLES PEARSON, Esq., unanimously resolved as follows :—

That the Report now read be approved of, and that the matter be remitted back to the same Committee, to proceed as recommended in the Report.

APPENDIX IV (*b*)

MINUTES AND CORRESPONDENCE
(*Printed for private circulation.*)
BETWEEN THE
HONORARY SECRETARIES
OF THE INSTITUTE OF ACTUARIES
AND THE
SCOTTISH MEMBERS OF COUNCIL, 1854-55

EXTRACT from LETTER from Mr. EDWARD CHESHIRE, Assistant Secretary to the Institute of Actuaries, to Mr. IVORY, one of the Vice-Presidents.

INSTITUTE OF ACTUARIES,
12, ST. JAMES'S SQUARE,
LONDON, 10th November 1854.

DEAR SIR,—In reply to your favour of the 2d instant, you will observe that the Council have appointed the

Examiners nominated by the Members of Council resident in Scotland; also, that the Examinations have been fixed for the day and hour agreed to by previous arrangement.

The Examiners for London are,—

Mr. HARDY.   Mr. FARREN, V.P.
Mr. JELLICOE, V.P.   Mr. TUCKER, V.P.

I am, &c. &c.,
EDWD. CHESHIRE.

MINUTE of Meeting called at the request of the Members of Council resident in Scotland, and held on Tuesday the 21st of November 1854;

Present,—

Messrs.   Messrs.
HOLMES IVORY, V.P.;   HENRY D. DICKIE;
JAMES BORTHWICK;   G. L. FINLAY; and
ROBERT CHRISTIE;   WM. T. THOMSON;

The following statement was unanimously agreed to, and authorized to be transmitted to the Council in London :—

The Members of the Council resident in Scotland, not having the advantage of personal communication with their Colleagues in England, are thus to some extent ignorant of their views and opinions as to matters of general and particular interest which occur from time to time; they trust, therefore, that their Colleagues will communicate with them on points of importance, which they themselves discuss, and give their Scottish brethren the benefit of their views and opinions on matters which may occasionally be brought before them.

The Scottish Members consider it highly important, if not essential, for the welfare of the Institute, that there should be undivided opinions in the Council, so as to secure harmony in the whole proceedings; and they do not hesitate, in accordance with these views, now to bring before the Council two matters which have of late been much discussed both in England and Scotland.

The first of these has reference to the circumstances connected with Mr. Farren's resignation of the office of Actuary to the Asylum Office, and his re-election as a Vice-President of the Institute. It is understood that Mr. Farren has already furnished the Members of the Council in London with full explanations on the subject. These, however, have not been communicated to the Scottish Members of Council; and as it is observed that that gentleman points to further personal justification when legitimate occasion serves, the Scottish Members trust that Mr. Farren will consider them, as Members of the same Council, proper parties before whom to place the explanations referred to, and they doubt not the English Members will consider it right that he should do so.

The other matter is the Report of the Investigation of the Affairs of the Professional Life Assurance Company lately published. That Report has given much dissatisfaction in Scotland; and as it is signed by some prominent Members of the Institute, and in particular by one of the recently appointed Examiners, the Scottish Members request to be informed whether that Report has been brought under the notice of the Council, and if so, whether it be not such as, in their opinion, to call for remark or animadversion.

The Scottish Members regret that their first communication should refer to gentlemen so closely connected with them in office, but they are sure the Council will give them credit for a sincere wish to elevate the Profession and strengthen the Society.

LETTER, Mr. IVORY to the HONORARY SECRETARIES, transmitting the above Minute.

EDINBURGH, 2, SO. ST. DAVID STREET,
21st November 1854.

GENTLEMEN,—The enclosed statement was this day unanimously agreed to at a Meeting of the Members of Council resident in Scotland, and directed by them to be transmitted to the Council of the Institute. I have, therefore, to request that you will lay the same before the Meeting of Council to be held on the 23d inst.

I need scarcely repeat, both for myself individually, and the other Members of Council here, our deep regret that our first communication should not have been of a more agreeable nature. You are no doubt aware that they (the Scottish Members) are most anxious to give their support to the Council, as has been evinced on more than one occasion ; and it is only from a sincere desire to promote the continued success of the Institute, that they have been induced to make the present representation.

From the strong feeling which prevails here among the Members of Council, as well as among the Ordinary Members of the Institute, in regard to the matters alluded to in the statement, we are all satisfied that it is of the utmost importance for the interests of the Institute, that satisfactory explanations should be furnished ; and it is hoped that the Council will favour us with their views with as little delay as possible. I remain, Gentlemen, &c.

HOLMES IVORY.

The Honorary Secretaries
of the Institute of Actuaries.

LETTER from the HONORARY SECRETARIES to Mr. IVORY.

INSTITUTE OF ACTUARIES,
12, ST. JAMES'S SQUARE,
LONDON, 8*th December* 1854.

DEAR SIR,—We have now to acquaint you, that your letter of the 21st ultimo, with the Minute of the Meeting at which you presided that day, has been submitted to the Council of the Institute, the President in the Chair, specially convened to consider that and other matters, and we are instructed to communicate the following as the result of the deliberation thereon.

The Council have ever been anxious that as perfect a unanimity should prevail among the Members as is to be expected among members of any deliberative body, and they have always done, and will continue to do, the utmost in their power to promote so desirable an object.

With regard to Mr. Farren's re-election as one of the Vice-Presidents of the Institute, the Council are not aware that they have anything to communicate beyond the following facts :—

In April last, Mr. Farren, who had recently left the Asylum Life Assurance Office, tendered his resignation as a Vice-President, and afterwards withdrew it at the request of the Council, who at the time recorded the fact ; and that, in originally recommending Mr. Farren as a Vice-President, they had not been in any way actuated by the circumstance that he represented any Life Office whatever, but grounded their recommendation solely on his well known talents and acquirements as an Actuary.

At the Anniversary Meeting in July last, Mr. Farren was unanimously re-elected a Vice-President, and the Council have the pleasure to add, for the satisfaction of their Colleagues in Edinburgh, that they have not had any reason to question the propriety of the unanimous vote of the Members of the Institute assembled in General Meeting.

At the time of his retiring from the Asylum Office, Mr. Farren furnished some of his more intimate friends with explanations of the circumstances under which he had resigned the appointment of Actuary to that Company, but no explanation was ever furnished to, nor indeed required by, the Council on that subject.

In answer to your inquiry respecting the recent Report of the Investigation of the Affairs of the Professional Life Assurance Company, the Council have to state, that such Report has not been brought under their consideration, and to add their opinion, that by the Rules and Constitution of the Institute, they are entirely precluded from expressing either commendation or censure upon any Life Assurance Company or its official Reports. We are, &c.

SAMUEL BROWN, *Honorary*
J. HILL WILLIAMS, *Secretaries.*
Holmes Ivory, Esq., V.P.

MINUTE of Meeting of the Members of the Council of the Institute of Actuaries resident in Scotland, held at Edinburgh on the 12th December 1854.

Present,—

Messrs.   Messrs.
  H. IVORY, V.P. ;   H. D. DICKIE ;
  R. CHRISTIE ;   G. L. FINLAY ; and
                  Mr. W. T. THOMSON.

Mr. Ivory submitted to the Meeting a letter dated the 8th inst., received by him from the Honorary Secretaries of the Institute in London, in reply to the communication made by him to the Council of the Institute, in accordance with what passed at the Meeting on 21st November last.

Mr. Thomson then stated, that he had seen Mr. J. Hill Williams, one of the Honorary Secretaries, when in Edinburgh, on Monday, and had received from that gentleman some further explanations, which he repeated to the Meeting.

The Meeting, after a careful and anxious consideration of the letter and subsequent explanations, were of opinion,—

1. That while they admit the difficulties of Mr. Farren's position in connexion with the Asylum Office, it does not appear to them that the explanations now given are altogether satisfactory, and they conceive that it would have been better if Mr. Farren had not been proposed for re-election as a Vice-President till the whole matter had been specially investigated.

2. That it is much to be regretted that Mr. Hardy, one of the Examiners, and formerly a Vice-President of the Institute, should have been a party to the published Report of the Investigation into the Affairs of the Professional Assurance Company, that Report being, in the opinion of the Scottish Members, calculated not merely to weaken the public confidence in such investigations, even when conducted by neutral and professional Actuaries, but as emanating from one of its leading Members, to injure in some degree the character of the Institute itself.

The Scottish Members are quite aware that the Council would not be warranted in attempting to exercise a censorship on the Management or the official Reports of Life Assurance Institutions generally, or even of those with which the Members of the Institute may be officially connected ; but they are of opinion that gentlemen belonging to the Council should, in circumstances such as those under discussion, be amenable to their brethren, to the extent of affording explanations when the propriety of their official conduct has been publicly called in question.

They are further of opinion, that in the selection of office-bearers for an Association, which was established for the purpose of elevating the character of the Profession, as well as the attainments of its Members, there are other and important considerations to be attended to besides their mere talents and acquirements as Actuaries ; and it is with deference submitted, that no Member should be recommended for official appointment in the Institute whose professional conduct has been the subject of public animadversion or discussion, unless the Council should have previously satisfied themselves on due inquiry of the groundlessness of the charges or objections made against such Member.

It is with extreme regret that the Scottish Members have felt themselves called upon to make these remarks, but the principles involved in the discussion are so important, that they cannot close the subject until a clearer understanding is come to on the matter. They sincerely hope, however, that their English Colleagues will at once concur with them in regard to the principles by which the Council should be guided, so that a common resolution on the subject may be come to, thus bringing the present unpleasant discussion to a close, and preventing the risk of permanent disunion, which may otherwise ensue.

N.B.—The above Minute was transmitted by letter dated 15th December 1854.

LETTER from the HONORARY SECRETARIES to Mr. IVORY.

INSTITUTE OF ACTUARIES,
12, ST. JAMES'S SQUARE,
LONDON, *5th January* 1855.

DEAR SIR,—Your letter of the 15th ult., and the Minute enclosed in it of the Meeting held in Edinburgh on the 12th, have been under the careful consideration of the Members of the Council in London.

It appears to them that the statements therein made have for the most part been replied to in their letter of the 8th ult.; nevertheless, for the satisfaction of their Colleagues in Scotland, they will endeavour to explain further their views as to the matter under discussion.

As regards Mr. Farren, the non-acceptance, in April last, of his resignation as a Vice-President, and his subsequent recommendation for re-election to that office, were the Acts of the then Council; and these acts of their predecessors, the London Members of the present Council have certainly no desire to call in question, nor do they see how they could call them in question, even were they so disposed.

For the reasons alleged in their previous communications, the Members of the Council here decline to pronounce any opinion upon the Report made by certain Actuaries on the Affairs of the Professional Life Assurance Company, or upon the propriety of Mr. Hardy's being a party to such report; neither do they think it advisable to commit themselves to any particular course with reference to the recommendations which they or their successors may hereafter be called upon to make of gentlemen as office-bearers in the Institute.

These recommendations, as you are aware, can be only in accordance with the decisions of a majority of the Council; and in like manner, the acceptance or rejection of these recommendations, and the consequent election or non-election of any individual to an office in the Institute, must depend upon the decision of a majority of its Members at a General Meeting legally convened.

The Council in London trust, that upon reviewing the whole subject, their Colleagues in Edinburgh will be led to the same conclusion. We are, &c.

SAMUEL BROWN, } *Honorary*
J. HILL WILLIAMS, } *Secretaries.*
Holmes Ivory, Esq., V.P.

MINUTE by the Scottish Members of Council, agreed to at a Meeting held on the 17th January 1855.

Present,—

Messrs.   Messrs.
  H. IVORY ;   GILBT. L. FINLAY ;
  JAS. BORTHWICK ;   W. T. THOMSON ;
              Mr. R. CHRISTIE.

The Scottish Members of Council have considered the letter dated 5th January current, addressed to them by the Council of the Institute, in reply to their Minute of 12th December last.

The Scottish Members have no desire to continue the present painful discussion, in so far, at least, as the two gentlemen named in former Minutes are personally concerned. They cannot, however, but express their extreme regret, that their London Colleagues should have declined, and apparently on merely formal grounds, to join in any general expression of opinion as to the principles which ought to guide the Council in recommending Members for election to prominent offices in the Institute. These principles the Scottish Members consider absolutely essential to the wellbeing of the Institute ; and unless they can entertain some hope of seeing them practically carried out, they feel that, in justice to themselves and the profession to which they have the honour to belong, no other course is open to them but to tender their resignations as Members of Council.

But before taking this decisive step, they have with deference to suggest, for the consideration of the English Members of Council, whether it might not be advisable, at the present crisis, to call in the aid of some neutral and influential parties, possessing the confidence of the Council, for the purpose not merely of bringing about a better understanding on the immediate subject of discussion, but of obtaining their counsel and assistance with reference to the present position of the Institute and the Profession generally, and as to whether some means might not be devised for rendering the Institute of more practical benefit to the Members at large, and securing for it the confidence and support of the whole body of the Profession.

The Scottish Members trust that their English Colleagues will give them credit for being actuated by an anxious desire to elevate the Profession, and they beg to assure them that it was in that view alone that the present Correspondence originated. They have all along given the Institute their cordial support, in the hopes that it would be the means of effecting an improvement both in the status and acquirements of the Profession. It cannot be denied, however, that the Institute, although it has achieved success in some respects, has not attained that high position which its founders originally aimed at, and that many Members of the Profession still withhold from it their support, whom it would be most desirable to embrace within its ranks.

This is a subject which, it is believed, has been already not unfrequently discussed both in London and Edinburgh, and various plans have from time to time been suggested, with the view of invigorating the Institute, and bringing together a larger number of the Profession ; but no serious practical attempt has hitherto been made for effecting this desirable object. Were, however, four or five gentlemen, such as Lord Overstone, Sir W. Lubbock, Professor De Morgan, or others of like standing, to take up the matter with energy and zeal, the most satisfactory results might be confidently anticipated, not only in healing the present division, but in reuniting the whole profession in a combined scheme for their general benefit.

Should the Council concur in the propriety of the course now suggested, no time should be lost in putting matters in train for the reference ; and for this purpose the Scottish Members will, if thought proper, be glad to unite in the application to be made to the above gentlemen, or others who may be selected to undertake the reference.

LETTER, Mr. IVORY to the HONORARY SECRETARIES transmitting the above Minute.

EDINBURGH, 2, STEELE'S PLACE,
23d *January* 1855

DEAR SIRS,—Referring to my letter to you of the 17th instant,* I now beg to enclose copy Minute agreed to at the Meeting of the Members of Council resident in Scotland, which was held that day. I may add that Mr. Dickie, who was unable to be present at the Meeting, concurs with the other Members.

I sincerely hope that the Council will agree to the proposal now made, and proceed at once to take the necessary steps for the purpose of having the matter fully matured, if possible, before the Annual Meeting. I think it but right, at the same time, to say frankly, that unless the Scottish Members have the satisfaction of knowing that their Colleagues are prepared to carry out the proposed plan, or something similar, they will not feel themselves at liberty to delay their resignations, or to allow matters to remain in their present unsatisfactory state till the Annual Meeting in July. I am, &c.

HOLMES IVORY.

J. Hill Williams, Esq.,
    Hon. Sec. Institute of Actuaries.

* The letter referred to intimated that resolutions had been agreed upon, and that a copy would forthwith be transmitted.

———————

LETTER, the HONORARY SECRETARIES to Mr. IVORY.

INSTITUTE OF ACTUARIES,
12, ST. JAMES'S SQUARE,
LONDON, 9th *February* 1855.

DEAR SIR,—The Council have had under their careful consideration your letter of the 23d ultimo, and the Minute enclosed therein of the Meeting held on the 17th ultimo, and they have instructed us to say in reply, that they observe, with much satisfaction, that the questions raised by their Colleagues in Scotland are relieved of the personal considerations by which their discussion has been hitherto embarrassed. They regret, however, that it should be thought, that any resolution they have come to has been based on merely formal grounds ; and they beg to assure you, that it has been their anxious desire to be influenced only by a due regard to the principles upon which the Institute was originally founded. These principles, they have thought, forbade them to enter into the questions here referred to as originally proposed, but they are quite prepared to give every possible consideration to any proposition that may be made, not inconsistent with the laws of the Institute, for the wellbeing of that body.

The Council fully recognise the importance of securing to the Institute, as far as possible, the confidence and support of the whole body of the Profession to which they belong.

They have made many attempts in this direction, and are quite prepared to renew their efforts in any way that may appear likely to bring about so desirable an object ; but they feel that it would be in the highest degree objectionable to place the destinies of the Institute in the hands of non-professional persons, who could hardly be expected to take charge of them under any circumstances, and would certainly be reluctant to do so, after such an avowal of incompetency as the application itself would obviously involve. We are, &c.

SAMUEL BROWN,   } *Honorary*
J. HILL WILLIAMS, } *Secretaries.*

Holmes Ivory, Esq., V.P.

MINUTE of Meeting of the Scottish Members of the Council of the Institute of Actuaries, held at Edinburgh, the 21st day of February 1855.

A letter of date the 9th of February, addressed by the Honorary Secretaries of the Institute to Mr. Ivory, as one of the Vice-Presidents, was submitted to the Meeting, and having been considered, along with the whole correspondence which has recently passed between the Members in Scotland and their English brethren, it was unanimously resolved,—

That the views and suggestions of the Scottish Members, with reference to important principles, the adoption of which appeared to them essential for advancing the interests and promoting the prosperity of the Institute, have not been received in such a manner as to leave them any ground for anticipating improvement in the constitution of the body by their means as Members of Council.

That without such improvement the Institute must, in their opinion, necessarily fail to a great extent in fulfilling its original design of elevating the profession, and becoming the nucleus of extended professional association among its members, on such a basis as would render it worthy of general confidence.

That with these views the Scottish Members cannot consistently remain connected with the Institute as Councillors, and now beg accordingly to place their resignations in the hands of the President and Council.

The Scottish Members do not consider it necessary at once to resign all connexion with the Institute, nor do they propose for the present to bring the subject before the general body of the Institute. They feel, however, that it is but due to the Fellows and Associates resident in Scotland, that they should be made acquainted with the reasons which led to the present resignation, and it is accordingly intended to lay before them the whole correspondence.

HOLMES IVORY.	H. D. DICKIE.
WILL. THO. THOMSON.	ROBERT CHRISTIE.
D. LINDSAY.	JAMES BORTHWICK.

LETTER, Mr. IVORY to the HONORARY SECRETARIES.

22, ST. ANDREW SQUARE,
EDINBURGH, 21*st February* 1855.

GENTLEMEN,—I beg to inclose Minute of a Meeting of the Scottish Members of the Council of the Institute, held here this day, and which I have to request you will lay before the Meeting of Council on the 22d.

I have to mention that the Minute has not received the signature of Mr. Finlay, in consequence of that gentleman's absence from Edinburgh. From communication received from him, however, I am aware that he concurs entirely in the resolution come to by his Colleagues here, and that a separate letter of resignation will be forwarded by him in due time. I am, &c.

HOLMES IVORY.

Samuel Brown, Esq.,
J. Hill Williams, Esq.,
    Hon. Secs. Institute of Actuaries.

LETTER, the HONORARY SECRETARIES to Mr. IVORY and
Others.

INSTITUTE OF ACTUARIES,
12, ST. JAMES'S SQUARE,
LONDON, 23*d February* 1855.

GENTLEMEN,—Mr. Holmes Ivory's letter, and the Minute of the Meeting of the 21st inst. of the Members of Council resident in Scotland, were submitted to the Council of the Institute at their Meeting yesterday, when we received instructions to inform you that your resignations were accepted by the Council with deep regret. We have the honour to be, &c.

SAMUEL BROWN, } *Honorary*
J. HILL WILLIAMS, } *Secretaries.*

To Holmes Ivory, Esq.,
    W. T. Thomson, Esq.
    D. Lindsay, Esq.,
    H. D. Dickie, Esq.,
    Robert Christie, Esq.,
    J. Borthwick, Esq.,
        Edinburgh.

Note.—Since the date of the last communication, Mr. Finlay's resignation as a Member of Council has likewise been transmitted.

APPENDIX IV (*c*)

PROSPECTUS of the FACULTY presented to Meeting of 4th January, 1856.

It is proposed to form an Association under the Title of " The Faculty of Actuaries in Scotland " with the view of uniting the Members of the profession there resident and of promoting the acquisition of those professional attainments which are essential to the efficient performance of the duties of an Actuary.

The present Managers, Actuaries and Secretaries in Scotland of Life Offices, and Professional gentlemen practising there as Actuaries, (although not connected with Life Offices) who have been Fellows or Official Associates of the Institute of Actuaries of Great Britain and Ireland, shall be admissible as Members on their intimating their wish to join the Faculty on or before the first day of January next.

The number of gentlemen at present qualified as above

for admission may be taken at about 50, of whom nearly all were formerly Members of " The Institute of Actuaries of Great Britain and Ireland " but have resigned their connection with that Association.

Among the objects contemplated by the proposed Faculty in addition to uniting the Scottish Actuaries in one body, the following may be specified :—

1. The formation of a Library of Professional works for the use of the Members.

2. The diffusion among the Members of information on all subjects of interest to Actuaries, including the publication from time to time, for the use of the Faculty, of additional data on the subject of Life Assurance, and of such Tables and other documents as may appear to be valuable.

3. The appointment of a duly qualified Lecturer, who shall deliver an occasional course of Lectures on the theory and practice of Life Assurance ; and who shall undertake the instruction of those who intend to adopt the profession of an Actuary, with a view to their being examined and admitted into the Faculty when duly qualified.

The preparation of the Bye Laws and Rules of the Faculty shall be intrusted to a Committee to be named by the Members, and shall be submitted for the society's approval before being adopted.

(This " Prospectus " (undated) was signed by the 38 original members named in Resolution 1 of the Minute which follows (Appendix IV (d)) and in Law No. 2 of the original Constitution (Appendix V). A reduced facsimile of the actual signatures will be found facing page 225).

APPENDIX IV (*d*)

MINUTE of MEETING of the FACULTY OF ACTUARIES held
within Messrs. Cay and Black's rooms 45 George
Street, Edinburgh, on 4th January 1856

Present

Messrs.	W. T. THOMSON	Messrs.	ESSON
	A. BORTHWICK		PEARSON
	MOINET		RAMSAY
	T. G. DICKSON		SANG
	W. FINLAY		SMITH
	BALFOUR		McCANDLISH

On the motion of Mr. Borthwick, Mr. W. T. Thomson
was called to the chair.

The Chairman then explained the preliminary proceedings
which had taken place and he laid on the Table a short
prospectus of the proposed Faculty which had been signed
by 38 gentlemen.

Thereafter the following resolutions were moved by the
Chairman and unanimously adopted by the Meeting

1. That the Faculty of Actuaries be declared to be now
constituted, and to consist of the following Members, viz. :
James Borthwick, H. D. Dickie, D. Lindsay, Gilbert L.
Finlay, John Mackenzie, D. Walkinshaw, Charles F.
Griffith, Archibald Borthwick, David Chisholm, John
Moinet, William Dickson, William Spens, James Smith,
D. Clunie Gregor, Charles Pearson, James Watson,
William T. Thomson, John M. McCandlish, George
Ramsay, W. Smith, Robert Balfour, William Chalmers,
H. Ambrose Smith, Robert Christie Jr., George Todd,
James Barlas, John Ogilvie, Wm. Finlay, E. Erskine Scott,
George A. Esson, John Watson, William Lindesay, James
Howden, William Wood, Thomas G. Dickson, Edward
Sang, Samuel Raleigh, and Alexander W. Robertson.

2. That the following Members be appointed a Committee to report with all due expedition upon the
Constitution and Laws of the Faculty, viz. : Messrs.

H. D. Dickie, G. L. Finlay, John Mackenzie, W. T. Thomson, Archibald Borthwick, Charles Pearson, G. A. Esson and the Honorary Secretaries.

3. That Messrs. John M. McCandlish and Robert Balfour be appointed interim Honorary Secretaries.

WILL THOS. THOMSON.
C.

(A reduced facsimile of this Minute will be found opposite).

At a Meeting of the Faculty of
Actuaries held within Messrs Cay
and Black's rooms 45 George Street
Edinburgh on 4 January 1856.

Present

Messrs W. J. Thomson, Esson A. Borthwick, Pearson
Monet, Ramsay, J. G. Dickson, Sang, W. Finlay Smith,
Balfour McCandlish.

On the motion of Mr Borthwick Mr W. J. Thomson
was called to the chair.

The Chairman then explained the preliminary
proceedings which had taken place and he laid on
the Table a short prospectus of the proposed Faculty
which has been signed by 38 gentlemen.

Thereafter the following resolutions were moved by
the Chairman and unanimously adopted by the
Meeting

1. That the Faculty of Actuaries be declared to be now
constituted, and to consist of the following Members
viz James Borthwick, A. D. Dickie, D. Lindsay
Gilbert L. Finlay John Mackenzie, D. Wackinshaw
Charles F. Griffith, Archibald Borthwick David Chisholm
John Monet, William Dickson, William Spens, James
Smith, D. Clunie Gregor, Charles Pearson, James
Watson, William J. Thomson, John M. McCandlish
George Ramsay, W. Smith, Robert Balfour, William
Chalmers, F. Ambrose Smith, Robert Christie Jr
George Todd, James Barlas, John Ogilvie, Wm
Finlay, E. Erskine Scott, George A. Esson, John
Watson, William Lindsay, James Howden William
Wood, Thomas G. Dickson, Edward Sang, Samuel
Raleigh & Alexander W. Robertson.

2. That the following Members be appointed a Committee
to report with all due expedition upon the Constitution
and Laws of the Faculty viz. Messrs A. D. Dickie
L. L. Finlay, John Mackenzie, W. J. Thomson,
Archibald Borthwick, Charles Pearson, G. A. Esson
and the Honorary Secretaries.

3. That Messrs John M. McCandlish and Robert Balfour
be appointed interim Honorary Secretaries

Will J. Thomson
C.

The original document constituting the Faculty

Geo. Ramsay

W. Smith

Robert Barbour

Wm. Finlay

Jno. Watson

Wat. Morton

Jas. Watson

Geo. Gould

James Barclay

Wm. Guthrie

Wm. Findlay

George Smith

James Watson

APPENDIX V

FACULTY OF ACTUARIES IN SCOTLAND
CONSTITUTION AND LAWS
1856

MEMBERS OF COUNCIL
FOR THE YEAR 1856-57.

JAMES BORTHWICK, Esq., *Chairman.*
CHARLES PEARSON, Esq.
HENRY DAVID DICKIE, Esq.
JOHN MACKENZIE, Esq.
ARCH. BORTHWICK, Esq.
WILL. THOS. THOMSON, Esq.
WILLIAM CHALMERS, Esq.
GILBERT LAURIE FINLAY, Esq.
ROBERT BALFOUR, Esq., } *Honorary Secretaries.*
JOHN M. M'CANDLISH, Esq., }
GEORGE AULDJO ESSON, Esq., *Honorary Treasurer.*

COMMITTEE ON LIBRARY
WILL. THOS. THOMSON, Esq.,—*Convener.*
DAVID CHISHOLM, Esq.   WILLIAM SMITH, Esq.
EDWARD SANG, Esq.   WILLIAM WOOD, Esq.

LECTURER
EDWARD SANG, Esq.

EDINBURGH, 20*th March* 1856.—*The Constitution and Laws of the Faculty of Actuaries in Scotland were approved of and adopted at a General Meeting of the Faculty, held here this day.*

ROBERT BALFOUR,
JOHN M. M'CANDLISH,
Honorary Secretaries.

FACULTY OF ACTUARIES IN SCOTLAND

THE FACULTY of ACTUARIES in SCOTLAND is constituted—

For the purpose of associating professionally those gentlemen who are engaged in the management of Life Assurance Institutions, or who are otherwise following the profession of an Actuary : and

For promoting the study of the Doctrine of Probabilities ; of vital Statistics and Statistics in general ; of Finance, as bearing on fluctuations in the value of money ; and of all cognate subjects a knowledge of which is essential to the efficient discharge of the duties of a Life Assurance Manager and Actuary.

The following are the Constitution and Laws of the Faculty :

1. The Faculty shall consist of Fellows, Honorary Fellows, Non-resident Members, and Associates.

FELLOWS.

2. The following gentlemen are Fellows of the Faculty:—

BALFOUR, ROBERT, City of Glasgow Assurance Company, Edinburgh.

BARLAS, JAMES, Scottish Union Insurance Company, Edinburgh.

BORTHWICK, JAMES, North British Insurance Company, Edinburgh.

BORTHWICK, ARCHIBALD, St. David Street, Edinburgh.

CHALMERS, WILLIAM, Northern Assurance Company, Aberdeen.

CHISHOLM, DAVID, North British Insurance Company, Edinburgh.

CHRISTIE, ROBERT, JUN., Northern Assurance Company, Edinburgh.

DICKIE, HENRY DAVID, Caledonian Insurance Company, Edinburgh.

DICKSON, WILLIAM, Edinburgh Life Assurance Company, Edinburgh.

DICKSON, THOMAS G., Scottish Amicable Assurance Society, Edinburgh.

ESSON, GEORGE A., George Street, Edinburgh.

FINLAY, GILBERT L., Edinburgh Life Assurance Company, Edinburgh.

FINLAY, WILLIAM, Scottish Equitable Assurance Society, Edinburgh.

GREGOR, D. CLUNIE, Colonial Assurance Company, Edinburgh.

GRIFFITH, C. F., Scottish Provincial Assurance Company, Aberdeen.

HOWDEN, JAMES, National Insurance Company, Edinburgh.

LINDESAY, WILLIAM, Scottish Widows' Fund, Edinburgh.

LINDSAY, DONALD, George Street, Edinburgh.

MACKENZIE, JOHN, Scottish Widows' Fund, Edinburgh.

M'CANDLISH, JOHN M., National Insurance Company, Edinburgh.

MOINET, JOHN, Caledonian Insurance Company, Edinburgh.

OGILVIE, JOHN, North British Insurance Company, Edinburgh.

PEARSON, CHARLES, George Street, Edinburgh.

RALEIGH, SAMUEL, St. David Street, Edinburgh.

RAMSAY, GEORGE, Scottish Union Insurance Company, Edinburgh.

ROBERTSON, ALEXANDER W., Great King Street, Edinburgh.

SANG, EDWARD, George Street, Edinburgh.

SCOTT, E. ERSKINE, Colonial Assurance Company, Dundee.

SMITH, JAMES, Northern Assurance Company, Glasgow.

SMITH, WILLIAM, English and Scottish Law Life Association, Edinburgh.

SMITH, H. AMBROSE, Northern Assurance Company, Aberdeen.

SPENS, WILLIAM, Scottish Amicable Assurance Society, Glasgow.

THOMSON, WILL. THOS., Standard Assurance Company, Edinburgh.

TODD, GEORGE, Standard Assurance Company, Edinburgh.

WALKINSHAW, DANIEL, City of Glasgow Assurance Company, Glasgow.

WATSON, JAMES, Scottish Provident Institution, Edinburgh.

WATSON, JOHN, Scottish Provident Institution, Edinburgh.

WOOD, WILLIAM, St. Andrew Street, Edinburgh.

3. The Manager, Actuary, or Secretary of any Scottish Life Assurance Institution, at its principal establishment, and any professional Actuary practising in Scotland at the date of the Constitution of the Faculty (4th January 1856) and any gentleman who shall have been an Associate of the Faculty for not less than one year, shall be eligible as a Fellow of the Faculty upon the recommendation, in writing, of any four of the existing Fellows. His application, addressed to the Council, shall be submitted to the first ordinary Quarterly Meeting of the Faculty, and at the ordinary Quarterly Meeting immediately following, the Fellows then present shall ballot on such application, the number present and voting not being less than eight, and if three-fourths of the votes shall be in favour of the applicant, he shall be admitted as a Fellow of the Faculty, but not otherwise; and it shall be incompetent to receive another application from him until the expiry of twelve months, at least, from the date of ballot.

4. Gentlemen not falling within the description of the preceding article, but who may be distinguished by scientific acquirements on subjects connected with the objects of the Faculty, or who may have rendered important service in promoting those objects, may be elected Fellows, or Honorary Fellows, at any meeting of the Faculty, upon the unanimous recommendation of the Council, and the approval of three-fourths of the whole existing Fellows, expressed in writing.

NON-RESIDENT MEMBERS.

5. Any gentleman not resident in Scotland, but connected with a Scottish Life Assurance Institution as a principal Officer at a Branch Establishment, shall be eligible as a Non-resident Member. His application, accompanied by the recommendation of two Fellows, must be addressed to the Council, and shall thereafter be disposed of in the same way as an application for admission as a Fellow in terms of Law No. 3.

ASSOCIATES.

6. Gentlemen resident in Scotland, who are not eligible for election as Fellows, may apply, on or before the Thirty-first day of May 1856, for admission as Associates of the Faculty, and if their official position or previous education shall, in the opinion of the Council, entitle them to be so admitted, their applications shall be submitted to the first Quarterly Meeting to be held after the above date, and shall then be disposed of by ballot, in the manner provided in Law No. 3.

7. Any Matriculated Student of the Faculty, or any gentleman who has been engaged for four years in the Office of a Scottish Life Assurance Institution, or of a Member of the Incorporated Society of Accountants in Edinburgh, and who has attended the Classes and Lectures established by the Faculty during, at least, two Sessions, and who shall have attained the age of 21, shall be eligible as an Associate ; but previous to admission, he shall be required to undergo two examinations, the one at an

interval of not less than twelve months after the other, on such subjects as may be prescribed by the Council ; and if these examinations are passed to the satisfaction of the Council, he shall be admitted as an Associate.

MATRICULATED STUDENTS.

8. Any gentleman desirous of prosecuting his studies in connexion with the Faculty, may apply to be entered as a Matriculated Student. He shall undergo a preliminary examination on such elementary subjects as may be prescribed by the Council. In the event of this examination being passed to the satisfaction of the Council, he shall receive a Certificate of Matriculation.

9. All Matriculated Students shall be entitled to attend the Lectures and Classes established by the Faculty, at such fee as shall be named by the Council. They shall also have access to the Faculty Library, under such regulations as the Council may from time to time resolve on.

OFFICE-BEARERS.

10. The business of the Faculty shall be conducted by a Council, consisting of eight Members, two Honorary Secretaries, and an Honorary Treasurer, all of whom shall be chosen at the first ordinary Quarterly Meeting of the Faculty each year, and at all Meetings of Council three Members shall form a quorum. A Chairman shall be annually elected by the Council from their own number.

11. Two Members of Council, whose names stand at the top of the list, shall each year become ineligible for re-election till after the expiry of one year, but the other Members of Council may be re-elected.

12. The Council shall manage and direct all matters which concern the Faculty in terms of the Regulations and subject to the control of the Faculty.

13. The Council shall have power to make from time to time such regulations, not inconsistent with these Laws, as may be found necessary, which shall remain in force

until the next Ordinary Meeting, when they shall be either affirmed or annulled.

14. They shall superintend the studies of the Matriculated Students—they shall prescribe the examinations which have to be undergone before admission to the Faculty,—and they shall appoint Examiners to conduct such examinations.

15. They shall watch over all Parliamentary or other proceedings affecting Life Assurance or the interests of the Profession ; and they may submit a Report thereupon to any Meeting of the Faculty, it being in the power of the Council to determine whether such Report shall be brought under the consideration of the Fellows alone, or under the consideration of all the Members of the Faculty, including Non-resident Members and Associates as well as Fellows.

16. The Honorary Secretaries shall conduct the correspondence of the Faculty, under the direction of the Council ; and one or both of them shall attend all the Meetings of the Faculty and of the Council and shall preserve minutes thereof.

17. The Honorary Treasurer shall receive all monies due to the Faculty. He shall keep an account of his receipts and disbursements ; which account shall be audited every year by a Committee to be named by the Council.

MEETINGS.

18. Ordinary and Special Meetings of the Faculty shall consist of Fellows only—eight to be a quorum.

19. There shall be Four Ordinary Meetings of the Faculty each year for the transaction of business, in the months of January, April, July, and October, upon such days as may be fixed by the Council. Intimation of such Meetings shall be given by circular, or by advertisement, at least Ten days previously to the day of Meeting.

20. Special Meetings of the Faculty for the transaction of business, may be summoned by the Council at such

times as they may consider advisable ; and upon a requisition addressed to the Council, signed by not less than one-fourth of the Fellows of the Faculty, and stating the subject to be brought forward, the Council shall be bound to call a Special Meeting of the Faculty, due notice of such Meetings being given as before provided.

21. The Chairman of the Council shall preside at all the Ordinary and Special Meetings of the Faculty, and in his absence the other Members of Council, according to seniority.

22. The Chairman of any Meeting shall have a deliberative vote upon all questions coming before the Faculty, and he shall also have a casting vote in the event of equality.

23. Occasional Meetings of the Faculty may be summoned at such times as seem fit to the Council for the purpose of hearing communications read upon subjects of interest to the Profession, and the Associates and Non-resident Members shall be entitled to attend these Occasional Meetings, but it shall not be competent on such occasions to enter upon the business of the Faculty.

FUNDS.

24. The Fellows shall pay to the Funds of the Faculty an Entrance-fee of £3, 3s. ; and thereafter an Annual Subscription of £1, 1s.

25. Non-resident Members and Associates shall pay to the Funds of the Faculty a fee of £2 2s., ; and thereafter an Annual Subscription of 10s. 6d.

26. Associates, on becoming Fellows, shall pay to the Funds of the Faculty an Entrance-fee of £1, 1s. ; and thereafter an Annual Subscription of £1, 1s.

27. Matriculated Students, on receiving their Certificates of Matriculation, shall pay to the Funds of the Faculty a fee of £1, 1s.

28. The Annual Subscription shall be payable on the 1st of January in each year, in advance ; and any Member whose subscription shall be in arrear for six months, shall

be applied to in writing by one of the Secretaries, and shall be incapacitated from exercising his rights as a Member till such subscription be paid ; and if the sum be not paid within two years from the date on which it became due, he shall cease to be a Member of the Faculty.

29. After payment of Current Expenses, the Funds of the Faculty shall, from time to time, be applied and invested by the Council to such purposes as a majority of Fellows present at any Ordinary or Special Meeting may determine.

COURSE OF STUDY.

30. The Faculty shall establish and superintend such Classes and Lectures as they may deem suitable for promoting the study of the subjects already referred to ; and it shall be the duty of the Council to appoint the number and order of such Classes and Lectures in each year ; and to report to the Faculty at the Quarterly Meeting in the month of July the arrangements they propose to adopt for the ensuing Winter Session.

31. It shall be part of the objects of the Faculty to form a Library of professional works for consultation and reference ; the arrangements in regard to which shall be intrusted to the Council, subject to the approval and control of the Faculty.*

32. Communications upon subjects of interest to the Profession proposed to be submitted to an Ordinary or Occasional Meeting, shall be laid before the Council for their consideration ; and they shall have the power of receiving or declining such communications.

GENERAL REGULATIONS.

33. No motion relating to the Laws of the Faculty shall be considered, unless twenty days' notice shall have been given by the Council by circular addressed to each Fellow ; and it shall be imperative on the Council to give such

* The Council will be happy to receive for the library donations of books and pamphlets on professional subjects. These may be sent to the care of the Hon. Secretaries, or to the members of the Library Committee, and will be acknowledged in the minutes of the Faculty.

intimation immediately on receiving a requisition to do so from any two Fellows.

34. Such motion, when duly intimated, shall be considered at the next ordinary Quarterly Meeting of the Faculty, or at a Special Meeting to be called in terms of Law No. 20.

35. Until a Member shall have paid up all his arrears, and given notice of resignation in writing to one of the Secretaries, he shall be liable for all subscriptions due.

APPENDIX VI

ROYAL CHARTER OF INCORPORATION

Victoria, by the Grace of God of the United Kingdom of Great Britain and Ireland Queen, Defender of the Faith ; To all to whom these presents shall come, Greeting : **Whereas, We considering** that an humble petition has been presented to Us by Donald Lindsay, William Thomas Thomson, Samuel Raleigh, William Spens, John M'Gregor M'Candlish, David Maclagan, George Ramsay, David Smith, William Smith, James Watson, Andrew Hugh Turnbull, William Wood, Robert Balfour, George Auldjo Esson, Charles Fox Griffith, Charles Pearson, Kenneth Mackenzie, David Chisholm, Robert Christie junior, William Dickson, Thomas Goldie Dickson, William Finlay, David Clunie Gregor, James Howden, James Maclean Macandrew, John Ogilvie, Robert Rainie, Alexander Weir Robertson, Edward Sang, Henry Ambrose Smith, George Todd, John Watson, James Meikle, Walter Brown, George Auldjo Jamieson, David Robertson Williamson Huie, James Wilkie, David Pearson, James John Philip Anderson, Frederick Hayne Carter, Frederic James Hallows, Hunter Douglas Prain, Thomas Robertson, Alexander Stables junior, Andrew Wood Stewart, John Stott, Charles Prentice, David John Surenne, Spencer Campbell Thomson, David Deuchar, James Ritchie Macfadyen, and Alexander Henderson Whytt, all members of the Faculty of Actuaries in Scotland ; **Setting forth ; That** the profession of Actuary to which the petitioners belong, has been called into existence mainly by the requirements of Life Assurance Institutions, the sound management and prosperity of which depend to a great extent on correct observations and calculations in regard to the duration of human life, and the probable rate of interest to be realised over a prolonged tract of future time : 𝕿𝖍𝖆𝖙 the business of Life Assurance has been extensively and successfully carried on in Scotland, and from the time of its first introduction, in the beginning of the century, to the present time, it has continued steadily to develop, and a very large amount of the savings of the people of the United Kingdom, for the future benefit of their families, is entrusted to such Institutions : 𝕿𝖍𝖆𝖙, apart from the schemes which have been in existence for many years for the benefit of the Widows of Members of the different learned professions, there are Assurance Institutions established in Scotland whose aggregate obligations to the public now probably exceed Eighty Millions Sterling, and whose invested funds amount to upwards of Twenty Millions ; 𝕿𝖍𝖆𝖙 it is mainly in connection with the proper regulation of the affairs of these Institutions the skill and services of an Actuary are called into requisition ; his special duties being, *Firstly*, to take care that the Institution under his charge, or which may at any time desire his opinion and advice, is founded on a safe basis, both as regards the rate of Mortality assumed for any particular country, class, or sex, and the rate of Interest at which it may be calculated the money entrusted to the care of such Institution can be safely improved ; *Secondly*, to ascertain from time to time as the Institution makes progress, by appropriate calculations, whether the rate of Mortality actually experienced, and the rate of Interest realised, are in accordance with the data assumed ; for the performance of these duties it is evident that not only a sound knowledge of mathematical principles is required, but also the practical application of financial judgment and experience : 𝕿𝖍𝖆𝖙, in addition to the require-ments of Life Assurance Institutions, the profession of Actuary is largely called into requisition, in the same manner as that of Advocate or Barrister, in advising and directing the public in regard to a great variety of pecuniary interests, frequently involving interests of large amount : 𝕿𝖍𝖆𝖙 the responsibility attaching to the profession of an Actuary is consequently great, requiring the services of well-educated and trustworthy men, specially trained in Actuarial business and calculations, more especially as the subject of their professional study is one with which the general public are almost entirely unacquainted, and in which, therefore, they must be wholly dependent upon the skill and integrity of the Actuary employed : 𝕿𝖍𝖆𝖙 the Actuaries of Scotland, in the year One thousand eight hundred and fifty-six, formed themselves into an Association or Faculty, with the object of uniting in one body those practising the profession, and of promoting the studies necessary thereto, and generally of furthering the objects in which, as Members of the same profession, they have a common interest : 𝕬𝖓𝖉 𝖙𝖍𝖆𝖙 the petitioners humbly conceive that it would tend greatly to promote and facilitate the attainment by the Members of their profession of the qualifications which are essential to the proper performance of their important duties ; and consequently, that it would conduce much to the benefit of the public, if the Petitioners who form the existing Body of Actuaries in Scotland were 𝖀𝖓𝖎𝖙𝖊𝖉 into a Body Corporate and Politic, having a Common Seal, with power to make Rules and Bye-Laws for the qualification and admission of Members and otherwise : 𝕬𝖓𝖉 the Petitioners therefore humbly prayed that 𝖂𝖊 would be graciously pleased to grant them a Royal Charter, incorporating them, and such persons as may hereafter be duly admitted Members, into one Body Corporate and Politic, by the name, style, and title of " 𝕿𝖍𝖊 𝕱𝖆𝖈𝖚𝖑𝖙𝖞 𝖔𝖋 𝕬𝖈𝖙𝖚𝖆𝖗𝖎𝖊𝖘 𝖎𝖓 𝕾𝖈𝖔𝖙𝖑𝖆𝖓𝖉 " with perpetual succession and a Common Seal, and power to acquire and hold Property, and to make Rules and Bye-Laws, and with such other powers, privileges, and authorities as are usually given to other Bodies Politic and Corporate, of the like nature, in such manner as to us in our Royal Wisdom shall seem proper : 𝕬𝖓𝖉 𝖂𝖍𝖊𝖗𝖊𝖆𝖘 such petition has been referred to the Lord Advocate of Scotland to consider thereof, and report his opinion what may properly be done therein : 𝕬𝖓𝖉 𝖂𝖊 having taken the said Petition and Report thereon into Our Royal consideration, and being satisfied that the intentions of the

Petitioners are laudable and deserving of encouragement : Therefore, We have constituted, erected, and incorporated, as We by Our prerogative Royal and of Our special grace, certain knowledge, and mere motion, by these presents, for Us and Our Royal Successors, Constitute, erect, and incorporate the said Donald Lindsay, William Thomas Thomson, Samuel Raleigh, William Spens, John M'Gregor M'Candlish, David Maclagan, George Ramsay, David Smith, William Smith, James Watson, Andrew Hugh Turnbull, William Wood, Robert Balfour, George Auldjo Esson, Charles Fox Griffith, Charles Pearson, Kenneth Mackenzie, David Chisholm, Robert Christie junior, William Dickson, Thomas Goldie Dickson, William Finlay, David Clunie Gregor, James Howden, James Maclean Macandrew, John Ogilvie, Robert Rainie, Alexander Weir Robertson, Edward Sang, Henry Ambrose Smith, George Todd, John Watson, James Meikle, Walter Brown, George Auldjo Jamieson, David Robertson Williamson Huie, James Wilkie, David Pearson, James John Philip Anderson, Frederick Hayne Carter, Frederic James Hallows, Hunter Douglas Prain, Thomas Robertson, Alexander Stables junior, Andrew Wood Stewart, John Stott, Charles Prentice, David John Surenne, Spencer Campbell Thomson, David Deuchar, James Ritchie Macfadyen, and Alexander Henderson Whytt, and such other persons as shall hereafter be admitted as Members of the said Society, into one Body Politic and Corporate by the name of "The Faculty of Actuaries in Scotland," unto which name they shall have perpetual succession, and shall have a Common Seal, with power to alter and renew the same at discretion ; and shall by the same name sue and be sued, implead and be impleaded, and answer and be answered in all Our Courts : As also, We will and ordain that the said Society shall be capable in law to take, purchase, and hold, to them and their successors, any goods, chattels, or personal property whatsoever, and shall also be capable in law to take, purchase, and hold, in the said Corporate name, such lands, buildings, and heritages as may be necessary for the purposes of the Society, with power to alienate, dispone, and dispose of all or any such lands, buildings, and heritages, goods, chattels, or personal property, and also to raise and receive such sums of money for the purposes of the Society, as they may think necessary, by annual contributions, fees on Entrants, or otherwise from the Members thereof ; and to do all other acts or things incidental or appertaining to a Body Corporate : **Declaring** that all Deeds and other Writings whatsoever affecting heritable or moveable property shall be valid and effectual in all respects, if conceived in the name of the Corporation, and sealed with the Seal and subscribed by three Members of Council, and by the Secretary and Treasurer of the Corporation for the time being : **And We also,** for Ourselves and Our Royal Successors, **give and grant** to the Petitioners and to those persons who shall hereafter compose the said Society, full power and authority, at their ordinary General Meetings as after appointed, to **constitute, make, and ordain** such Bye-Laws, Rules, and Regulations as to the majority of the Society present at such Meeting shall seem proper, provided that the same are not inconsistent with this Charter, or contrary to the laws of the Realm ; and to **alter and abrogate** the said Bye-Laws, Rules, and Regulations as to the majority of the Society present at such Meeting shall seem proper : **And We will and ordain** that such Bye-Laws, Rules, and Regulations shall be duly kept, observed, and obeyed : **And We hereby will and ordain** that a stated General Meeting of the Corporation shall be held once in every year in Edinburgh, in the month of January, or at such other time and place as the Society shall from time to time determine, with the power of adjournment as to the said General Meeting shall seem expedient, and that General Meetings of the Society may also be held at such other times and places as may from time to time be fixed, and that Special Meetings may also be held (provided the same are duly called in terms of the Bye-Laws, Rules, and Regulations for the time) at such times and places as may be necessary or expedient ; and that at each Annual General Meeting, or at any adjournment thereof, the Society shall choose out of the Members thereof a Council, Secretary, and Treasurer (the same person being eligible for both of the last-mentioned offices), and such other Officers as the Society may find hereafter to be necessary and proper : 𝕬𝖓𝖉 𝖂𝖊 𝖜𝖎𝖑𝖑 𝖆𝖓𝖉 𝖔𝖗𝖉𝖆𝖎𝖓 that the Society shall have power from time to time, and in such manner as may be fixed by the Bye-Laws, Rules, and Regulations, to constitute and appoint a Committee of Examiners for the purpose of conducting and regulating such examination of Entrants and others as the Corporation may from time to time direct, and in such manner as they may appoint, in furtherance of the objects of the Society ; and that the course of Education to be pursued, and the amount of general and professional acquirements to be exacted from such Entrants, shall be such as the Corporation shall from time to time fix : 𝕬𝖓𝖉 𝖂𝖊 𝖋𝖚𝖗𝖙𝖍𝖊𝖗 𝖍𝖊𝖗𝖊𝖇𝖞 𝖜𝖎𝖑𝖑, 𝖌𝖗𝖆𝖓𝖙, 𝖆𝖓𝖉 𝖉𝖊𝖈𝖑𝖆𝖗𝖊 that the present Council, Secretary, and Treasurer of the said Faculty shall hold their offices and discharge their functions respectively as Council, Secretary, and Treasurer of the Society hereby incorporated, until the stated Annual General Meeting in January One thousand eight hundred and sixty-nine, and that they and their successors in office to be chosen according to the Bye-Laws, Rules, and Regulations of the Society, shall have full power to manage, direct, order, and appoint in all matters and things touching and concerning the said Society, in terms of, and conform to, the Bye-Laws, Rules, and Regulations thereof ; 𝕬𝖓𝖉 𝖂𝖊 for Ourselves and Our Royal Successors, 𝖉𝖊𝖈𝖑𝖆𝖗𝖊 that this our present Charter shall be in and by all things valid and effectual in law, according to the true intent and meaning of the same ; and it shall be accepted and understood in the sense most favourable and beneficial to the said Corporation, notwithstanding any misrecital, defect, uncertainty, or imperfection in the same. 𝕴𝖓 𝖜𝖎𝖙𝖓𝖊𝖘𝖘 𝖜𝖍𝖊𝖗𝖊𝖔𝖋, WE have ordered the Seal appointed by the

The Royal Charter of Incorporation (1868)

Treaty of Union to be kept and made use of in place of the Great Seal of Scotland, to be appended hereto.

> 𝕲𝖎𝖇𝖊𝖓 𝖆𝖙 𝕺𝖚𝖗 𝕮𝖔𝖚𝖗𝖙 𝖆𝖙 𝕾𝖙. 𝕵𝖆𝖒𝖊𝖘'𝖘 the twenty-first day of September in the year One thousand eight hundred and sixty-eight, and in the thirty-second year of Our Reign.
>
> Per Signaturam manu S. D. N. Reginæ supra scrip^t.
>
> Written to the Seal and registered the fifteenth day of October 1868.
>
> (Signed)   JAMES P. HALLEY,
>   *Depute Director of Chancery.*

Sealed at Edinburgh the fifteenth day of October in the year One thousand eight hundred and sixty-eight.

    (Signed)   COLIN MACKENZIE,
                        Depute Keeper of the Seal.

    £LXXX. Scots.

APPENDIX VII

RULES AND BYE-LAWS
(as amended 28th June 1954)

RULES
Members

1. The Faculty shall consist of Fellows, Associates and Honorary Fellows.

2. Anyone possessing qualifications fitting him for the duties of an actuary and which render his admission to the Faculty desirable, may be elected a Fellow on the nomination of the Council. Such nomination must be concurred in by at least three-fourths of the Members of Council present at a meeting thereof, of which notice, specifying the nominee, shall have been issued not less than seven days previously. The nomination shall be submitted to the first General Meeting of the Faculty thereafter, at which a ballot shall be taken, and if a majority of votes be in favour of the admission of the nominee, he shall be held duly elected.

3. Anyone of distinguished attainments in mathematical, statistical, or financial subjects, or who has rendered important service in promoting the objects of the Faculty, may be elected an Honorary Fellow at any General Meeting of the Faculty, upon the recommendation of the Council. It shall also be in the power of the Council to recommend to the Faculty that a Fellow who has retired from the profession after long service be elected an Honorary Fellow.

4. (*a*) Any Student of the Faculty (see Rule 6) who has attained the age of twenty-three years and has passed, to the satisfaction of the Council, such examinations as the Council may prescribe, may on application within six

months of passing the final examination or within six months after attaining the age of twenty-three years (having previously passed such examination) be admitted a Fellow, subject to the approval of the Council. His application shall be considered at a meeting of Council of which notice, specifying his name, shall have been issued not less than seven days previously ; and if a majority of the Members of Council present approve of his admission he shall be declared duly admitted, and his admission shall be reported to the first General Meeting of the Faculty thereafter.

(*b*) Any Student of the Faculty (see Rule 6) who has attained the age of twenty-one years (but who has not attained the age of twenty-three years) and has passed to the satisfaction of the Council such examinations as the Council may prescribe, may on application within six months of passing the final examination or within six months after attaining the age of twenty-one years (having previously passed such examination) be admitted an Associate, subject to the approval of the Council in the same manner as is required in the case of the admission of a Fellow (see Rule 4 (*a*)).

(*c*) An Associate of the Faculty, having attained the age of twenty-three years, shall at a meeting of Council within six months thereafter be admitted a Fellow subject to the approval of the Council in the same manner as is required in the case of the admission of a Student to the Fellowship (see Rule 4 (*a*)).

5. A Fellow, Associate or Honorary Fellow may use after his name the initials F.F.A., A.F.A. or Hon. F.F.A. respectively.

Students

6. (*a*) Anyone desirous of prosecuting his studies in connection with the Faculty must be enrolled as a Student. Application shall be made on a prescribed form with the recommendation of two Fellows and shall be subject to the approval of the Council.

(*b*) The applicant shall furnish evidence that he has passed either—

> (i) The Scottish Leaving Certificate Examination provided that three subjects at least, including English and Mathematics, have been passed on the Higher Standard, or alternatively a sufficient number of subjects, including Mathematics on the Higher Standard, as would enable the applicant to obtain an attestation of fitness certificate for entry into a Scottish University ;

or (ii) the Preliminary Examination for Scottish Universities provided that passes in English and Higher Mathematics have been obtained ;

or (iii) such other Examinations as in the opinion of the Council are equivalent to the above ;

or shall produce such other evidence of general education as may be accepted by the Council from time to time after individual enquiry.

(*c*) The Council shall have power to remove a Student from the Roll, provided that at the Meeting of Council when such removal be proposed not less than five-sixths of the Members of Council present shall vote in favour of such removal.

Council

7. The Faculty, at the Ordinary General Meeting to be held each year as hereinafter provided, shall elect by ballot from among the Fellows a President, not more than four Vice-Presidents, one or more Honorary Secretaries, Honorary Treasurers, Honorary Editors, Honorary Librarians, such other additional Office-Bearers as may be required, and not more than twelve other Members to act along with them as the Council of the Faculty for the ensuing year. The Council shall have power to co-opt the Chairman of the Board of Examiners and the Chairman of any Committee it may have appointed.

8. Of the Members of Council who are not Office-Bearers the three whose names are highest on the list as adjusted at the last Ordinary General Meeting, or such smaller number than three as, taken along with the number of vacancies by death, resignation, or other causes, make three in all, shall each year become ineligible for re-election till after the expiry of one year, except to fill any office referred to in Rule 7 or any other existing office.

In the application of this Rule it shall be a condition that of the Members of Council (including Office-Bearers) elected in any year there shall be at least three who were not Members of Council in the previous year.

9. When a vacancy occurs among the Office-Bearers or other Members of Council in the interval between one Ordinary General Meeting and the next, the Council may make an interim appointment to fill such vacancy.

10. The Council shall manage and direct all matters which concern the Faculty in terms of the Rules and subject to the control of the Faculty. The Council shall have power to appoint a Secretary and such assistants as may be required, with such remuneration, if any, as it may see fit, and also to appoint Committees, and to delegate any of its powers to such Committees.

11. The Council shall have power from time to time to make such Bye-Laws or such alterations on existing Bye-Laws as are not inconsistent with these Rules or with the Charter of Incorporation and as may be found necessary. Any new or altered Bye-Laws shall remain in force until the next General Meeting of the Faculty, when they shall be confirmed or annulled.

12. The Council shall prescribe the Examinations to be undergone by a Student before admission to the Faculty. It shall appoint a Board of Examiners to conduct such Examinations and, on the report of the Board, shall decide as to which candidates have passed such Examinations.

13. The Council shall watch over all parliamentary and other proceedings affecting the interests of the profession

and shall report thereon to a General Meeting of the Faculty when such proceedings appear of sufficient importance.

14. The Honorary Secretaries and the Secretary shall conduct the correspondence of the Faculty under the direction of the Council, and minutes of the Meetings of the Faculty and of the Council shall be preserved.

15. The Honorary Treasurers or the Secretary shall receive all moneys due to the Faculty. An account shall be kept of receipts and disbursements, which account, made up to 31st December in each year, shall be audited by an Auditor to be appointed by the Council, and shall be submitted to the Faculty at the next Ordinary General Meeting.

Meetings

16. Ordinary and Special General Meetings of the Faculty shall consist of Fellows only—eight to be a quorum. At Meetings of the Council, five Members shall form a quorum.

17. One Ordinary General Meeting of the Faculty shall be held each year, on the fourth Monday in the month of June, or upon such other date as may be fixed by the Council. Notice of such Meeting shall be issued by circular to each Fellow and given by advertisement in at least one Edinburgh newspaper not less than seven days previous to the day of meeting.

18. A Special General Meeting of the Faculty may be summoned by the Council at any time it may consider advisable. Notice of such Meeting, stating the subjects to be brought forward, shall be issued by circular to each Fellow not less than seven days previous to the day of meeting.

Upon a requisition addressed to the Council, signed by not less than ten Fellows and stating the subject to be brought forward, the Council shall within twenty-eight days of the receipt of such requisition call a Special General

Meeting of the Faculty, but for consideration only of the said subject.

19. The President, or in his absence the senior Vice-President present, shall take the chair at all Meetings of the Faculty and of the Council. In the absence of the President and of all the Vice-Presidents, the Meeting shall elect a Chairman.

20. The Chairman of any Meeting shall have a deliberative vote and shall also have a casting vote in the event of equality.

21. Sessional Meetings of the Faculty shall be held at such times as may be approved by the Council, for the purpose of receiving papers and communications upon subjects of interest to the profession, and of engaging in discussion thereon, such papers and communications having previously received the approval of the Council, and the Council shall have power to print and publish, at the expense and for behoof of the Faculty, any communications read at such Sessional Meetings, reports of the discussions thereon, and any other matters which it considers likely to be of use to the profession. Students and Library-members (see Rule 32) shall be entitled to attend such Sessional Meetings, to contribute papers (subject always to the approval of the Council as aforesaid) and to take part in the discussions. At such Sessional Meetings it shall not be competent to enter upon any business of the Faculty other than as aforesaid.

Funds

22. (a) Students shall pay upon enrolment an entrance fee of £1, 1s. The subscriptions payable by Students on enrolment and on 1st January in each succeeding year shall be £2, 2s. until Part I of the Examinations has been passed, after which the annual subscription shall be £3, 3s.

If the subscription of any Student shall be in arrear for two months, notice thereof shall be sent to him, and such Student shall not be entitled to exercise his rights as a Student till such subscription be paid. If the subscription be not paid within six months from the date on which it became due, the name of the defaulter shall be removed from the Roll, but the Council shall have power to suspend the operation of this rule or to reinstate such defaulter on such terms as it may see fit if in its opinion the circumstances so warrant.

(*b*) During any period when a Student is performing whole-time National Service the Council may, on written application by the Student, reduce the amount of subscription payable.

(*c*) A Student on each occasion of giving in his name for Examination shall pay a fee or fees according to a scale. The scale of fees shall be decided by the Council and may be altered from time to time by the Council.

23. Students on becoming Fellows or Associates shall pay the excess of the annual subscription of a Fellow or Associate over that of a Student for the year then current.

24. Fellows elected in terms of Rule 2 shall pay the annual subscription for the year then current.

25. (*a*) Fellows and Associates shall pay an annual subscription of £9, 9s., which subscription shall be payable in advance on 1st January of each year.

(*b*) During any period when a Fellow or Associate is performing whole-time National Service the Council may, on written application by the Fellow or Associate, reduce the amount of subscription payable.

(*c*) Fellows who have attained the age of sixty and have permanently retired from their normal business and from any form of actuarial practice shall on application to the Council be entitled to a reduction in the amount of annual subscription payable by them. Any Fellow who has not attained the age of sixty, but who has retired from active business and from any form of actuarial practice on account of ill-health, should also apply to the Council to have his annual subscription reduced. The amount of the reduction in the subscription will be at the discretion of the

Council and will take effect as from the first subscription falling due after the application has been received unless the Council decide otherwise.

26. If the subscription of any Fellow or Associate shall be in arrear for two months, notice thereof shall be sent to him, and such Fellow or Associate shall not be entitled to exercise his rights till such subscription be paid. If the subscription be not paid within six months from the date on which it became due, the name of the defaulter shall be removed from the Roll, but the Council shall have power to suspend the operation of this rule or to reinstate such defaulter on such terms as it may see fit if in its opinion the circumstances so warrant.

27. Until a Fellow or Associate shall have paid up all his arrears and given written notice of resignation, he shall be liable for all subscriptions due.

28. On any Fellow attaining the age of seventy years his annual subscription shall cease.

It shall be in the power of a Fellow at any time to commute his annual subscription by a single payment calculated on such basis and subject to such regulations as may from time to time be made by the Council. The single payment received shall be carried to a separate " Commutation Fund Account," and the income from the investments forming such account shall be included in the ordinary revenue account. There shall also be transferred from the " Commutation Fund Account " to the ordinary revenue account such annual amounts as shall extinguish each single payment in the year equal to the Fellow's year of birth plus seventy.

29. After payment of current expenses the Funds of the Faculty shall from time to time be applied by the Council in promoting the objects of the Faculty or be invested for like purpose in such manner as the Council may determine.

30. The Council may, with the consent of a General Meeting and under such conditions as may then be prescribed, devote a sum or annual sum to any object tending

in the opinion of the Council to promote the study of actuarial or cognate subjects.

Library

31. The Faculty shall maintain a Library of professional works for consultation and reference, the arrangements in regard to which shall be entrusted to the Council, subject to the approval and control of the Faculty.

32. Anyone resident in Scotland who possesses actuarial qualifications or such other qualifications as may be approved by the Council may, on the recommendation of a Fellow and subject to the approval of the Council and to such regulations (including the payment of an annual subscription) as may from time to time be made by the Council, be admitted as a Library-member ; but the Council shall have power to terminate such Library-membership at any time.

33. Students and Library-members shall have access to the Library with consent of the Council and under such regulations as it may from time to time determine.

Faculty Hall

34. For the purpose of Meetings and for the preservation of the Faculty's Library it shall be competent to the Council to rent or purchase suitable premises.

General Regulations

35. The Rules of the Faculty may be repealed, altered, or added to, at an Ordinary or Special General Meeting, provided notice shall have been issued by circular specifying the proposed changes not less than fourteen days previous to the day of meeting.

36. On receiving a complaint that the conduct of a Fellow or Associate is unprofessional or otherwise of such a nature as may be justly considered likely to bring discredit to the Faculty, the Council shall have power to take action on such complaint. The Council shall make such investigation and require such information and explanations from such Fellow or Associate as it may think proper, and

thereafter, if the Council shall deem it necessary, a Special Meeting of the Council shall be called to consider the complaint. At least fourteen days' notice of such Special Meeting shall be given to the Fellow or Associate in question. If at such Meeting less than twelve Members shall be present the Meeting shall stand adjourned to a place and time to be then determined, of which the Fellow or Associate in question shall receive at least one week's notice. If at least twelve Members of Council be present at such Special Meeting or adjourned Meeting the Fellow or Associate in question may, if he so desires, appear at the Meeting and state his case, and if the Meeting shall decide by a majority of at least three-fourths of the Members present that the complaint is well founded, and that it would be discreditable to the Faculty that the Fellow or Associate in question should continue as a Fellow or Associate of the Faculty, the Council shall call upon such Fellow or Associate to resign, and if he shall fail to do so within fourteen days of being so called upon the Council shall report to a Special General Meeting of the Faculty that in its opinion such Fellow or Associate ought no longer to be a Fellow or Associate of the Faculty. At such Meeting a ballot shall be taken among all the Fellows present, and if three-fourths of the votes then given are for his expulsion, and the number of votes for expulsion is not less than fifteen, it shall be declared that he is no longer a Fellow or Associate, and he shall thereupon *ipso facto* cease to be a Fellow or Associate and his name shall be removed from the Roll.

In the event of the resignation or expulsion of a Fellow or Associate as aforesaid, the Council may, if it sees fit, cause notice thereof to be published in such newspapers or journals as it may select.

37. To the intent that women may be admitted to the Faculty on the same conditions as men, in the foregoing Rules and in the following Bye-Laws the masculine shall include the feminine.

BYE-LAWS

Examinations

1. Examinations of candidates for admission as Fellows or Associates shall take place annually in the month of April or at such other times as the Council may think desirable. In addition an Examination in Part I, Section A, shall be held in the Autumn of each year.

2. Not less than one month's public notice of the days on which the Examinations will take place shall be given by advertisement in at least one Edinburgh newspaper.

3. Each candidate must give the Secretary notice in writing of his intention to come forward for Examination. Such notice must reach the Secretary at least fourteen days before the date of the Examination, unless the candidate wishes to be examined elsewhere than in Great Britain or Ireland, in which case the notice must reach the Secretary not later than the 20th of that month which is three calendar months previous to the month in which the Examination is being held. The notice must be accompanied by the appropriate fee or fees.

4. The Examinations may be conducted in writing, or *viva voce*, or both, at the discretion of the Board of Examiners. Candidates are not allowed any means of information, except such as the Board of Examiners may supply.

5. The Examinations are distinguished as Parts I, II, III, and IV respectively. Part I is divided into two Sections A and B, and Part IV into three Sections A, B, and C. The subjects of Examination are as follows :—

(*Here follows the Examination Syllabus, which is printed in Appendix IX, page* 267).

6. The following rules shall apply in regard to the order of sitting for the Examinations :—

(i) The candidate must commence with the Examination in Part I, Section A (unless exemption has been granted in terms of Bye-Law 8 (*b*)), but may take Part I, Section B, at the same time.

Where a candidate takes both Examinations at the same time, success or failure in each will be determined independently.

The candidate must have passed in both Sections of Part I before proceeding to take Part II (except as provided in Bye-Law 8 (*b*)).

(ii) Part II must then be taken.

(iii) A candidate who has passed Part II will then take Part III and may take any one Section of Part IV at the same time. Where a candidate takes a Section of Part IV at the same time as Part III, success or failure in each Examination will be determined independently. In the event of failure in Part III the candidate must take that Part again on every subsequent occasion of sitting until it has been passed.

(iv) A candidate who has passed Part III may then take any one or two Sections of Part IV at the same Examination, and success or failure in each Examination will be determined independently.

Note.—*Nos. (iii) and (iv) above should be read in conjunction with Bye-Law 7.*

7. Subject to the provisions of Bye-Law 6 as to the order of sitting the Examinations (except to the extent that these provisions are varied by paragraph (iv) below), a system of " Credits " will apply to Part II, to Part III and to Sections A, B and C of Part IV, *e.g.* in Part II a candidate who passes in " Theory of Interest and Annuities Certain," but who fails in " Theory of Life and Other Contingencies," will not require to take the " Theory of Interest and Annuities Certain " portion again and *vice versa*.

(i) For the purposes of these " Credits " the division will be as follows :—

PART II   (*a*) Interest and Annuities Certain.
(Subject No. 1 in Syllabus.)

          (*b*) Life Contingencies.
(Subject No. 2 in Syllabus.)

PART III   (*a*) Statistics.
(Subject No. 1 in Syllabus.)

          (*b*) Mortality and other Investigations.
(Subject No. 2 in Syllabus.)

PART IVA   (*a*) Office Premiums, etc. ; Surrenders
and Conversions of Contracts of Life
Assurance Companies.
(Subject No. 1 in Syllabus.)

          (*b*) Valuation and Income Tax—Life
Assurance Companies.
(Subject No. 2 in Syllabus.)

PART IVB   (*a*) Pension Funds, Widows' Funds and
Friendly Societies.
(Subject No. 1 in Syllabus.)

          (*b*) Social Insurance.
(Subject No. 2 in Syllabus.)

PART IVC   (*a*) Stock Exchange and other Investments.
(Subject No. 1 in Syllabus.)

          (*b*) Life Interests and Reversions.
(Subject No. 2 in Syllabus.)

          (*c*) Law affecting Life Assurance Con-
tracts.
(Subject No. 3 in Syllabus.)

(ii) In arriving at a decision as to whether a candidate
merits a " Credit " in any of the foregoing Parts
or Sections, all the papers returned by the candidate
for that Part or Section will be taken into account.

(iii) Where a candidate has obtained a " Credit " in a
Part or Section, the remainder of that Part or

Section must be taken on every subsequent occasion of sitting until it has been passed.

(iv) Subject to the preceding paragraph, a candidate with a " Credit " in Part II (Life Contingencies) may take Part III at the same Examination. A candidate who has passed Part II and who has a " Credit " in Part III may take any one Section of Part IV at the same Examination. A candidate who has passed Part III and who has a " Credit " in any one Section of Part IV may also take one other Section of Part IV at the same Examination. A candidate with " Credits " in two Sections of Part IV who has still one complete Section of Part IV to take may take that Section at the same Examination.

8. (*a*) Any person who has obtained the Diploma in Actuarial Mathematics granted by the University of Edinburgh shall be exempted from Parts I and II of the Examinations.

(*b*) Any Student who has graduated with Mathematical Honours at any University approved by the Council may, in the discretion of the Council, be exempted from Part I, Section A, and be allowed to present himself for Part I, Section B, and Part II in the same year. Success or failure in Part I, Section B, or Part II will be determined independently.

(*c*) Members of the Institute of Actuaries who have completed the Examinations for the Fellowship of that body may be admitted as Students of the Faculty and will be deemed to have passed Parts I, II and III of the foregoing Examination Syllabus.

9. Unless a Student shall have passed, or been exempted from, Part I, Section A of the Examinations within three years from the date of enrolment, his name shall be removed from the Roll. Students are required to take the subsequent Examinations in the prescribed order. Unless for cause shown to the satisfaction of the Council, a Student is

expected to appear for examination within three years from the date of passing or being exempted from Part I, Section A, and subsequently at intervals of not more than three years, failing which his name may be removed from the Roll. Allowance shall be made in calculating the above periods for any time during those periods when the Student has been on full-time National Service.

Sessional Meetings and Publications

10. The Council may annually nominate Fellows who are not Members of Council to act along with it, or with any Committee appointed by it, in carrying out the objects contemplated by Rule 21.

11. Except as may be otherwise arranged by the Council, a Sessional Meeting shall be held on one Monday in each month from November to March inclusive.

12. Every paper or other communication intended to be read at a Sessional Meeting shall be submitted before the date of such Meeting and the Council shall determine whether or not it shall be published or issued in printed form at the expense and for behoof of the Faculty.

13. Every paper or communication submitted for reading at a Sessional Meeting, or for inclusion in the published *Transactions* of the Faculty, shall, in the absence of any previous agreement to the contrary, be the property of the Faculty. The Council shall, if required by the Author, decide within three months from the date when such paper or communication is submitted whether or not the same is to be published or issued in printed form by the Faculty. If its decision is in the negative, or if in any case a paper or communication so submitted is not published or issued in printed form by the Faculty within twelve months from the said date, all right and property in the same shall be held to have been relinquished by the Faculty.

14. In the absence of any special arrangement, the Author of any paper shall be entitled, free of charge, to twenty-five copies of the part of the *Transactions* of the

Faculty containing his paper, when issued; and to additional copies at half the published price.

15. Each Fellow, Associate, Student and Library-member shall be entitled to receive one copy of each current part of the *Transactions* of the Faculty free of cost.

Library

16. The Library shall be open at such times as the Council may determine.

17. No one shall be allowed to borrow more than four volumes at one time, except with the sanction of the Council.

18. Books shall not be borrowed for a longer period than one month; but when a book is returned it may be re-borrowed, provided it has not been bespoken in the meantime. If a book is not returned within the prescribed period the borrower shall pay a fine of one shilling per volume for each additional week or part of a week that the volume is retained by him, and no other book can be borrowed by him until such a volume has been returned and the fine paid.

19. Books shall be lent only on the receipt of the borrower or on the receipt of a messenger bearing a written order signed by the borrower.

20. A borrower losing, injuring, or defacing any book shall supply another copy, or shall pay such sum as the Council may determine.

21. Cyclopædias, works of reference, and unbound numbers of scientific journals and periodicals (except the *Transactions* of the Faculty or the *Journal* of the Institute of Actuaries) shall not be lent, except with the sanction of the Council, but may be consulted in the Library.

APPENDIX VIII

Excerpt from Report by the Special Committee on Sessional Meetings as to the issue of Publications by the Faculty, and as to the interest of members in papers read by them.

The Council having by their Minute of 26th November 1901, remitted to this Committee to consider what rule should be adopted as to the interests of members in papers ready by them, the Committee met on 4th December to consider the subject.

Present—Mr. Low (in the Chair), Mr. Wallace, Mr. Deuchar, Mr. Warden, Mr. Chatham, Mr. Fraser, Mr. Sim and the Secretary.

It appeared to the Committee that in order to deal with the question remitted to them it was desirable to consider the whole subject of the Faculty's publications and the form these should take, and they submit the following suggestions to the Council as their unanimous recommendations :—

1. That each paper read before the Faculty and approved by the Council for publication should be issued as soon as ready, with the discussion appended and with any other matter that the Council may decide to publish at the same time. These issues should be under the title of " Transactions of the Faculty of Actuaries." They should be in octavo form, similar to the *Transactions* of the late Actuarial Society of Edinburgh, but with a distinctive cover ; and the parts should be numbered consecutively in arabic numerals.

2. That the printing of the *Transactions* should be done in Edinburgh, but as to their publication the Committee desired the Secretary to communicate with

Messrs. C. & E. Layton, London, whose reply will be laid before the Council.

3. That the price to be charged for each part should be fixed by the Council, according to circumstances, it being however provided (*a*) that the author of any paper shall be entitled to 25 copies gratuitously for his own use when issued; (*b*) that every Fellow and Associate of the Faculty shall be entitled to receive a copy of each part of the *Transactions* free of cost, and one additional copy at half the published price; and (*c*) that one copy at half price shall also be allowed to each student of the Faculty, and to each member of the late Actuarial Society of Edinburgh who is not a member or student of the Faculty, but is a contributor to the funds of the Faculty in terms of Rule 21.

4. That the Council should appoint an Editorial Committee to superintend the Faculty's publications, and to whom may be entrusted, if the Council see fit, and always subject to reference to the Council in cases of dubiety or difficulty, the decision as to whether any particular paper or communication shall or shall not be published.

5. That in order to promote discussion, papers intended to be read at the Sessional Meetings, and to be afterwards issued in printed form, should be put in print beforehand, and proof copies be furnished to gentlemen who propose to attend the reading of the paper, or to take part in the discussion.

6. On the subject specially remitted to them the Committee are of opinion that the rule to be adopted should be similar to that expressed in Nos. 24 and 25 of the Bye-Laws of the Institute of Actuaries, but giving right to an author to require a decision within three months as to whether his paper is to be published by the Faculty or not. They recommend the adoption by the Council of the following Bye-

laws which, in terms of Rule 11 will fall to be submitted for confirmation to the next General Meeting of the Faculty, viz.:—

" Every paper or other communication intended to
" be read at any sessional meeting of the Faculty
" shall be given in at least fourteen days before the
" date of such meeting, and if the Council approve
" of the same, they will at the same time, or sub-
" sequently, determine whether or not it shall be
" published or issued in printed form at the expense
" and for the behoof of the Faculty."

" Every paper or communication given in to be
" read at a sessional meeting or to be included in
" any publication issued by the Faculty shall, in the
" absence of any previous agreement to the con-
" rary, be the property of the Faculty : provided
" that the Council shall if required by the author
" decide within three months from the date when
" such paper or communication is given in whether
" or not the same is to be published or issued in
" printed form by the Faculty, and, if their decision
" is in the negative, or if in any case a paper or
" communication so given in is not published or
" issued in printed form by the Faculty within
" twelve months from the said date, all right and
" property in the same shall be held to have been
" relinquished by the Faculty."

APPENDIX IX

EXAMINATION SYLLABUS
1885

First Examination

Arithmetic	Binomial Theorem
Equations	Nature and use of Logarithms
Series	Finite Differences
Permutations and Combinations	Theory of Probabilities

Second Examination

Theory of Logarithms.

Interest and Annuities-certain, with Construction of Monetary Tables.

Probabilities of Life and Survivorship.

History, Characteristics and Uses of Mortality Tables.

Theory of Life Annuities and Assurances, with Construction of relative Tables.

Third Examination

Mortality Investigations. Construction of Tables from actual or assumed data.

Graduation of Tables.

Life Assurance Finance and Practice, viz.:—

Calculation of Office Premiums.

Valuation of the Liabilities and Assets of a Life Office.

Distribution of Surplus.

Repurchase and Conversion of Policies and Bonuses.

Book-keeping and Accounts.

Miscellaneous Questions in Life Office Practice.

Law of Life Assurance. Elements of the Law of Scotland in relation to Property.

Valuation of Reversions, Life-rents, and other Contingent Interests.

Rates and Valuations of Widows' Funds and Friendly Societies.

EXAMINATION SYLLABUS
1899

First Examination

Arithmetic.

Equations.

Series.

Permutations and Combinations.

Binomial Theorem.

Theory and use of Logarithms.

Elements of the Calculus of Finite Differences.

Theory of Probabilities.

Second Examination

Interest and Annuities-certain, with Construction of Monetary Tables.

Probabilities of Life and of Survivorship.

Theory of Life Contingencies, including Annuities and Assurances, with Construction of relative Tables.

History and Characteristics of Mortality Tables.

Application of the Calculus of Finite Differences to Life Contingencies.

Elements of the Differential and Integral Calculus.

Third Examination

Mortality, Marriage and Sickness Investigations, including Construction of Tables from actual or from hypothetical data.

Graduation of Tables.

Formulas for Summation and Interpolation.

Application of the Differential and Integral Calculus to Life Contingencies.

Life Assurance finance and practice, viz.:—

    Calculation of Premiums.

    Valuation of Assets and Liabilities.

    Distribution of Surplus.

    Surrender and Conversion of Policies and Bonuses.

    Book-keeping and Accounts.

    Investments.

    Miscellaneous questions.

Law of Life Assurance.

Reversions, Life-interests and other Contingencies.

Widows' Funds, Superannuation Funds and Friendly Societies—Calculations of Rates and Valuations.

EXAMINATION SYLLABUS

1915

(used immediately after 1914-18 War)

PART I.

Arithmetic.

Algebra up to and including Quadratic Equations.

Plane Analytical Geometry, up to and including Elementary Conic Sections.

Arithmetical and Geometrical Progressions.

Permutations and Combinations.

Binomial Theorem.

    (No questions necessitating the use of Trigonometrical functions will be set).

PART II.

Theory and use of Logarithms.

Series.

Theory of Equations.

Curve-Tracing.

Theory of Interest and Annuities-Certain, with Construction of Relative Tables.

Theory of Probabilities.

The Mortality Table, Probabilities of Life, Expectations of Life, Probabilities of Survivorship, and Statistical Applications of the Mortality Table—

being the subjects dealt with in the first five chapters of the Institute of Actuaries Text-Book, Part II.

Elements of :—

Calculus of Finite Differences,
Calculus of Operations,
Differential Calculus,
Integral Calculus,

and their applications to the Theory of Interest and Annuities-Certain, or to the Mortality Table.

(No questions necessitating the use of Trigonometrical functions will be set).

PART III.

Theory of Life Contingencies, and Formulas of Summation and Interpolation, including Applications of the Calculi mentioned in Part II.

Mortality, Marriage, and Sickness Investigations (including the History of existing Tables), and Construction of Relative Tables.

Graduation of Tables.

Money Market and Foreign Exchanges, including the principal classes of Stock Exchange Securities, and practical questions arising in connection with their Purchase and Sale.

PART IV.

Life Assurance Finance and Practice, including :—

Calculation of Office Premiums ; and Assessment of Extra Risks due to Family and Personal History, Residence, and Occupation,

Valuation of Assets and Liabilities,

Distribution of Surplus,
Surrender and Conversion of Policies and Bonuses,
Drafting of Contracts and Endorsements,
Book-keeping and Accounts,
Investments.

Law affecting Life Assurance, National Health Insurance, Friendly Societies, and Joint-Stock Companies.

Reversions, Life Rents, and other Contingent Interests.

Sickness Insurance, Widows' Funds, Superannuation Funds, and Friendly Societies—Calculation of Rates and Valuations.

Employers' Liability Insurance—Valuation of Outstanding Claims.

EXAMINATION SYLLABUS
1923

PART I.

Section A.

Arithmetic and Algebra, including the Progressions, Permutations, Combinations and the Binomial Theorem.

Plane Analytical Geometry up to, and including, Elementary Conic Sections.

Section B.

Advanced Algebra, including Logarithms, Probabilities, Series and Theory of Equations.

Curve-tracing.

Finite Differences, including Interpolation and Summation.

Elementary Differential and Integral Calculus and the Calculus of Operations.

Candidates are expected to have a knowledge of Elementary Trigonometry.

Part II.

Section A.

Theory of Interest and Annuities-Certain with Construction of Relative Tables.

Section B.

Theory of Life and other Contingencies.

Part III.

Section A.

Compilation of Tables from Mortality, Marriage, Sickness and other Statistics. The history and features of the more important existing Tables and the methods of Construction and Graduation of Tables generally.

Section B.

Calculation of Office Premiums or Rates of Contribution in respect of Life Assurance, Sickness Insurance, Annuity and other Contracts, including those of Friendly Societies, Pension Funds and Widows' Funds.

Assessment of Extra Risk due to Family and Personal History, Residence and Occupation.

Book-keeping, particularly with reference to Life Office Accounts.

The Money-Market and Foreign Exchanges—Stock Exchange and other Investments (excluding Reversions and Liferents), their purchase, sale and valuation.

Part IV.

Valuation of Life Assurance, Sickness Insurance, Annuity and other Contracts, including those of Friendly Societies, Pension Funds, Widows' Funds and Employers' Liability Companies — problems connected therewith.

Analysis and Distribution of Surplus of Life Assurance Companies, Friendly Societies, Pension Funds and Widows' Funds—The Board of Trade Returns.

Reversions, Liferents and Contingent Interests.

Surrender and Conversion of Policies.

Law affecting Life Assurance, Friendly and Approved Societies, Pension Funds, Widows' Funds and Joint-Stock Companies, including Income Tax Law.

EXAMINATION SYLLABUS

1954

(still in force in Centenary Year)

PART I.

Section A.

(1) Arithmetic, including Fundamental Operations; Contracted Methods; Approximations; Relative Errors; Calculation of Averages; Practical Use of Logarithms; Application to General Problems.

(2) Algebra, including Remainder Theorem; Solution of Equations; Theory of Quadratic Equations; Easy Partial Fractions; Simple Series; Proportion; Indices; Surds; Permutations and Combinations; Binomial Theorem for a Positive Integral Exponent; Use of the Binomial Theorem for any Exponent; Theory of Logarithms; Induction; Graph of y where y or y^2 is a Rational Function of x, and Approximations to the Form of the Graph at a given Point.

(3) Trigonometry, including the Radian Measure of Angles; Trigonometrical Ratios; Periodicity; General Solution of Equations; Graphs of Trigonometrical Functions; Addition Theorems and Applications thereof; Inverse Trigonometrical Functions.

Section B.

(1) Advanced Algebra, including Theory of Equations and Numerical Approximations to the Roots of Equations; Inequalities; Elementary Convergence

and Summation of Series (including Recurring Series) ; Exponential, Logarithmic, Sine and Cosine Series ; Complex Numbers and Demoivre's Theorem ; Probability (including Inverse Probability).

(2) Finite Differences, including Interpolation with Equal and with Unequal Intervals of the Argument ; Central Difference Formulae ; Inverse Interpolation ; Derivatives ; Numerical (including Approximate) Integration ; Applications.

(3) Differential Calculus, including Notion of a Limit and Differential Coefficients ; Leibniz's Theorem ; Rolle's Theorem ; Mean Value Theorem ; Statement of Taylor's and Maclaurin's Theorems ; Expansions ; Bernoulli's Numbers ; Indeterminate Forms ; Maxima and Minima.

(4) Integral Calculus, including Integration as Inverse of Differentiation ; Standard Methods of Integration ; Reduction Formulae ; Integral as Limit of a Sum ; Definite Integrals ; Repeated and Double Integrals ; Application to Areas, Mean Values and Probability.

PART II.

(1) Theory of Interest and Annuities Certain, with Construction of Relative Tables.

(2) Theory of Life and other Contingencies.

PART III.

(1) Statistics.—Classification and tabulation of data ; Measures of location, dispersion and skewness ; Binomial and normal distributions ; Elementary theory of correlation ; Elementary theory of sampling (large samples) ; Theory and tests of graduation.

(2) Mortality and Other Investigations.—Compilation and graduation of mortality and other tables including exposed-to-risk formulae and theory of selection ; Vital statistics including census, birth, death, marriage, and migration statistics and index numbers ; Sickness

rates ; Fertility rates ; Population estimates and trends ; History and features of the more important existing tables.

Part IV.

Section A.

(1) Calculation of Office Rates of Premium for the Contracts of Life Assurance Companies, including the assessment of Extra Risks ; Surrender and Conversion of the Contracts of Life Assurance Companies.

(2) Valuation of the Contracts of Life Assurance Companies and Problems connected therewith ; General Provisions of the Acts relating to Life Assurance Companies, including the relative Schedules and the Certificates required thereunder ; Analysis and Distribution of Surplus of Life Assurance Companies and Problems connected therewith ; Income Tax in relation to Life Assurance Companies and the Contracts of Life Assurance Companies.

Section B.

(1) Pension Funds, Widows' Funds and Friendly Societies ; Law, Rates of Contribution, Valuation, Analysis of Surplus, and, generally, Actuarial Problems arising in their administration.

(2) Social Insurance Schemes in their Actuarial aspects.

Section C.

(1) Stock Exchange and other Investments. (A general knowledge of current financial conditions will be expected.)

(2) Life Interests and Reversions.

(3) Law affecting the Contracts of Life Assurance Companies.

APPENDIX X

PROSPECTUS OF OFFICIAL COURSES OF TUITION HELD DURING THE WINTER 1922-23

(the first comprehensive system of official classes)

Number of Course.	Examination.	Subjects covered.	Approximate Period covered by Courses.	Tutor.
I.	First	Arithmetic, Algebra up to and including Quadratic Equations, Plane Analytical Geometry up to and including Elementary Conic Sections, Arithmetical and Geometrical Progressions, Permutations and Combinations, Binomial Theorem	Nov. to March	S. F. M. Cumming, F.F.A., Secretary, Scottish Life Assurance Company, and an Assistant or Assistants.
*II.	Second	Theory and use of Logarithms, Series, Theory of Equations, Curve-Tracing, Theory of Probabilities, Elements of:—Calculus of Finite Differences, Calculus of Operations, Differential Calculus, Integral Calculus	11th Oct. to Dec.	*University Lecturer.*
*III.	Second	Theory of Interest and Annuities Certain, with Constructions of Relative Tables : The Mortality Table, Probabilities of Life, Expectations of Life, Probabilities of Survivorship and Statistical Applications of the Mortality Table—being the subjects dealt with in the first five chapters of the *Institute of Actuaries Text Book*, Part II.	Jan. to March	G. O. Gunn, F.F.A., Edinburgh Assurance Company. *University Lecturer.*
*IV.	Third	Theory of Life Contingencies and Formulae of Summation and Interpolation, including applications of the Calculi.	Nov. to March	W. A. Robertson, F.F.A., Actuary, Friends Provident and Century Life Office. *University Lecturer.*

* These three courses are conducted under the auspices of the University of Edinburgh in connection with the Diploma in Actuarial Mathematics. Arrangements have been made that Students preparing for the Faculty Examinations may attend these Courses.

Number of Course.	Examination.	Subjects covered.	Approximate Period covered by Courses.	Tutor.
V.	Third	Mortality, Marriage and Sickness Investigations (including the history of existing Tables), and construction of Relative Tables and Graduation of Tables	Jan. to March	A. R. Davidson, F.F.A., F.I.A., Assistant Actuary, Standard Life Assurance Company.
VI.	Third	Money Market and Foreign Exchanges, including the principal classes of Stock Exchange Securities and practical questions arising in connection with their purchase and sale	Nov. to Dec.	J. A. Thomson, F.F.A., Investment Secretary, Scottish Widows' Fund Life Assurance Society.
VII.	Fourth	Calculation of Office Premiums and Assessment of Extra Risks due to Family and Personal History, Residence and Occupation, Valuation of Assets and Liabilities, Distribution of Surplus, Surrender and Conversion of Policies and Bonuses, Drafting of Contracts and Endorsements, Employers' Liability Insurance, Valuation of Outstanding Claims	Nov. to Jan.	C. S. Penn, F.F.A., F.I.A., Actuary, Scottish Life Assurance Company.
VIII.	Fourth	Book-keeping and Accounts	Nov. to Dec.	A. M'Intosh, F.F.A., Assistant Secretary, Scottish Equitable Life Assurance Society.
IX.	Fourth	Finance	Jan. to Feb.	J. Wybar, F.F.A., Assistant Secretary, Scottish Amicable Life Assurance Society, Glasgow.
X.	Fourth	Reversions, Life Rents and other Contingent Interests, Sickness Insurance, Widows' Funds, Superannuation Funds and Friendly Societies—Calculation of Rates and Valuations	Feb. to March	G. W. Melville, F.F.A., A.I.A., Consulting Actuary, Glasgow.

A fee of three guineas will be payable for each Course (other than Nos. II., III., and IV.), restricted to a maximum of ten guineas if all four Courses for the fourth Examination be taken. The fees for Courses II., III., and IV. will be three guineas each, together with a special entrance fee of 5s. in the case of other than Diploma Students. The fee for Course II. and the entrance fee will be payable direct to the University, and the fees for Courses III. and IV. will be payable to the Faculty except in the case of Diploma Students.

APPENDIX XI

(a) THE SCOTTISH ACTUARIES' CLUB

Office-bearers

Year	Chairman	Vice-Chairman	Hon. Secretary
1932	Charles Guthrie	S. E. Macnaghten	A. C. Murray
1933	S. E. Macnaghten	R. M. M. Roddick	A. C. Murray
1934	R. M. M. Roddick	A. Graham Donald	A. C. Murray
1935	A. Graham Donald	F. J. Cameron	R. Ll. Gwilt
1936	F. J. Cameron	W. A. Robertson	R. Ll. Gwilt
1937	W. A. Robertson	H. G. Sharp	R. Ll. Gwilt
1938	H. G. Sharp	A. C. Murray	R. Ll. Gwilt
1939	Office-bearers re-elected for the War period.		
1944	A. C. Murray	S. F. M. Cumming	J. D. Williams
1945	S. F. M. Cumming	J. G. Kyd	J. D. Williams
1946	J. G. Kyd	J. M. Ross	J. D. Williams
1947	J. M. Ross	A. R. Davidson	J. D. Williams
1948	C. S. Penn	R. Ll. Gwilt	J. D. Williams
1949	R. Ll. Gwilt	A. R. Davidson	J. B. Dow
1950	J. D. Williams	J. Davie	J. B. Dow
1951	J. Davie	K. K. Weatherhead	N. M. Law
1952	K. K. Weatherhead	A. R. Reid	N. M. Law
1953	A. R. Reid	F. J. McGregor	N. M. Law
1954	F. J. McGregor	R. Sullivan	D. W. A. Donald
1955	R. Sullivan	D. A. B. Scrimgeour	D. W. A. Donald

(b) FACULTY OF ACTUARIES (ENGLAND) CLUB

Office-bearers

Chairman		Hon. Secretary	
1933-34	J. W. More	1933-38	J. Jamieson
1934-35	G. H. Recknell	1938-51	G. Welch
1935-36	J. Murray Laing	1951-56	P. Geddes
1936-37	J. W. Robson		
1937-38	G. S. Campbell		
1938-48	Sir Thomas Frazer		
1948-49	D. A. Porteous		
1949-50	Sir William Elderton		
1950-51	A. Currie		
1951-52	T. F. Swift		
1952-53	D. G. McKelvie		
1953-54	M. D. W. Elphinstone		
1954-55	G. Welch		
1955-56	D. Drybrough		

INDEX

INDEX

INDEX

INDEX

INDEX

INDEX

INDEX

THE FACULTY OF ACTUARIES: 1856-1956

INDEX

INDEX

INDEX